FOUR EARLS AND A PLAYWRIGHT

THE STORY OF THE EARLS OF SOUTHAMPTON

BRYAN DUNLEAVY

FOUR EARLS AND A PLAYWRIGHT
THE STORY OF THE EARLS OF SOUTHAMPTON

Published by Magic Flute Publishing Ltd. 2022
ISBN 978-1-909054-69-1 hardcover
ISBN 978-1-909054-89-9 paperback

Magic Flute Publishing Limited

231 Swanwick Lane

Southampton SO31 7GT

www.magicflutepublishing.com

www.magicflutepublications.co.uk

A catalogue description of this book is available from the British
Library

MAGIC FLUTE
PUBLISHING

PREFACE

I had no knowledge of Titchfield until I moved into the district 25 years ago and I knew practically nothing about the earls of Southampton. I did know, as an English undergraduate that William Shakespeare's poem *Venus and Adonis* was dedicated to the Earl of Southampton but I had no curiosity to look further into this connection. This changed after my move to Hampshire.

The association between the third earl of Southampton and William Shakespeare has excited much interest over the centuries, especially in relation to the Sonnets. This interest increased in the 19th century and Mrs Charlotte Carmichael Stopes (1840-1929) became a pioneer. She devoted much of her considerable energy to Shakespearean scholarship, and published her singular work, *The Life of Henry, Third Earl of Southampton* in 1922. She stood out in a man's world, and it would appear, in an age before photocopiers and scanners, that she tirelessly copied every document relating to her subject that she could find. Her work remains, a century later, as an important landmark in this field of study.

In 1965, another tireless Elizabethan scholar, A. L. Rowse published *Shakespeare's Southampton: Patron of Virginia*. As the title suggest, this book places more emphasis on the earl's pioneering contribution to the opening of North America to European settlement, than his incidental connection to Shakespeare.

In 1968, G.P.V. Akrigg, Professor of English at the University of British Columbia. published his *Shakespeare and the Earl of Southampton*, a work focussed more upon the relationship between the two men. Incidentally, and in quite another context, I met Professor Phillip Akrigg in Vancouver in the 1980s. At the time I was unaware of his book, nor was I interested in the subject. An opportunity missed!

Many writers have speculated about the relationship between the two men, particularly those who wish to unravel the Sonnets.

The third earl has therefore been the subject of much attention, while the other three have been largely ignored. The 1st earl has always figured in the work of Tudor historians although he has always been presented as a secondary player. Perhaps this is right. Contrasted with the bright lights of More, Wolsey and Cromwell he does indeed appear as a supporting actor and it was not until Geoffrey Gibbons published his work *The Political Career of Thomas Wriothesley, First Earl of Southampton 1505-1550, Henry VIII's Last Chancellor,* in 2001, that the 1st earl received book-length attention The second earl died at the age of 36 and did not live long enough to make his mark. Surprisingly, the fourth earl, who was a loyal and steadying hand for a time at the court of Charles I and a senior statesman after the restoration of the monarchy, has attracted less attention that I feel he deserves.

The aim of this book is to tell the story of the earldom of Southampton through four generations from its foundation in 1547 to its demise in 1667, when the fourth earl died without a male heir. The necessary prelude to this story is the life of the first earl Sir Thomas Wriothesley who built a considerable fortune and who had established himself as a great landowner by the time of his death in 1550. This is not exactly a 'rags to riches' story, but it was a remarkeable achievement and I have placed more emphasis on that aspect of his life than his political activities. The second earl's temperament and upbringing would not allow him to adapt to mainstream opinion and his short life was conducted on the fringe of society. The third earl did not prosper during the time of Elizabeth, but did find favour during the reign of James I and put his energy into many projects that engaged his interest. The 4th earl, Thomas, who came into the earldom on the death of his father and older brother, turned out to be a man who could revive the fortunes of the house and show himself to be a man of considerable statesmanship.

Each of the successors to the earldom were minors and in the instances of the second and third earls, these minorities were lengthy periods, which did nothing to further the development of the estates. The third earl had to sell off many properties to make ends meet and left the estate encumbered at his death in 1624. The 4th earl was compelled to continue the sale of manors and at one point was on the verge of selling Beaulieu. It was the development of Bloomsbury after 1640 which rescued the fortune of the earldom.

Thus, the story is one of decline from the great portfolio assembled by the first earl. Neither Henry, the third earl, nor Thomas, the fourth earl, were inclined to marry heiresses, although each had that opportunity, and the only inherited manors, which came from Katherine Cornwallis in 1626, were sold three years later, to pay debts.

In the middle of this story there is an interlude with a man who became more famous than any of the earls, William Shakespeare. Much has been written and many have speculated on a close relationship between the third earl and the poet and playwright. My own view, for what it's worth, is that the relationship, whether transactional or more intimate. probably only lasted between 1592 and 1594. After 1594, Shakespeare was a sharer in the company of actors known as The Lord Chamberlain's Men, and was less reliant on patronage.

That was less true of John Florio, who was in the earl's service for a time and whose literary efforts very much depended on the patronage of the wealthy. He features in this narrative with connections to both the earl and William Shakespeare.

This has been a lengthy project. I started my research in 2013 and the work was often on the back burner while I was working on other books. After the first lockdown in 2020, I decided to pull together the material I had gathered and bring this to a conclusion.

I must foremost thank my wife for her patient support during this enterprise. Many have helped along the way, and those dedicated preservers of our documentary heritage at the Hampshire Record Office, the Nottinghamshire Record Office, the National Archives and the Bodleian Library should not be forgotten. I must in particular thank Dr. Peter Mills and Terence Ogden for a critical reading of a draft manuscript. I am also indebted to Lord Montagu of Beaulieu and his Research Team for a careful reading of the manuscript which led me to make several corrections and some structural changes. Finally, there is the Titchfield History Society, which has nourished the flame of its unique history for almost a half century.

CONTENTS

PART 4   THE LAST EARL

APPENDICES

THE FOUNDER

PART 1

1

A FAMILY OF SHOWMEN

She was greeted by painted wooden castles built upon stone foundations, columns and statues, fountains and artificial mountains, mechanical zodiacs and battlements. – Peter Ackroyd

On Friday November 12th 1501 a young Spanish Princess set out with her retinue from Lambeth Palace on the final leg of a very long journey. She had sailed north across the Bay of Biscay to land at Plymouth and from there travelled by stages to London, a journey across uncertain roads that took almost a month. She was betrothed to be married to the heir of Henry VII, Arthur, Prince of Wales. Everyone at court knew that this was a marriage of great importance to both England and Spain and diplomats had been working hard to secure an alliance against the French government which, at the time, was on hostile manoeuvres throughout Europe. From the point of view of Henry VII, still insecure after 16 years on the throne, the union was further designed to add legitimacy to the still precarious Tudor claim to rule England. The 16 year-old princess, named Catherine, was a product of the union between the kingdoms of Aragon and Castille, and herself a descendant of John of Gaunt. Henry could not have found a better match.

The importance of this occasion was not to be left to imagination. Catherine and her contingent were met by a large party of England's nobility dressed in their finest clothes and bedecked with jewels and plumes. Among them were the Duke of Buckingham, the Earl of Surrey, the Archbishop of York and no less a personage than young Henry, Duke of York, Henry VII's second son who, although nobody could know it at the time, was destined to become her second husband.

Once across London Bridge they were met by the Lord Mayor, dressed in scarlet satin and flanked by twenty-four aldermen also clothed in brilliant scarlet, but in the slightly less expensive material of velvet. The square they entered on the north side of the bridge was sumptuously decorated. A two storey wooden structure with a canvas covering painted to resemble stonework was draped with flags and banners with emblems of the Order of the Garter. On either side two large gold painted wooden posts held the badges and emblems of the English king. On the lower floor sat a figure costumed to resemble Saint Catherine and above her a second figure who played the part of Saint Ursula. Saint Catherine, the 4th century Alexandrian woman famous for being executed on a spiked wheel (commemorated by the Catherine's Wheel) was regarded as the patron saint of secular learning and thus had become an important saint in this new age of humanism. Saint Ursula was reputedly a 4th century British princess who was sent to the continent with her accompanying virgins to marry Conan the ruler of Armoraica, which approximated to the area known as Brittany. For reasons which have never been successfully explained, she and her retinue ventured into the Rhineland before her marriage, where they were set upon by an army of Huns who had them all beheaded. The facts of her life are extremely obscure and were probably embellished as interest in her grew over the centuries. One fact alone can be relied upon. A basilica was built in Cologne in the 4th century to honour a group of virgins who had been martyred at Cologne. The legend of Saint Ursula seems to have appropriated this event.

It is now difficult to determine the significance of Saint Ursula, who enjoyed some popularity at this time and there was a church nearby dedicated to Saint Mary the Virgin jointly with Saint Ursula. The story had lost nothing in its re-telling over 1,000 years and at the time of the wedding the reported number of virgins who lost their lives with Saint Ursula had reached the hugely inflated figure of 11,000. The site is now occupied by the Mayor of London's offices, popularly known as *The Gherkin*, and the street name is Saint Mary Axe. Apparently the axe which was claimed to have beheaded Saint Ursula was among the relics once preserved in the church.

The two actors taking the parts of saints immediately stepped forward to greet the future queen, mounted on her palfrey, a quality horse with a docile temperament, and described the six pageants that would follow. These would portray her on a quest for great honour and immortal fame through her marriage to Prince Arthur. And it was no accident that the Prince was named Arthur; he was the living embodiment of the legendary King Arthur, 'the once and future king', who (and this was important to the myth-making of the insecure Tudor throne) would once again unify the country in peace and harmony.

The procession slowly made its way through the narrow and crowded London Streets to a wider part of Gracechurch Street where a second pageant was enacted. A mock turreted castle was dressed with banners and escutcheons and once the party had arrived, an allegorical figure called *Policy*, dressed as a Roman senator, emerged to make a speech, representing Henry's good government which always had its "eye on the common weal".[1]

From this point the party turned into Cornhill to see more pageants, enhanced by the movements of mechanical constellations, which wondrously turned while musicians played. Each tableau was laden with astrological forecasts of the benefits that would flow from this union between England and Spain. Progress was slow through the narrow, crowded streets and with the afternoon light fading on this short November day, the procession now tried to hurry up Cheapside to reach the final pageants. Here King Henry and Prince Arthur had commandeered a spacious merchant's house for a prime vantage point. Out in the street another stage supported a group of choirboys, conducted by William Cornysh, Master of the Children of the Chapel Royal. They were dressed as a choir of angels surrounding a figure dressed in gold, intended to represent God but who bore more than a passing resemblance to Henry VII himself. Should anyone miss the point, one of the actors declaimed:

> Right so, our sovereign lord the king
> May be resembled to the king celestial
> As well as any earthly prince now living.[2]

Here again was another attempt to impress on his subjects the closeness of their king to divinity itself - an early representation of the divine right of kings.

The final stage of this elaborate pageantry was enacted before the church of Saint Michael le Querne at the eastern edge of Saint Paul's churchyard. A costumed figure representing *Honour* showed the princess two thrones containing crowns and sceptres that awaited the occupancy of the couple about to be wed. After receiving gifts of gold and silver from the merchants of the city, Catherine entered the Cathedral where she was blessed by the Archbishop of Canterbury. This marked the end of the day's proceedings and the various players went to their lodgings. The princess herself was hosted by the Bishop of London.

During the following morning the business side of the marriage was concluded between the king and the Spanish ambassador and the princess was introduced to Queen Elizabeth. According to contemporary accounts, the two women took to each other immediately, and one suspects that this was in large part due to Elizabeth's own diplomatic and personal gifts. The afternoon and evening were given over to feasting and entertainment at Baynard's Castle.

The appointed day, Sunday, November 14th 1501, duly arrived and the sixteen year old Princess Catherine of Aragon and Castille was married to Henry's fourteen year old heir to the throne of England, Arthur, Prince of Wales. The ceremony was conducted in the old cathedral of Saint Paul's in the centre of the city, the capital of the country which the young Arthur would some day rule. The occasion, like the previous days, and indeed those which followed, was steeped in pageantry.

The maestro behind much of this ceremonial and pageantry was John Writh, Garter King at Arms, possibly not knighted at the time, who was the forbear of the Wriothesley family. Writh had been summoned by Henry, together with William Cornysh, to manage the pageantry after he effectively sacked the two men to whom he had previously assigned the task. Henry would leave nothing to chance and clearly wanted every aspect of the occasion to run perfectly. Writh records a trip by boat to Richmond Palace to 'have the king's mind' on the colour of Prince Arthur's trumpets.[3] This example illustrates not only Henry's considerable attention to detail, but also his confidence that men like John Writh could carry out his wishes. This pageantry and the events of the three days could only be organised by people with special expertise. The planning, design, construction of sets, the hiring of builders, painters, actors and costumiers was the preserve of only a few men, and in the late 15th and early 16th century these men were heralds.

The Garter King at Arms, could bring a lifetime's experience to bear on the occasion. He was Falcon Herald before February 1474, and on 25 January 1477 Edward IV made him Norroy King of Arms. A year and a half later, on 6 July 1478, he was promoted to Garter King of Arms, in effect the head of the College of Heralds. Garter was a senior court official. Only three years prior to his appointment, Edward IV had sent his predecessor, John Smert, to Paris to negotiate terms with Louis XI prior to Edward's threatened invasion. The job required good administrative skills and an ability to arbitrate in sensitive matters of status, while at the same time ride serenely above court intrigue and faction without any risk of having his life terminated through being on the wrong side. His perceived neutrality meant that he could officiate at Edward IV's funeral in April 1483 and a few months later at Richard III's coronation. Richard confirmed his appointment as Garter on 30 November 1483. The only interruption in his career came in January 1485 when he resigned for unknown reasons. It is possible that he fell out of favour with Richard, but in any case, his resignation may have protected him from being tainted with Yorkist partisanship. Henry VII re-appointed him to Garter on 13 February 1486 with back pay to the date of the Battle of Bosworth. He was then able to officiate at the Coronation of Henry VII.

He held this position until his death in 1504 and thus enjoyed a career in this role spanning almost 30 years, surely a long time in that day and age. So secure was he that he was able to ensure family continuity, his son Thomas assumed the position of Garter and another son William became York Herald. One of his grandsons, Charles, continued to work in heraldry, while another grandson, Thomas, became, as we shall see, the Earl of Southampton.

I have described these days at some length to provide some flavour of the world that John Writh and his sons Thomas and William inhabited. Their work was in the world of presentation and display, of honour and dignity and moments like royal weddings were their high career points. The heralds, and in these instances the Wriths, were central to ceremonial functions, and later John Writh and his sons were to have roles at the funerals of Queen Elizabeth and Prince Arthur and at the coronation of the new king after the death of Henry VII. The events themselves were not peripheral to history and they are well recorded, but most histories tend to skip over the pageantry of the occasion to concentrate on the political consequences of the event.

This is a viewpoint that would be shared by most readers, and were I not describing the Writh family I might be tempted to do the same. However, let us consider the impact that these displays had on late medieval England.

We still retain pageantry and ceremonial and on state occasions gilded coaches are led by groomed horses and accompanied by polished liveried staff, but in an age of so much other competing visual display, these events may hold less importance for us. In 1501 this kind of pageantry was the only display on offer, and it was rare. In addition we should note that the science of heraldry held a place of high importance. The right to bear arms and the uniqueness of those arms were highly-valued status symbols. Nobody regarded them as trivial. The Wriths lived in a world of pageantry, ceremonial and heraldic propriety. They did not hold great offices of state but they did hold offices which upheld the majesty of kingship and communicated that to the greater public. It would not have occurred to anyone to suggest that heraldic positions were irrelevant. The Wriths were men of the court and presumably knew everyone at court, from the high to the low.

Pageantry and display was a social unifier. On such occasions the word could be visibly presented as it should be. Court and business rivalries were put aside as lords and merchants wore their finest clothes and presented themselves in harmony as the public had a right to expect. It also had a foreign policy impact. Observers would report back to their governments and the image of the English Crown depended on reports that royal celebrations were of a degree that befitted a king. The heralds were men with considerable specialised knowledge who were able to give authority to a person's lineage. Inherited social standing matters less today, but people are still conscious of their image and good name, and those in power hire spin doctors and public relations experts to protect the reputation of their business.

The arrival of Catherine signalled not only a new century, but also the expectations of a new dynasty. There had been no stable succession since 1422 when the infant Henry VI succeeded his father. Hopes were high that Catherine and her husband would provide for further generations.

The wedding festivities now moved to Westminster Palace, which was to be the venue for the entertainment of the citizens of London, two miles down river, and beyond. Crowds came from everywhere and were charged one shilling admission to come within the walls - a high price, equivalent to ticket prices at the opening ceremonies for the Olympic Games. The centrepiece of this afternoon's entertainment was a joust planned and organised by Henry's tournament planner, together with John Writh, Garter King of Arms. This was an event, as with all the other pageants of the day, intended to push through the message of the good and harmonious government of Henry Tudor.

John Writh was far from being the only player in the elaborate pageantry of this week, but he was a key player. He was the man with the detailed knowledge of heraldry and genealogy and he was the one who could add academic legitimacy to any presentation. Besides writing books himself he was the possessor of a library of several volumes, each expensively produced, which were key references for his trade.

There were two major occasions during the last years of Sir John Writh, each less joyous than the event just described. On 11 April 1502, the Prince of Wales, died at Ludlow, probably from influenza. He had been unwell for about two months but he fell off very rapidly in the last few days. He was only 16 years old and was expected to become the next king of England. His death came as a huge shock to the fledgling Tudor monarchy. Once more Sir John Writh's services were called upon. On this occasion he had to travel far beyond London to distant Shropshire, several days on horseback. The weather was stormy and the roads were in poor condition. On the 25 April, after a service in Ludlow parish church, just outside the castle, the funeral cortege made its way to Worcester. John Writh described the weather as 'foul' and the road 'as the worst way I have seen'. The cart bearing the coffin was repeatedly stuck in the mud and villagers along the route were often called upon to heave the wheels out of the ruts. It was a very hard two-day journey.[4] Worcester was an appropriate burial place for the prince as it was also the final resting place of one former king, John.

John Writh had an open purse. 2,400 yards of black cloth was ordered, a large cost in itself as black dye was very expensive. The cloth was allocated to some 550 mourners so that they could wear suitable clothing for the occasion and a brigade of tailors and seamstresses were employed to complete the rush job. The coffin was covered in a black cloth, edged with gold and embroidered with a white cross. It was carried into the minster under a canopy of purple damask sprinkled with golden flowers. At the entrance to the minster the coffin was transferred to a hearse, an impressive wooden structure, decorated with heraldic shields and various royal banners, 1,000 candles lit the cathedral. Writh observed that it was the best funeral he had ever seen.[5] A comment from one with a professional eye for such ceremonials.

He also had a prominent part to play at the funeral of Queen Elizabeth. She died on 11 February 1503, a week after giving birth to another daughter, Catherine, who only survived a further week. There was much sorrow at court and in the land as she was a much-loved queen, who had a more amenable personality than her beautiful, but somewhat flinty mother. Sir John rode alongside the Lord Mayor in the vanguard of lords leading the funeral cortege. The hearse was drawn by eight warhorses draped in black velvet and the coffin carried a painted effigy of the late queen. The experienced hand of Sir John arranged for this sorrowful occasion to be filled with light. The hearse was followed by a procession of 200 poor men bearing tapers, and over 4,000 flaming torches lit the streets as the procession travelled from the Tower through Cornhill and Cheapside all the way to Westminster Abbey. The main thoroughfares, such as Cheapside were lined with men dressed in white robes, each bearing a torch, and at the top of Cheapside 37 virgins, each symbolising a year of the queen's short life, stood silently dressed in white and holding lighted tapers.[6]

The procession was led by Carmelite and Augustinian friars singing anthems. The queen's ladies, knights, squires, chaplains, aldermen of the city, representatives of the London Guilds and the foreign communities joined the solemn procession to its destination, and there, on 22 February 1503 mourned the loss of a much-loved queen.

It was the second serious blow to the new Tudor regime in the space of a single year.

Sir John Writh's role as a herald was not merely ceremonial. There were diplomatic missions on behalf of the king and while most of them would be headed by a lord, it was prudent to send along a knowledgeable man such as Sir John to guide the talks. He was employed by Edward IV in Scotland in 1479 and 1480. Henry VII sent him to treat with Maximilian, elected king of the Romans, in 1485 and in 1487 sent him on an Irish mission. In 1488 he found himself in Brittany and again in 1491. In that same year he presented the insignia of the Garter to Maximilian and in 1492 did the same for the Duke of Burgundy and again in 1494 to Charles VIII, king of France.

Thomas Wriothesley's grandfather was therefore at the core of early Tudor court life. He was in effect, although the term was not used in those days, a senior civil servant, a man who could be depended upon to get things done and leave political aspirations to others. It was an environment in which his sons, and later grandsons were schooled and young Thomas, born in 1505, a year after the death of his grandfather, spent his formative years in this ambience.

2

THE RISE OF THE WRITHS

He was not precisely a novus homo. A.L. Rowse

It is ironic that for all the effort made in the 16th century to establish an aristocratic name, it was to die out in its fifth generation when the fourth earl could only produce daughters, who then married and gave up their names. The name did survive as a first name for some of the male descendants but it did expire after a few generations and in recent centuries is unknown. Difficult as it is to spell and pronounce, Wriothesley is the name which will guide us through four generations as we chart the accelerated rise to wealth and power of Thomas Wriothesley and the influence of his descendants.

The conventional way of telling a story about someone's rise to great power is to present it as a rags-to-riches tale. In these tales the humbleness of the subject's origins is often exaggerated to dramatise the story. In truth, many of these spectacular rises to wealth and power begin, not at the very bottom, but in the ranks of those we would now call middle class. Thomas Beckett and Thomas Wolsey both came from merchant families, and, while they could not boast an aristocratic pedigree, were none the less substantial citizens. The same is probably true of the great bishop of Winchester, William of Wickham, who, while growing up in the country, was not brought up by an indigent peasant family. So while people like Thomas Wriothesley appear to come from nowhere because they are not noticed until they earn their prominence, in actual fact they are almost always in a position to exploit their circumstances. This is true of Wriothesley. He was from a well-connected court family who had the means to send him to university and the inns of court for his education. Once he had completed this rite of passage he moved seamlessly into Court employment, at first working for Cardinal Wolsey.

The second son of John Writh, William held the position of York Herald in London. He married Agnes Drayton, the daughter of a London merchant and on December 21st 1505 she gave birth to a son. He was named Thomas and it is not known whether he had any siblings. The family was in comfortable circumstances although it was the junior branch of a dynasty of heralds established by John Writh in the previous century. Although it could not have been apparent at the time, this new baby was to pole vault the family into the first ranks of Tudor society.

The name which the family now bore was not the one they had inherited but was in fact a Tudor contrivance. The family name was never so complicated or grandly written. It was a plain, monosyllabic Writh, alternatively spelled Writhe or Wrythe, a name which apparently emerged from Wiltshire in the 14th century. The origin of the name is completely opaque as it bears no passing resemblance to any place or craft (a common origin of surnames) and this surname has not come down through the ages in any of its possible variant spellings. The word today commonly means to twist or wriggle and one possible source of the word is from the Anglo Saxon *rithe*, which means a rivulet or stream. The derivation of the modern word 'writhe' from the twisting of a stream seems plain, and a surviving clue in this regard is a Wrythe Green in Carshalton in Surrey. It may be that when surnames were taken up in the 14th century or earlier that this family lived beside or near a stream. Possible? Likely? We really have no idea. The only time the name appears, before it disappears under its Tudor adornments, is when used by the individuals of this unique family.

The Wriths were rising in the middle classes of those Tudor times and Sir Thomas Wrythe, by then the inheritor of his father's position as Garter King-of-Arms at the College of Heralds, and possibly more sensitive to the value of ancient names, apparently discovered a Wriothesley from the reign of King John and decided to claim descent from this man. He got agreement from his younger brother William and posthumously ascribed the name Wriothesley to his father Sir John Wrythe. The name Wriothesley seems like an extravagant piece of snobbery, but it was a fashion of the period and many names were supplemented by extra consonants, vowels and even syllables. Wriothesley may be one of the more outrageous concoctions.[7]

The pronunciation of Wriothesley is difficult. A. L. Rowse proposed that the name was pronounced *Risley*, to rhyme with 'grizzly,' and it may have come to that in time, but the Canadian scholar G. P. V. Akrigg offered one rhyme by Thomas Heywood as evidence that it may have been pronounced "rye-o-sley" with a silent "th".

> Wriothesley was such, in all things striving
> To gain a name, by Artes, and Armes: surviving[8]

It is a cumbersome hexameter, but as Akrigg points out, it only works if 'Wriothesley' is pronounced as three syllables. He also notes that the Titchfield Parish register records the burial on 24 December 1624 of Lord James Wryosley, which seems to indicate that the two vowels "i" and "o" were still articulated at this time.[9] As to its true pronunciation in the 16th century we can only guess. 'Roseley' is another pronunciation of the name that has been advanced. The veteran Imperial ambassador to London, Eustace Chapuys, wrote the name in his letters as 'Vristley', which we might imagine to be a phonetic rendition. When we allow for the fact that many continentals have difficulty with the English 'th' sound, it is not too much of a stretch to imagine that Chapuys was trying to render a name which in his time was pronounced 'Writhsley'. This may be close. As if to confirm that the name was down to two syllable, the poet John Phillip wrote a dedication to "Lord Henry *Risley*" in 1581. Perhaps in the minds of the 16th and 17th century Writh descendants the contrived name served its purpose of suggesting an ancient lineage, but like Cholmondley and Featherstonehaugh[10] the name was unwieldy for everyday use and became abbreviated to two syllables.

It is tempting to assume that because so little is known about the Writh family prior to the Tudor period that they rose rapidly from complete obscurity. The scarcity of records is something we have to live with, but the fragmentary clues we have suggests that the family was of some importance in the 15th century. William Writh, for example, was MP for Cricklade in the Parliament of 1450-1. This could not have happened were he not a man of substance, although the source of his prosperity is not known. His son John, who became Garter King of Arms, was a draper in London, so it would appear that he was the one who moved from Cricklade towards the greater economic opportunities

The Writh Family

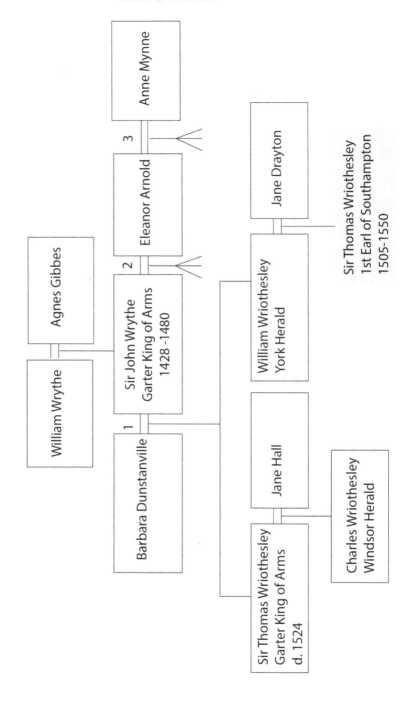

of London. The draper was a person of substance in every town and city in those days and doubly so in the economic environment of London. William Writh was also receiver for John Beaufort, Duke of Somerset and in this position was probably able to secure the economic base for the family's later fortune.

John Writh, his eldest son, must therefore have been well-placed to secure a position at court. He married Barbara Dunstanville (sometimes known as Castlecombe) and she was the heiress of Januarius (Janvier) Dunstanville of Castle Combe and presumably there was a useful inheritance of property that came with this marriage. The Wriths are known to have had at least four children, Thomas and William and two daughters, one of whom married John Mynne, the York Herald. Barbara Writh died between 1480 and 1483 and she was probably not beyond 30 years of age. John then remarried another heiress, this time Eleanor Arnold. Some sources say that he had a further son and three daughters although only one, Barbara, has a recorded marriage, and upon Eleanor's death he married for a third time to Anne Mynne, possibly a relative of his son-in-law.

At the end of what must have been a long life, John Writh, or Sir John Wrythe as he was later styled left lands in Cricklade, Wiltshire, Middlesex and Chichester, as well as a library, an expensive property in itself. He also made some genuine contributions to his profession, more lastingly in his book *Garter*. In it he records the adventures and deeds of some contemporary knights. It was of course part of the duty of heralds to observe and record the events of battle and note those who had shown especial courage and prowess, as well as to record the names of the dead and wounded. He wrote at least three books: *Wrythe's Book, Wrythe's Book of Knights and Wrythe's Garter Book.*

His fortune, which was later dwarfed by that of his grandson Thomas, was not insignificant. As a London draper his income must have been high and lands also came to him through his marriages. He had a house on Red Cross Street beside the Barbican where his family lived in some comfort. They could be accurately described as well-to-do. His duties as herald would not have been full time and he was able to attend to his business, as too, were his sons. While men like the Wriths were celebrating the old warrior class which had held sway over England for so many centuries, they themselves were emerging as the new governing class who were never required to raise a sword in battle.

Young men like his grandson Thomas, who were clever and literate and completely untrained for the battlefield, would emerge in the 16th century as the new men of the ruling class.

John's son, Thomas, succeeded him as Garter in 1505 but prior to that he had held heraldic positions. He was Wallingford Pursuivant to Prince Arthur and after his death to Prince Henry, later to become Henry VIII. He was also employed on various missions abroad and performed important ceremonial functions. He was knighted in 1523. Like his father he was industrious and proved to be an accomplished painter. He accomplished a considerable body of work in his lifetime - drawings of the great armoury and ordinary of English arms, and drawings of English monuments. He made additions to his father's Garter Book and expanded the pedigree of many families. He wrote in manuscript a *Westminster Tournament Roll* and a *Parliament Roll of 1512*. He is generally thought to have invented the modern presentational form of the pedigree, that is, a chart showing lines of descent. The old medieval practice simply presented a list of names, to show parentage.

The eldest son, Thomas, who must have inherited the larger share of his father's estate, was able to build himself a large mansion at Cripplegate, Garter House and appears to have been anxious at all times to emphasise his new status. It was he who, as noted above, transformed the family name from Writh to Wriothesley and persuaded his brother William to do the same. At the same time the appellation 'Sir' John Wrythe begins to appear. And it is to his son, Charles Wriothesley, that we owe the information that his grandmother Barbara Dunstanville was a lineal descendant of one of Henry I's illegitimate children. Since Henry I was extremely promiscuous and is known to have fathered at least twenty bastard children this is entirely plausible. Ten or eleven generations after Henry there were likely to be many who could make that claim. The only evidence we have for this is Charles Wriothesley's family tree which was most probably based upon hearsay. That is not necessarily a reason to dismiss the claim but its mention in this context tells us something of the ambition of the Wriothesleys.

Thomas married Jane Hall of Salisbury and apparently she bore ten children. The only male to survive was Charles who took the profession of heraldry into a third generation. He was also an active writer and compiled a chronicle of Tudor times, beginning with the accession of Henry VII. However Charles never had quite the success of his cousin and never seemed to be able to move beyond his position as Windsor Herald. His career stalled in the 1530s while that of his cousin Thomas was beginning to take off.

William was the younger son of Sir John Wrythe, although he is presented as the elder son in some genealogies, in particular the much-cited genealogy in the Hampshire Field Club guide of 1889.[11] Being named after his grandfather might suggest precedence in birth but it was not so. It was the elder brother Thomas who succeeded his father as Garter; William had to be content with the lesser job of York Herald. He married Joan or Jane Drayton, a daughter of Robert Drayton. Nothing is known about this family. William made less of a mark upon the world possibly because he did not live very long. He was appointed York Herald in 1509 but by 1513 he was dead, probably dying before he was 40. At the time of his death his son Thomas was 8 years old. There is no information about the cause of his death; there was a more fatalistic approach to death in those times and therefore less curiosity than we might show today. We might note however that his son Thomas only made it to 45 and his grandson Henry met his end at the age of 36. Was there some genetic flaw here?

Even so, this early death does not seem to have impacted on the young Thomas's upbringing. There is no evidence that the mother remarried, so one must assume that she had sufficient resources as a widow to continue to bring up her children. Thomas was provided with a good education and like his cousin Charles went to Trinity Hall at Cambridge.

These founder members of the Wrythe family were intelligent, hard working and anxious to improve their social and economic standing. In this they were successful and nowhere is there any question about their competence. Indeed their written legacy demonstrates their high ability in these endeavours. English government, as it was in the rest of Europe, was moving out of the grasp of the warrior class who depended on clerics for administration, into the hands of clever men who could interpret and implement policy. The Medici family of Florence were an outstanding manifestation of this trend. They were bankers, and very successful ones too, who were able to use their new wealth to achieve power and influence. If they needed an army and a general they simply hired the best they could find. They had no need, as English kings were still doing up to the time of Bosworth, to lead their troops into battle.

There was much more to government than military success in the field. Young Thomas Wriothesley never had any training in arms nor, as far as we know, was ever required to undertake military service. The world was changing and there were new men ready to fulfil new roles.

One innovation of Tudor government was the promotion of able men from secular ranks to high office who did not have an aristocratic lineage that might challenge the Tudor monarchy. Churchmen had been a safe bet in earlier centuries but the rise of an educated middle class created a wider talent pool. Thus there was real opportunity for men like Thomas More, Thomas Cromwell, Sir Thomas Writh and William Cecil to advance themselves and assume positions in government without being schooled by the church. The old feudal world, based on land tenure, provided for a stable society until the fourteenth century when poor harvests at the beginning and the Black Death in the mid-century destabilised the old order and brought about an economy where goods and services were bought and sold for money. The dynastic struggles of the 15th century in England, commonly known as the *Wars of the Roses,* brought about a further complication that delayed social reform in England, which might have been undertaken prior to the revolutionary Tudor years.

The Tudor period has often been viewed as the beginning of our modern era. This is partly due to Tudor propaganda which was active in smothering the history of the Plantagenet regime, and partly due to a European cultural change which resurrected classical texts from Greece and Rome and generated an increased interest in humanistic thought. The new thinking, styled as a *Renaissance* gave man a role in controlling his own destiny rather than supinely succumbing to fate. These factors contributed to a new energy, which can be clearly seen with the benefit of hindsight, but although this society was making new experiments in government and religious life they were still at core medieval men and women. Conservation of tradition became the business of heralds, and it was in this field that society was most recognisably medieval.

Heraldry became highly formalised and regulated during the 14th and 15th centuries. It grew from a need to systematise the markings that knights and some of their followers would wear on their shields and banners so that they could more easily differentiate between friend and foe. The heralds, whose original function was to make announcements prior to battle became the custodians of this information. In the high middle ages arms had become codified and held a surprising consistency across Europe. It did become highly complex. Colours were codified and the practice of quartering arms and dividing arms between father and son led to highly elaborate designs. It has been suggested that coats of arms were more appropriate to the tournament than of any practical use on the battlefield, although heralds were required to act as observers or even umpires on the battlefield. As early as 1200 the right to bear arms was prized as a status symbol, a characteristic that it retained for many centuries after its original purpose had been forgotten. By the end of the 16th century, families who had made some money and achieved status in their communities were queuing up at the door of the College of Heralds for a grant of a coat of arms. John Shakespeare was one of many.

Garter King of Arms, regarded as the most senior herald, dates from 1348 when Edward III created an exclusive order of chivalry, known as the Order of the Garter. Membership of that order was, and is, strictly limited to twenty four, and a herald's office was required to document membership and record acts of chivalry. Other heralds came into being as the demand for arms increased.

A L Rowse observed that the Wriths had a respectable genealogy, and that they were hardly *arriviste* when Sir Thomas Wriothesley emerged at the court of Henry VIII.[12] The family were part of the court establishment and it was probably very easy for young Thomas Wriothesley to move seamlessly into a court position.

3

THE APPRENTICESHIP

Why come ye not to court?
To which court?
To the King's Court,
Or to Hampton Court?
Nay, to the King's Court.
The King's Court
Should have the excellence;
But Hampton Court
Hath the pre-eminence. – John Skelton

There may have been no better opportunity for an ambitious young man in 1524 than to enter the service of the outrageously grand Cardinal Wolsey. At the age of 19 Thomas Wriothesley's career was off to a flying start.

Thomas Wriothesley was born on 21st of December 1505 in London. There was a younger brother Edward and two sisters, Helen and Anne who proved their recorded existence by getting married in later years, otherwise very little is known about them. We have to remind ourselves that the record of births and even burials was not a public requirement until 1538 and although births may have been recorded within the family, the prospect of those records surviving was entirely accidental. One of the reasons we have some sort of pedigree for the Writh family is that the Tudor Wriths (or Wriothesleys) took a personal and professional interest in the subject.

Thomas was first educated by William Lily, master of St Paul's School, which had only been founded in 1512, seven years after Thomas's birth. Lily. then in his 40s, was a widely travelled and erudite man who is thought to have been the first man to teach Greek in

England. He was a friend of Sir Thomas More. As well as the young Wriothesley, several other boys, who later became eminent figures in Tudor times, passed under his tutelage, among them William Paget, John Leland, Edward North and Anthony Denny. Each of these young men went on to favoured careers in government. Paget, Denny and North rose to senior positions and were elevated to peerages. Leland concentrated on his antiquarian and academic interests but is possibly better known to posterity because of his *Itineraries*. Lily's school was a leader in the new humanist movement that was beginning to open up the intellectual life of the early 16th century.[13] Humanism, during the Renaissance, was broadly speaking an educational movement which intended to extend the scope of learning away from the prescriptive learning of the Scholastic tradition. Scholastic studies were very much directed towards a trade: law, medicine and theology. There was little interest in opening up the mind to new ideas. Humanism, by contrast sought to educate people to communicate effectively through proper use of language, and its proponents placed emphasis on grammar, rhetoric, history, poetry and moral philosophy, subjects which formed a broader curriculum, known today as the Humanities. This ushered in a new age which was willing to take a fresh look at the classical texts and led them to speak of a re-birth (renaissance) of learning.

New powers were emerging in Europe. The seafaring merchants of Venice and Genoa, and the banking families of Florence founded their wealth and power on money rather than land. Even in England, there were signs of this change. The Hull merchant family, who took the name 'de la Pole' started to take the national stage in the late 14th century. By the time of Henry VIII their descendants were senior members of the aristocracy and there were some living who had a respectable claim to the throne. Some of these new men did distinguish themselves in bearing arms in battle, but they were also keen to sponsor art and intellectual interests to embellish their own pretensions to power. They became masters of a propaganda that held newness to be a virtue and this has led subsequent historians to see the middle ages as completely reactionary. The Renaissance was presented as that period between the great classical age of Greece and Rome and the long intermediate period of history - a millennium in fact - was presented as the "middle ages" - a dismal age between two periods of enlightenment. Even so, it is fair to observe that there was change. A capitalist economy was developing to replace the old feudal economy; the invention of the printing press assisted the propagation of knowledge and ideas; new technologies enabled seafarers to cross oceans and colonise newly discovered parts of the world.

However, some of these new men were revolutionary, even avant garde, and the humanists were sowing seeds which directly led to change. The Protestant reforms in parts of Europe were a product of a willingness to embrace fresh ways of thinking. Not least of these revolutions was the translation of the Bible into vernacular languages, aided of course by the invention of the moveable type printing press, first introduced to England in 1476 by William Caxton through the sponsorship of Earl Rivers. Ideas could spread remarkably quickly and Wriothesley was part of the new generation that was fully exposed to this new medium of communication. Old conservatives like the Duke of Norfolk could assert that he had never read the Bible in his life nor did he intend to, but newer government figures of the time, including Thomas Cromwell and Henry VIII's last wife, Catherine Parr, were keen to devour and discuss the new texts. This did not in the least undermine Christianity. These humanists were only humanists in the sense that they were interested in the study of humanity as a creation of a Christian God. Not for one moment did they question Christianity which was *sine qua non*. They certainly had issues with the church and they also questioned theological ideas, but in their fundamentals they were still unquestioning believers in God and Christianity.

Wriothesley was therefore exposed to these ideas from the earliest and they cannot be discounted when assessing his political activities of the 1530s. It could be argued that Wriothesley, schooled as he was, was able to live comfortably with the monastic dissolution precisely because his education had humanist foundations, although there are other arguments, as we shall see, which may attribute other motives to his actions.

From St Paul's he was sent to Trinity Hall, Cambridge for his university education, possibly when he was about 14 years of age. The Master of the college at this time was Stephen Gardiner, the man who later became Bishop of Winchester and a conservative opponent of the Reformation. Gardiner was about ten years older but it was the start of a relationship that was to last Wriothesley's life, and, but for a brief falling out over Wriothesley's selection as MP for Hampshire in 1539, the two men remained on good terms. The careers of both men were often closely linked.

Stephen Gardiner was born between 1495 and 1498, the son of a clothmaker in Bury St Edmunds. He was sent to Cambridge in 1511 where he studied at Trinity Hall. By the time Thomas Wriothesley arrived Gardiner was an established figure and would be elected master of the college in 1525. He first met Cardinal Wolsey in 1523 and Wolsey increasingly employed him on his various projects. Along the way, Wolsey was able to grant Gardiner various benefices, which of course added to his wealth and influence. He became, in quick succession, archdeacon of Taunton, Worcester, Norfolk and Leicester and a prebend of Salisbury. Before too long Henry VIII had taken note of his talents and in 1529 he became principal secretary to the king and after the fall of Wolsey Henry appointed him to the plum bishopric of Winchester.

These young men were sufficiently robust and extravert to take part in play productions. At least one was recalled by Gardiner in later life, a production of the Plautus comedy, *Miles Gloriosus*, when he reflected that he appeared in that production with Wriothesley and Paget. Who took which part is unknown, but John Leland, who reported this, also recalled the performance of Gardiner, so it is likely that he took a leading role. In Plautus's play it is the slave, Plotinus, who is the smart one, doing his master's bidding and helping him out of his difficulties. This may be the thought that Gardiner had in mind after the three of them had spent a lifetime serving their king.

Wriothesley probably left Cambridge in 1522 when he was about seventeen. There is no record of him taking a degree and perhaps he did not think it important. He was not destined for a career in the church which was the only practical advantage in holding that honour. Plainly he knew, because of his father's connections, exactly where he was going. Stephen Gardiner must have found a position for him and took him to Paris during the winter of 1522-3 and it was there that young Thomas, with his quick intelligence, gained some competence in the French language, which he was able to call upon in later years. He may then have worked in Thomas Cromwell's office, in or about 1524, and from that platform he found a place in Cardinal Wolsey's office on the recommendation of Stephen Gardiner. Thomas Wolsey, by then aged about 50 and at the peak of his power, never entirely forgot his own humble origins and that he was once an aspirant in search of position.

He therefore made a practice of hiring bright and precocious young men. Thomas Wriothesley was a young man of promise who proved himself worthy; before too long he was entrusted with important documents.

Clerkly work, the writing and transcribing of documents, was the staple of his working life in these early years and it is not surprising that we do not hear very much of him, but it was a period of expanding government and the legal documentation of almost every activity was critical.

Within a few years he was given larger assignments. By 1525 he was employed in Wolsey's grand plan to build a new college at Oxford. In July of that year he prepared a detailed set of instructions about which buildings should be demolished at St Frideswide's monastery, which was to be the site of the new college. In December of that year he drew up a patent for the sale of seven monasteries and their lands and manors to pay for the expensive work of the new building. These were clerical tasks but they required a good and detailed understanding of the work involved. Land acquisition and building works appears to have been as complex in the 1520s as they are today and it was essential to employ an official who could work with intricate legalities. It is worth recalling that another Hampshire man, the great William of Wykeham, began his government career by managing public works.

This gives us some idea of the versatility that the young Wriothesley was beginning to demonstrate. That he was marked out as a rising young man might be illustrated by this anecdote. At the end of 1526 Dr John London wrote to Wriothesley seeking his support to maintain some Oxford Colleges, "sixteen have decayed in these few years."[14] The new college, with its large and attractive new buildings, was having a negative impact on the enrolments of older colleges and Dr London wished to get his case across to the Cardinal. Wriothesley was expected to place the matter before the Cardinal for his consideration and if we remember that Thomas Wriothesley was only 21 years old this incident is noteworthy in that a senior figure like John London believed that this bright young man could gain him access to the great Cardinal.

This access came at a price. Wolsey had been Henry's Lord Chancellor since 1515 and was the fulcrum of government. All despatches, whether to local officials or to foreign governments passed through his hands. No policy could be formulated without the involvement of the Cardinal.

He also approved, and therefore controlled, all senior positions. He also helped Henry to create a new judicial body known as the Star Chamber, so-called because the meeting room had a ceiling decorated with stars. This body, which included the king and council, operated as a kind of Supreme Court. The Star Chamber was not entirely new, but what was new was the range and scope of its jurisdiction. Under Wolsey's management the number of cases multiplied tenfold and with this increased activity an expansion of income opportunities.

As another sign of his increased power, there was also the court of Chancery, over which the Cardinal, as Lord Chancellor presided. Each day he would walk to Westminster Hall in a formal procession, preceded by men carrying two large crosses and the grey seal of his office. He was dressed splendidly in scarlet carrying in his hand half an orange filled with vinegar so that he could smell something more pleasant than the odours of the men grouped on either side of the path to the hall. Behind him his officials, such as Thomas Wriothesley, followed carrying books and papers.

Government was visible and personal. Men who sought a judgement, an award or preferment made their case in person before the man who could make a decision. Amidst this great press and clamour for a judgement of one kind or another, there would be young officials like Thomas Wriothesley who drew up the list of who should speak to the Cardinal. Therefore the officials who made these lists and determined priority became important and a payment or gift to the official would ensure that your case was moved higher up the list. Those who could afford more got greater priority. This was not seen as corrupt in Tudor England. It was simply the way things were done, and if you had more wealth it was self evident that you had greater access to 'justice.' In time such practice, or the abuse of such practice, was understood to be corrupt and you can see this emerging during the lifetime of Thomas Wriothesley's great grandson, the fourth earl, who struggled against a quagmire of corruption when he was Lord Treasurer to Charles II.

The significance of this move to Peckham's office was to be appreciated in his later career, when he became much valued for his expertise in financial administration. Under Peckham he learned much about the finances of the state, surely good preparation for his later financial offices, and not incidentally to the skills he acquired in establishing his own fortune.

At the same time he was spending more time on Cromwell's work. Cromwell did not at that time hold any office at court. He was a lawyer with recognised skills who would be consulted from time to time to check and develop the legality of various transactions. The example given above of the acquisition of St Frideswide may give us a general idea of how things worked. Young Wriothesley did much of the legal spade-work and prepared documents relating to the various properties. These were then submitted to Thomas Cromwell to check over. Once amended and approved by Cromwell the Cardinal could proceed with his project.

The Cardinal's influence over Henry VIII was waning in these years, although that probably mattered little to a junior employee. Cromwell, however, was becoming more prominent and at some point before 1529 Wriothesley was seen to be working directly for Cromwell rather than the Cardinal.

In 1530 he was appointed Clerk of the Signet. This job, as we now understand it, was to take letters patent (i.e. documents from the king's office that made a grant or deed) and prepare a document which would then become signed by the king or affixed with his seal. The work required care and accuracy and clearly the young Wriothesley had demonstrated his competence. He was one of four clerks to the Signet. Once Thomas Cromwell came to power he recruited the young man into his office where he spent a decade beside the Principal Secretary while he conducted his reformation of the English church.

The overall picture that emerges from the wealth of documents where Wriothesley's hand is visible, presents the image of a conscientious, dependable worker who became in time indispensable. One is tempted to draw parallels with crown ministers in recent times who have moved seamlessly through various government departments, doing sound, if unspectacular work, and eventually rising to one of the top jobs. This appears to be true of Wriothesley. He was clever and hard-working but unspectacularly so and it is perhaps for this reason that Tudor historians have not rated him highly. His reputation has also suffered in comparison with four other men in the 16th century, who for different reasons were colossi in Tudor government - Cardinal Wolsey, Thomas More and Thomas Cromwell before him and William Cecil in Elizabeth's reign.

Thomas Wolsey, Archbishop of York, holder of innumerable

benefices in England and Ireland, Cardinal, Lord Chancellor, was an extraordinarily ambitious man who became, next to the king, the most powerful political figure in England for 15 years during the reign of Henry VIII. He was certainly instrumental in creating the unitary state that was the legacy of the Tudors and along the way was not reticent about his own enrichment and aggrandisement. He was not a creative thinker however, and it was his inability to see beyond the status quo that led to his eventual downfall. Thomas Cromwell, who succeeded him as Henry's factotum, showed much greater flexibility in thinking and was able to engineer Henry's divorce from Catherine and enrich the state hugely through the dissolution of the monasteries. It was Wriothesley's good fortune to take his apprenticeship under these two men and by the time he was thirty he was thoroughly schooled in the art and practice of government. This period, from 1527-1536, although nobody at the time realised it, was one of the most momentous in 16th century history.[15] In this decade Henry VIII broke with the church of Rome, took a succession of wives in the desperate search for a male heir, and dissolved all monasteries, and accidentally created a new class of aristocracy.

In 1529 he was placed in the household of Sir Edmund Peckham, who was then Cofferer of the King's Household. Peckham, who married a cousin of Jane Cheyney, remained a friend for life and was one of the executors of Wriothesley's will. It is probable that while working for Peckham he gained the introduction to the woman who was to become his wife. Jane Cheyney was a daughter of William and the relationship with John Cheyney (the father of Anne - Peckham's wife) is indistinct. William may have been a nephew. Sir William Cheney held lands in the Chalfont area of Buckinghamshire. The Cheyney family were probably (although we cannot know for certain) from an ancient Norman Conquest family. Isenhampstead, later known as Chenies, was a manor with a knight's fee attached to the Barony of Wolverton, held by Mainou the Breton, so it is possible, that the manor was given to one of Mainou's knights and through either male or female lines, came to the family that took the name of Cheyney. At any rate it was a good match for Wriothesley.

However, to make the relationships of this circle even closer, Jane Cheyney's mother was also the mother of Germaine Gardiner, the nephew of the redoubtable Stephen Gardiner. Therefore Thomas

Wriothesley was related by marriage to Stephen Gardiner and Edmund Peckham. Each of these men and women held out as defenders of the old faith when the reform movement became too extreme for their taste after 1547.

As to when they married we can only guess. Some say before 1533 but it could have been earlier. His daughter Elizabeth married in 1545 to Thomas Radcliffe, later Earl of Sussex. This marriage had been arranged in 1543 so the actual date two years later might suggest that they waited until at least she was 14, or possibly 16. If it was 14, her birth would be 1531, offering us a potential wedding year of 1530 between Thomas Wriothesley and Jane Cheyney. Since Wriothesley was appointed Clerk of the Signet in 1530, this date may be about right.

As to their children some names can be pieced together from various sources. There was a William, most likely the first born son named after his two grandfathers, and Anthony. Both died in infancy or as small children and we only know of their existence through a notebook left by the Countess. William died in August 1537 at about the age of two and Anthony died in 1542. The third son, Henry, was born in 1546 and lived to become the second earl and inherited his father's estates upon his majority.

The remaining survivors were daughters. Again we know little of their birth dates, but we do know who they married from the Wriothesley tomb in Titchfield. Each of them married into fairly prominent families. Mary married Richard Lister, grandson of Sir Richard Lister of Southampton. Catherine married Thomas Cornwallis of East Horsley in Surrey and Mabel married Sir Walter Sands of the *Vyne* near Basingstoke. It is not clear if there was any issue from these marriages. A further daughter, Anne, was betrothed to Sir John Wallop, but he died before the wedding and it is unclear how her life developed from this point.

Our curiosity must remain unsatisfied and this is a problem with early Tudor and Medieval genealogies. Daughters only find themselves in records if they marry and sons only if they live to inherit. In this respect the Wriothesley family is typical of the times.

In the same way we can only guess at the Wriothesley's domestic life. The omnipresence of Wriothesley in state papers would suggest that he was rarely away from London, only visiting his growing Hampshire estates on occasion. He was also sent abroad on occasion on diplomatic missions. After 1540 the splendid pile at Titchfield was used as a country seat.

4

CROMWELL'S RIGHT HAND

Cromwell is constantly rising in power, so much so that he now has more influence with his master than Cardinal ever had. Nowadays, everything is done at his bidding. – Eustace Chapuys.

The decade which began in 1530 was a remarkable one for English history, but it was also the decade which transformed Thomas Wriothesley from a junior court official into a wealthy and influential man. By 1540 he was a substantial landowner with the prospect of doubling his wealth before the end of the next decade. He was also rising on the coattails of one of the great figures of English history.

Thomas Cromwell came from an obscure but not necessarily humble family. His father Walter had been a blacksmith and an innkeeper and one of his sisters married a successful lawyer. Thomas appears to have left England for the continent as a young man and after a period as a soldier created a name for himself as a useful advocate. He returned to England circa 1516 and developed a career as a money lender and lawyer. His portfolio of influential contacts grew steadily and by about 1522 he had met Cardinal Wolsey who immediately sought to use his talent. He arranged for Cromwell to be returned as an MP in 1523. In 1524, he was elected as a member of Gray's Inn, which underscores his recognition by a profession in which (as far as we know) he had no formal training. Increasingly he undertook work for the Cardinal in the 1520s. Thus his own career in government service began at the same time as the young Thomas Wriothesley.

Wriothesley's position as one of the Clerks of the Signet moved him to a senior position at the heart of government, a position he was to hold for a decade. The Cardinal's power was waning fast. Cromwell continued to serve Wolsey and remained loyal to him to the very end, but, in January 1530 he sought, and was granted a position in the king's service. Up to that point he had worked as a freelance lawyer This brought him into closer association with Wriothesley, who may at this date have moved into Cromwell's office. About a year later Cromwell became a junior member of the king's council.

Cromwell is often presented in popular fiction as a shadowy, somewhat sinister figure, lurking in the background, ready to pounce, once his master was disgraced. This fiction is far from the truth. Cromwell stood by his former mentor to his death, even at the expense of losing favour with Henry VIII. Cromwell was always prepared to be principled and fearless. Indeed, he fully expected to lose position alongside Wolsey in 1529 and had prepared his will. He need not have worried; he continued to work steadily from 1530 onwards and in time Cromwell became Henry's chief councillor.

Once the Cardinal's downfall had been decided, the dukes of Norfolk and Suffolk were sent to Wolsey to demand that he hand over the Great Seal. The Cardinal dug in his heels and would not comply unless he had the order in writing from the king. Accordingly, Wriothesley was enjoined to prepare the document and the two dukes returned the following day, 17 October 1529, to complete their mission. The cardinal recognised that he was out of options and surrendered the seal. Legal proceedings against Wolsey may have been intended but he died a year later and his huge estates were confiscated by the Crown, including his great college project at Oxford.

Cromwell has often been presented as the originator of the idea that the king could be the head of the church, but John Schofield has successfully made the argument that these ideas were being bruited long before Cromwell entered the king's service, and came to fruition before Cromwell was promoted to a position of real power.[16] Anti-Papal sentiment was evident in England in 1529 when Cromwell was out of favour immediately after the fall of Wolsey. Henry told Eustace Chapuys, the Ambassador to the Holy Roman Emperor, that he was dissatisfied with the Pope and if Luther had confined his attack on Rome to the abuses and vices of the church instead of condemning the sacraments he would have had Henry's full support. A month later Chapuys reported that 'the English will not care much for Rome.

Neither the leaders nor the rest of the party can refrain from slandering the Pope.'[17] In September 1530 the Duke of Suffolk, himself a staunch catholic, together with Anne Boleyn's father, newly ennobled as Earl of Wiltshire, told the papal nuncio bluntly that England cared nothing for Popes, 'even if St Peter should come to life again.'[18] In January 1531, the Duke of Norfolk, another catholic stalwart, told Chapuys that 'Kings of England in times past had never had any superior but God only.'[19] The tide was flowing against the Pope and in favour of a marriage between Henry and Anne Boleyn, so when Cromwell became part of the government he was joining a movement that was more-or-less set on a break with Rome. It became a question of how could that be achieved.

Henry remained indecisive. For all the bluster, a break with Rome was a massive step to take and he needed a push. Anne Boleyn's pregnancy in 1532 made the 'great matter' urgent and Cromwell's clever mind presented a solution. It may also be true to say that Thomas Wriothesley made a contribution. There is a letter, written by Wriothesley in February 1532 that developed the point that a judge was only able to bring into effect judgements within his own jurisdiction, and therefore Henry, in this case, could not be compelled to obey judgements from Rome as England was not within Rome's jurisdiction.[20]

Matters moved forward. Henry sought and received support from King Francis of France for his divorce from Catherine. The French at the time had a political interest in scoring points over Spain, but it is unlikely that he imagined that the English church would break from Rome. After this events moved quickly. Henry married Anne Boleyn in January 1533 and in May Archbishop Cranmer announced the divorce from Catherine. On 25 May 1533 Henry's marriage to Catherine was declared illegal and void. Anne was crowned queen of England on 1 June 1533. Later that year, on 7 September, she gave birth to her first child. It was a girl and she was named Elizabeth. Anne went through two more pregnancies and both were stillborn; the last, a son, was born on 29 January 1536. Anne's time on earth was very short after this and she was executed on Tower Green 19 May 1536.

There was no popular acclamation for the new queen. Catherine had been queen since 1509 and had lived in the country from 1501 onwards, almost a lifetime for many, and she had done nothing in that time to blemish her reputation. The people took her side entirely and felt she had been unjustly treated, and there was not much to argue against this popular view. Anne did not help her cause through a tendency to be haughty and imperious, but neither she nor Henry cared much about popular opinion, but whereas Henry was secure as king, her position was more tenuous than she realised, and so it proved a few years later.

England was still a catholic country and Henry was very much a catholic in his beliefs and remained so for the rest of his life. The rupture with Rome, came eighteen months later with the passing of the Act of Supremacy, which made the king the head of the church. England became at that point a Protestant country, although doctrinally little had changed. These were momentous times and there were fresh intellectual currents. Lutheran thinking, which began in a protest against the corruption of the church, was forced by the conservative push back into a new breakaway movement. Lutheran ideas, such as *sola fide* (justification by faith alone),[21] were gaining some currency in England in the 1530s and Thomas Cromwell was certainly under their influence. However, dividing lines began to develop between the leading figures of the day. Both Cromwell and Thomas Cranmer, archbishop of Canterbury, were Lutherans. Thomas Wriothesley remained true to his faith. Although he was prepared to acknowledge his king as head of the church in England, there is no sign that he deviated from conventional Christian doctrine, a matter that was to create trouble for him and his family after the king's death in 1547. For the time being, and and for the remainder of Henry's life he was prepared to serve his king unquestioningly.

Apart from dissatisfaction with the papacy there was no swell for a Protestant church. What brought about the creation of the Church of England was Henry's desire to secure his dynasty with a son and heir. The break from Rome was an entirely political matter where the dispute with Rome became caught in the tangle of European politics. The Act of Supremacy of 1534 changed the head of the church from the bishop of Rome to the king of England; there were no doctrinal or sacramental changes at this time. To the average Englishman the change was little different from a manor coming into new lordship. The head changed but otherwise everything continued as before.

Wriothesley, as we have noted, was orthodox in matters of religion and not at all receptive to new fashions of Lutheran thought. He appears to have been intellectually incurious, unlike his colleague and master Thomas Cromwell. Henry, equally, remained orthodox and this may explain why Wriothesley and his fellow conservatives were content to implement some policies which grew out of the independence of the English Church.

During the early 1530s, although Wriothesley had official positions at court, he increasingly undertook work for Cromwell. As it became apparent that Wriothesley was dependable, his work for Cromwell grew in quantity. In the latter part of 1533 he became, in effect, Cromwell's representative in the privy seal office.[22] Henry appointed Cromwell as his principal secretary in April 1534 to replace Stephen Gardiner, bishop of Winchester. The powerful prelate was always a difficult man, and Henry had had enough, and Cromwell was then obvious alternative to replace him. Nevertheless, Gardiner resented Cromwell for the rest of his days for usurping his position and took his revenge in 1540. Wriothesley was also one of Henry's secretaries, so the two men now worked together on a daily basis.

Wriothesley was a useful man. He was highly intelligent and hard working and he had the necessary skills to get things done. Therefore he became Cromwell's second in command during these years. In effect he managed the office and saw to the day to day transactions while Cromwell looked after higher matters of state. Wriothesley's function was to draft deeds and documents, which Cromwell would inspect and amend if necessary. Cromwell was prepared to delegate but would always want the final say. Elton comments on "the outstanding importance of Wriothesley - more than chief clerk, perhaps, but definitely a subordinate and not the head of the office: Cromwell alone was that."[23]

And after the Act of Supremacy one of the highest matters of state was religious reform. These were momentous years and the radical reform of religious houses created the conditions for a more vibrant economy. Wriothesley may not have foreseen the long term impact of his efforts, but he was intimately involved in the implementation of this policy.

After Catherine had been repudiated, their only daughter Mary remained a problem. She took her mother's side in the argument and could not in any case champion a law that made her illegitimate. In 1533 she was 17 years old - old enough to know her own mind and royal enough to be able to stand her own ground. She was pressured to sign the oath of allegiance, which would have required her to renounce her own legitimacy. She was adamant about her position as was her father's opposite stance. In this whole difficult process he could not be seen to make exceptions to the rule he was applying to every other citizen of the country. The Duke of Norfolk headed a delegation to persuade Mary to sign, without success. Cromwell wrote to her that "I think you are the most obstinate and obdurate woman" and hinted that her continued stand-off might lead to a traitor's death.

At this point he sent Wriothesley to work with her and he appears to have gained her trust. He was not a doctrinal reformer. Mary's commitment to the old religion would not allow her to look kindly on any man who promoted the new faith. In Wriothesley she found a sympathetic ear, and she must have intuitively understood where his religious sentiments lay. In 1533 Mary had lost her household cook for one reason or another and her father, in order to put pressure on her to conform, would not provide the funds for her to recruit a new cook. This may seem trivial but the position of cook for a Tudor household (and Mary's would not have been small) was critical. Without a cook and kitchen staff it was practically impossible to eat! There were no easy ways to prepare meals in the 16th century and the position required a high level of knowledge as well as the organisational skills to manage staff. After talking with her, Wriothesley was able to find the money to pay her cook but he was also able to bring his diplomatic skills to bear on Mary's dilemma.[24]

There was the more difficult matter of the Act of Supremacy of 1536 which made Henry head of the church. Mary refused to take this oath which made her a traitor in the eyes of the law, but as Henry's daughter this made it once again a delicate issue. One of her supporters, Sir Anthony Browne, whose granddaughter was to marry the second Earl of Southampton, was arrested in consequence. Wriothesley's diplomatic skills were once again called upon and his consultation had the effect of persuading her to agree to take the oath without putting her immortal soul in peril. She agreed to take the oath and was rewarded by Henry with kinder treatment.

> "My body I do wholly commit to your mercy and fatherly pity, desiring no state, no condition nor no manner or degree of living but such as your grace shall appoint unto me."[25]

We might consider that Thomas Wriothesley played a large part in helping her to come to this sensible decision, even though her conscience fought against it.

Anthony Browne then had no reason to hold out his submission to the Act and was accordingly released.

In November 1536 she wrote to Wriothesley:

> "Good Master Secretary how much I am bound to you, which have not only travailed, when I was drowned in folly, to recover me before I sunk."[26]

Later, in 1539, he was asked for help in obtaining clothing for one of her footmen. Again he was able to oblige and received another letter of thanks signed "Your assured frend duryng my lyfe Marye."[27] And later that year when a proposed marriage was bruited between Mary and Phillip Duke of Bavaria it was Wriothesley who was sent to sound her out about the prospect. She did not warm to the idea since Phillip was a declared Lutheran and for Mary religion was always a sticking point, but again it illustrates that Wriothesley's good relationship with Mary was well known and he was inevitably the messenger when the tactful broaching of difficult issues was required.

We might safely assume that had Wriothesley lived longer he would have been prominent in Mary's reign once she came to the throne.

When Henry spoke out in defence of the sacraments and the authority of the Pope in 1521 a grateful pope awarded him the title Defensor Fidei, Defender of the Faith, a title that has been proudly displayed by successive monarchs. The Pope understandably revoked the title in 1530 yet it was restored by Parliament to the king in 1544, but this time with application to the Church of England. After 1530, despite Henry's doctrinal orthodoxy, moves were made to curb the power of the church and already by 1532, some religious institutions were becoming nervous. The prior of the Crutched (Crossed) Friars in London asserted that the king was determined to put down some religious houses and sneered that he should be called "Destructor Fidei" instead of "Defensor Fidei." It was Wriothesley who recorded this intelligence.[28]

Wriothesley's hand can also be discovered in a document he wrote for Henry proposing that the income of bishops should be limited and the surplus handed over to the crown. This was written in October 1534.[29] At the time this was little more than a 'bright idea' by an ambitious young man. The prospect of implementation against uproar from powerful bishops was practically nil. However, once attention turned to the monasteries, the crown was on firmer ground.

Church reform was overdue in the 1530s. Religious houses had increased in number and in wealth during the middle ages without contributing much to the economy. The core of the ancient city of Winchester, for example, was occupied by three large monasteries, four friaries and a hospital, with a second large hospital on the outskirts. Once free of Rome, a movement to dissolve monasteries became very strong.

Closing religious houses was not new in the 1530s. Many had been closed in the 15th century or had their income diverted to other purposes. In the 14th and 15th centuries, the so-called "Alien Houses", those which belonged to a parent house in Normandy, frequently had their funds sequestered during times of war with France. In the 15th century some houses were closed and their lands granted to another house or hospital, or, increasingly, in the 15th century, their assets were used to found colleges at Oxford, Cambridge or Eton. Cardinal Wolsey continued this practice when he closed down several small religious houses in 1524 in order to create his massive college at Oxford, now known as Christ Church College. The lack of outcry at the time may have emboldened those implementing the greater dissolution of the 1530s.

Thomas Cromwell is usually seen as the architect and prime mover in the General Dissolution of the 1530s, and to some extent there is truth in that view. But his initial intention was to reform houses rather than close them down. Commissioners were sent out in 1535 to assess and value all religious houses, and they compiled what is known as the *Valor Ecclesiasticus*. Some houses were completely corrupt, some were inefficient and most could benefit from reform, although it should be added that many houses had conducted themselves in a blameless and responsible fashion - Titchfield for one. One of the reports was quite comic. Richard Layton, one of the commissioners, tried to get access to the abbot's lodging at Langden in Kent. He banged on the door repeatedly but could get no response other than a dog barking. He broke in and found the abbot busy servicing his 'whore'. The woman tried to escape through a passageway but was intercepted. She was imprisoned for 8 days. The abbot was taken to Canterbury for judgement by his churchmen but it is not known what punishment, if any, was administered. Such stories were not new. The nunnery at Romsey was in trouble in 1286 because one of the chaplains was pimping for some of the nuns, and almost two centuries later, in 1472, there were concern that some of the nuns were able to slip out to frequent taverns and participate in lewd behaviour. Many houses were well-regulated, but the publication of sensational stories swayed public opinion. By 1535 there was widespread belief that the religious houses had strayed very far from the monastic rule that had been set several centuries earlier. The commissioners were motivated to expose instances of corruption and immorality, but most of the instances they discovered came as no surprise to the general population.

While many houses were free from corruption, there was general agreement that the smaller monasteries should be suppressed and the proposed bill had an easy passage through Parliament. The Act of Suppression received royal assent on 14 April 1536. A Court of Augmentation was set up to handle the process and administer the acquisition of properties. Only houses with an income of less than £200 a year were to be suppressed. The work proceeded immediately, and, for the most part, the process was benign. Legal form was observed and the monks were suitably compensated with alternative livings, transfer to larger houses, or pensions. Some of the higher placed individuals did very well out of it.

1536 was a tipping point. England was in the throes of one of its periodic revolutions and this one, however accidentally it came about, went to the cultural and spiritual core of most English people. For good or ill, the Christian church, governed by the vicar of Christ in Rome, had been central to the lives of the English for almost 1,000 years and it was difficult to imagine alternatives. Lutheranism had certainly captured the minds of forward-thinking intellectuals, but the majority of the population were probably content with the status quo. Henry's new church was in urgent need of definition. What constituted true faith and what were the limits of tolerance?

Ten Articles developed by Cranmer and promoted by Cromwell and others were devised to establish "Christian quietness and unity among us." Henry found them too extreme for his own taste and watered them down to a much more conservative document, and they were published in 1536. On the whole they re-affirmed the principal sacraments and quietly introduced Lutheran thinking. For example, the veneration of saints and various ceremonies were not condemned but acknowledged, provided that they did not distract from God's monopoly on Grace. The concept of Purgatory, which enabled the Pope to intervene to ensure swift admission to heaven was ditched, although, if people wished to pray for the dead, this practice was not condemned.

Such changes, however much they tried to steer a middle course, would inevitably attract opposition. Rumours of increased taxation and confiscation of property got people excited. A sermon preached at Louth in Lincolnshire on 1 October 1536 prompted riots in the town, which spread to Caistor and Horncastle. The mob killed the bishop of Lincoln's chancellor and one of Cromwell's agents. The Duke of Suffolk was sent in with a force and the uprising was quickly suppressed. Further north, Robert Aske, from the East Riding of Yorkshire had been in Lincolnshire at the time of the uprising and on 4 October initiated his own rebellion, which he styled the 'Pilgrimage of Grace'. His success was spontaneous and within a few days had attracted a large force, estimated between 20,000 and 40,000. York quickly surrendered, as did Pontefract a few days later. Soon, virtually the whole of England north of the Trent and Ribble. stood in armed opposition to the government. The situation was now very dangerous.

The Duke of Norfolk was despatched with a force of about 8,000, and it was soon evident that he was outnumbered. He met with the rebel leaders, Aske, Lord Darcy and Sir Robert Constable. Articles were drawn up and agreed to on 2 December. A few days later, with assurances of the king's pardon, and that all of their demands would be put before Parliament, the great rebel hosts dispersed. The steam from the rebellion had been released.

On December 15 the king sent a message to Robert Aske that he would like to meet him. Aske, having been given assurances that he was safe, agreed and was greeted by Henry in a most friendly manner and put it to him that he could help suppress the holdout rebels. Aske, now charmed by the king, assented, and a small force raised by the Duke of Norfolk managed to completely squash the uprising. The Reformation could have ended, or at least have been set back by several years, had the Pilgrimage of Grace been successful. The force raised in the north in support of the uprising was huge and far outnumbered the king's hastily assembled army. But Aske and the other leaders of the rebellion hesitated and chose to believe Henry's offer of conciliation, and the moment passed.

Whether or not Henry ever intended to honour the pardons is arguable, but a few weeks later Henry was given the excuse he needed to squash any challenge to his authority. In January a smaller uprising by die-hards in Carlisle, Scarborough and Hull gave Henry the excuse he needed to move in with a punitive force. By March the rebellion had been crushed and by May and June, the leaders, including Aske, Darcy and Constable, had been legally condemned to death. Overall the number of casualties from this uprising was very low. Few men died in actual fighting and the large majority of deaths, by legal execution, amounted to about 130.

The uprisings were a threat to government but their effect was counterproductive. In the end the Pilgrimage of Grace was not a great setback and the monastic dissolution was highly successful from a government perspective. Henry's ruthless suppression of disagreement terrified enough people that public outcry was minimal and in the majority of cases the abbots and priors were bought off with rewarding positions or pensions. Lower down the scale the majority of monks were placed as parish priests or provided with pensions. The Abbot of Beaulieu was certainly happy to settle. "Thank God," he is reported to have said, I am rid of my lewd monks."[30] There were a few hold-outs. The abbots of Reading, Colchester and Gloucester refused to cooperate and paid the penalty of execution. The treasury was enormously enriched during the process.

Henry now saw the monasteries as the enemy and it became easier for the reformers to persuade themselves that a complete end to monasticism was the best solution. Early takeovers were deliberately punitive. The priory at Lewes was razed to the ground. Seventeen hands, three carpenters, two plumbers and "the one that keeps the furnace" were brought down from London. The lead from the roof was melted down, the vaults destroyed and the pillars and walls demolished. Much of the stone, timber and lead was sold. No respect was given to the libraries of manuscript rolls and books. This was paper, a commodity, and as such was used to scour candlesticks or clean shoes. Unused paper was nailed up in latrines so that people could wipe their bottoms. Nothing survived to suggest that Lewes ever had a priory. Titchfield Abbey also had a very fine library which disappeared without trace, One wonders if the monks sold the books or whether these books met a similar fate to those in Lewes.

The richer establishments were asset-stripped. The shrine of St Thomas Becket in Canterbury was probably the richest in Europe and Erasmus had earlier written that 'every part glistened, shone and sparkled with rare and very large jewels, some of them exceeding the size of a goose's egg.'[31] The Royal treasury was not ndisappointed; it took 26 wagons to transport this haul to safe-keeping in London.

The larger houses were dissolved in 1538 and 1539 and then attention focussed on the friaries. An act of 1539, which was applied retrospectively, legalised voluntary surrender and assured tenants of their rights. By 1540 the process was complete. Minsters where there was a bishop were translated into cathedrals. At Winchester, for example, the priory of St Swithun became Winchester Cathedral and the prior became its first Dean. The other monasteries and friaries, of which the city of Winchester had many, were suppressed. Wriothesley acquired Hyde Abbey in north Winchester and quickly demolished most of the buildings to sell off the materials. Some former monasteries, such as those at Romsey and Twynham, were acquired by the surrounding town as a parish church. Many were snapped up by the well-to-do to create splendid country houses. Sir Edwin Sandys transformed Mottisfont into a huge country mansion and Sir William Paulet did the same at Netley. Wriothesley himself converted Titchfield into his country seat. Beaulieu, possibly too far from London to be a prospect for development, was largely left as a hunting lodge. Quarr Abbey, on the Isle of Wight, was also dismantled and much of the stone was used to build defensive blockhouses at Cowes.

The land associated with many of these monasteries was the most worthwhile asset. Hyde Abbey held many manors in north and central Hampshire and Titchfield held many associated manors in the Meon Valley. All of these became part of Wriothesley's land portfolio and the basis for his family's future wealth.

Part of the rationale for dissolving monasteries was a growing impatience with various cults that were promoted over the use of relics. Fragments of the true cross, often just splinters of wood, were common, as were glass vials of the blood of Christ. Locks of hair, bones, fragments of cloth were all displayed with varying claims about their miraculous powers. Better education and the new humanism, in which Wriothesley himself had been schooled his early days, led people to question the value of some of these dishonest practices, and often the first acts of the men who took over the monasteries was to destroy the relics.

Wriothesley was nothing if not hard-headed when it came to effecting the new policy. He personally supervised the confiscation of the treasures of the shrine of St Thomas Becket at Canterbury and at St Swithun's at Winchester. The former was the most politically sensitive and probably needed a senior figure, such as Wriothesley had now become, to ensure that Crown wishes were put into effect. At no time, however, was Wriothesley freelancing. He was under direct instructions from Henry to confiscate all the treasures of Beckett's shrine and to publicly burn his bones. Henry and his government wanted to eliminate any ambiguity; no part of the Church of England was to be used as a shrine to undermine Henry's authority. Thomas Beckett in any case was a saint who challenged the authority of the king, just as had the recently executed Thomas More, a future saint of the Roman Catholic church.

It was Wriothesley's task to carry out some of the dirty work of the Reformation. One such, for which he was much criticised, was to dismantle the shrine of St Swithun's at Winchester. As with most controversial acts, there is more than one side to the story. Much of the so-called treasure was, as it turned out, fake. The monks and priests of the middle ages were not above making a counterfeit of a golden object and selling off the gold and several instances of fakery emerged as the monastery's were systematically decommissioned.

They discovered less actual treasure than they might have expected in the ancient minster. This would not sway those who believed that the tomb and all its relics were holy objects and that the dismantling was a violation of sacred space.

Thomas Wriothesley knew this and planned his coup carefully; his men arrived at three o clock in the morning when most of Winchester's population were still sleeping. He arranged for the Mayor and eight aldermen to be present as witnesses together with representatives of the priory and convent. Apart from the counterfeit gold and precious stones they did salvage silver worth 2,000 marks, a cross of emeralds, two gold chalices, a gold cross and something called the Jerusalem cross. They also salvaged the stonework from the altar. In his report he reckoned that this work would take two days. He then moved on to Hyde Abbey, where he had secured the lease for himself and proceeded to dismantle the entire abbey. During this process, or possibly later, the bones of

King Alfred, which had been re-interred there after being moved from the old minster, were lost.[32] This quote from his report illustrates the attitude of some toward the edifice of medieval religion:

> Which done we intend both at Hyde and Saint Mary's to sweep away all the rotten bones that be called relics: which we may not omit lest it should be thought we came more for the treasure than for the avoiding of the abomination of idolatry.[33]

Similar action was taken at Chichester in December 1538 when the bones of St Richard, a former bishop, were disposed of.

Most medieval relics - vials of the blood of christ, bones, splinters of the true cross, were completely, and to us self-evidently, fake, but to true believers (and there were many in the middle ages) everything was plausible. Boxley Abbey in Kent was known for a cross with the head and body of Christ carved on it. Those who prayed in front of the cross could see the eyes move and sometimes the body trembled, as if in response to the prayer. The intricate mechanical movement behind this apparent miracle was of course exposed. The blood of Christ held at Hailes Abbey was discovered to be a mixture on honey and saffron. The dissolution ran a steam-roller over all relics.

The church had itself to blame. It had grown too powerful, too rich and too corrupt. There had been stirrings against the church in the 14th century but by the time of Henry VIII there was no doubt in the minds of many that the church needed to be stripped down. The monasteries, intended as places for the quiet contemplation and worship of God had become venal institutions with little moral hinterland. Henry and his ministers were motivated by money and power, but there were intellectual underpinnings to the exercise.

The credit for the efficient stage management of the dissolution must lie with Thomas Cromwell, but in turn, he was equally dependent on the efficient implementation of the policy by his lieutenants, like Thomas Wriothelsey. There is no doubt that once given a task his masters could depend on Thomas Wriothesley to perform zealously and to perfection.

That is one side of Wriothesley, but in the same period we see other aspects. He is clearly seen as an influential figure in Cromwell's office and he received letters from many who looked to him to help them acquire new property. The Earl of Northumberland wrote to him to ask him to arrange a meeting with Cromwell. The Earl of Rutland also wrote a letter expressing his interest in Croxton Abbey. In June 1536, John Husee, chief agent for Viscount Lisle was angling to get Quarr Abbey and Netley Abbey for his master. He was becoming frustrated.

> I wrote your lordship what answer Mr. Secretary made me therein: but since that time, whether it were by the means of Mr. Wriothesley or some other, he never made me good countenance nor would give scant ear to what I would open or say unto him in that or in your own suit to the king.[34]

Arthur Plantagenet, Lord Lisle, was an illegitimate son of Edward IV, and his mother was Elizabeth Lucy, who came from a Hampshire family. His date of birth is unknown and is estimated at any date between 1461 and 1475. He was lucky that he was not a contender for the crown and he was able to live a long and prosperous life. He had a middling career at court and in 1533 was appointed Constable of Calais, a position he seems not to have been up to. In 1540 he was arrested on a charge of plotting to betray the Calais garrison to the French. He was most likely innocent, but he spent the last two years of his life in the Tower of London, dying of a heart attack on being given the news that he was about to be released. His agent, John Husee, was the son of a Southampton wine merchant.

One benefit to history was that all of his correspondence was confiscated by the state in an effort to prove his complicity in the Calais plot and these letters therefore became part of the state collection of papers.

In December 1536 Sir John Tregonwell wrote to ask for assistance in obtaining the nunnery of St Giles in Hertfordshire. Husee again wrote to Lord Lisle in February 1537 advising his patron to "make a friend of him; the man standeth in a place where he may please or displease."[35] It sounds as if Hussee (and Lord Lisle) were disappointed because 18 months later he was writing that Wriothesley's promises were about as dependable as holy water - in other words worthless.

In the end Quarr Abbey was one of the properties that Wriothesley himself picked up and Netley Abbey went to Sir William Paulet, another of Cromwell's commissioners. Viscount Lisle had strong Hampshire interests and would have dearly loved to expand hus estates in that county, but the rising men like Wriothesley had the inside track. Outsiders, even one as well-connected as Viscount Lisle, stood little chance.

We also have an insight into Wriothesley's diplomatic skill and powers of persuasion. Edward Bacheler of St John's College Cambridge, presumably a fellow of that college, wrote to him:

> "I am so much bound to you who pulled me out of the darkness of the old religion and brought me to the light … and a house which continues to set forth the unfeigned verity of Christ's gospel."[36]

Wriothesley was clearly successful in persuading Edward Bacheler that his best interest lay in adapting to the tenor of the times, a story I suspect that was often repeated. Despite the bad press that presented the monastic dissolution as an act of unparalleled vandalism, the large majority received adequate (and sometimes generous) pensions or other positions within the church. One could argue that the monasteries and their assets were not sold at a fair price. Estimates of their worth were often made by the same people who were the principal buyers and they were unable to resist the temptation to place a value on the asset that was under its market price.

One group who were seriously disadvantaged were the nuns, and this was entirely due to the position of women in Tudor England. A woman had limited life choices: she could marry or not. If unmarried she could stay at home and look after her parents or she could move to a nunnery. Unlike their male counterparts at the dissolution there were no positions for women in the church. The abbesses and probably some of the senior nuns received pensions, and those from well-to-do families could at least go home, but the general run of the mill nuns may have been left stranded. There appears to be no record of complaint, which may reflect contemporary disinterest in the position of women in society. Some may have found work in hostelries or as servants in large houses. Marriage may have been an option for younger nuns, but only if they renounced their vows of chastity.

Thomas Wriothesley emerges from this revolution as a large landowner. A lot of the money he had been collecting in secure chests at his London home was carried to the Treasury in payment for these newly acquired monastic lands. The land was the real value and future rents would become the source of the wealth of the earls of Southampton. His insider status no doubt allowed him to get what he wanted at a knock-down price, and it is likely that he recovered his investment within a few years. The inflationary years of the reign of Edward VI further enhanced the value of his estate.

In 1539 Wriothesley was nominated by the king (meaning he was chosen by Cromwell) as one of the MPs for Hampshire. Cromwell intended to have his own men in Parliament to support his proposals. In this instance he was bitterly opposed by Stephen Gardiner, at one time Wriothesley's patron, who wanted his own men in Parliament. Cromwell prevailed in this instance but it did open up a division between Wriothesley and Gardiner who was becoming increasingly conservative. It is probable that Wriothesley was more in sympathy with Gardiner's world view than with Cromwell's; however, Cromwell was in the ascendent in 1539 and Gardiner was complaining from the fringe. Wriothesley knew how to keep out of trouble.

He was becoming a man of rising power and importance, particularly in Hampshire. He became justice of the peace in 1537 and in November 1538 was made sheriff for the county. In January 1539 he was appointed to the Commission of the Peace in Hampshire.

The fact that Wriothesley and Gardiner were old friends and were both of the same mind on religious matters, meant that their spat was over by the spring of 1539. Wriothesley was becoming increasingly important in Hampshire life through his property acquisition and Gardiner must have been ready to acknowledge that he was no longer the only man with Hampshire interests.

But the Parliament of 1539 affirmed Henry's position and stopped the reform movement dead in its tracks. Henry was becoming concerned that the publication of the Bible in English was not bringing about harmony and instead led to dispute and disunity. Above all, Henry wanted no dissension and was determined to enforce unity. He established a committee of four conservative bishops and four reforming bishops, with Thomas Cromwell as vice-regent in the chair. They were, understandably, unable to reach any conclusions. Henry intervened. He drew up six questions to which the only answer was agreement. On his behalf, the conservative Duke of Norfolk presented the questions to Parliament. Nobody was foolhardy enough to object and the Act of the Six Articles was duly passed. Archbishop Cranmer became fearful since priestly celibacy was now affirmed as central to faith in the Church of England, and sent his wife and children into exile. Radical reforming bishops such as Hugh Latimer at Worcester and Nicholas Shaxton at

Salisbury were forced to resign.

Cromwell himself had embraced Lutheranism intellectually and was in full sympathy with the reformers. Could his time be over?

5

SURVIVING CROMWELL

These laws I made myself alone to please
to give me power more freely to my will,
even to my equals, hurtful sundry ways
(Forced to things that most do say were ill)
upon me now as violently seize
by whom I lastly perished for my skill.

– Michael Drayton, History of the Life and Death of Lord Cromwell

The downfall of Thomas Cromwell in 1540 was very swift, and quite arbitrary. He must have wondered himself where he went wrong. Some have speculated that the marriage to Anne of Cleves, which he promoted, was the trigger, but although the arrival of Anne in England and Cromwell's fall from grace was a mere six months, it is difficult to tie the two together. She was a daughter of John, Duke of Cleves, a group of states in what is now the North Rhine-Westphalia region of Germany. Anne was born circa 1515 in Dusseldorf. The proposed union had a diplomatic purpose as it brought a number of German states into an alliance with the English against France, and considerable care went into the appraisal of Anne as a suitable consort for Henry. Thomas Cromwell was not the only councillor who promoted the union with Cleves.

Several diplomats gave her a favourable report and Hans Holbein was sent over to paint her portrait. The result we can see today and there is no reason to take exception. Some later commentators have imagined that Holbein made her look pretty in the portrait when in fact she was rather plain. One argument is that he painted he in full frontal mode to de-emphasise her lack of character. It must be said that it is doubtful that Holbein (a highly skilled and accurate painter) would dare to perpetrate such a deception unless he was sure of the backing of powerful figures. The written accounts too describe her as very presentable, demure and having all the qualities to be queen. The one quality she lacked was that she was not sexually attractive to Henry. The demure and bland expression in the Holbein portrait may, after all, reflect the fact that little personal liveliness lay behind it.

On New Years Day 1540, Henry left Greenwich to meet his bride to be at Rochester. Nothing seemed untoward at the time but when Cromwell asked the king how he found his prospective wife, he was astonished at the response. "She is nothing so fair as she has been reported."[37] Henry certainly discussed with his councillors ways of avoiding the marriage but reluctantly went ahead with it anyway. From later reports it is understood that he made no serious attempt to consummate the marriage.

For a time the issue died and everyone returned to normal business. Cromwell was elevated to the earldom of Essex in April, which surely would not have happened if he had been out of favour with the king. What really disrupted the equilibrium was that the youthful and vibrant Catherine Howard was intentionally dangled before the king. Norfolk and others had seen their opportunity. If (and they did succeed) they could tempt the king to take the bait and divorce Anne, then the marriage to Catherine would restore the Howards to the centre of power. It would also enable them to proceed against Cromwell and the reformers and return the church to the old faith.

There was no deficiency in Cromwell's statesmanship; he was acting in the best interests of the state and in fashioning this marriage he was certainly doing something which would strengthen England's hand in European alliances. Henry was by now becoming increasingly autocratic and identified his personal wishes with statecraft. He began to feel resentful that he had been engineered into this marriage. He blamed Cromwell to an extent, but were it not that Cromwell's enemies, Norfolk and Gardiner, were steering Henry towards an alternative, the matter might have passed.

On 15 April 1540 Henry created the earldom of Essex for Thomas Cromwell and made him Lord Chamberlain. This left an opening for the king's Principal Secretary, a position Cromwell had formally held since 1534. Henry, rather quixotically, appointed two men in his place,

Ralph Sadler and Thomas Wriothesley. Both men were knighted. No formal division of responsibilities is evident from the papers prepared by the two men, so it seems likely that work was undertaken as it came by whomever was free. Both men were highly experienced administrators and it is doubtful that the office suffered at all from these new appointments.

By May Wriothesley was appointed one of the king's secretaries, certainly an indication that some of Cromwell's power was slipping away. Cromwell saw the looming danger and remarked to Wriothesley that "the king liketh not the queen."[38] but at the same time appeared paralysed by inaction over the matter. Had he been assiduous in arranging a divorce he might well have kept his head, as he was well aware that Norfolk was engineering a union with his niece Catherine. He also understood that once Norfolk was back into power his own neck might be on the block. He may have felt he could trust to the mercy of the king, who had, when all said and done, been kind to Wolsey in his downfall. But the Henry of 1540 was not the Henry of 1530. Some historians have speculated that a bad fall while riding in 1536 led to a personality change that caused him to be more arbitrary and vicious than he had been in his youth and middle years.

Cromwell was arrested on June 10th in the Council chamber. Norfolk led the party but Cromwell's former associates, FitzWilliam, Paget and Wriothesley were also involved in the reduction of their former master. Paget and Wriothesley were assigned to interrogate Cromwell, which they did without showing any deference to their former patron. Wriothesley wrote a letter on behalf of the council to Sir John Wallop informing him of Cromwell's treasons:

> So it is that the lord privy seal ... hathe not only...wroughte clene contrary to this his Graces most godly entent...for whiche apparent and detestable treasons...he is commytted to the Tower of London"[39]

The swiftness in Wriothesley's action in turning his personal craft into the prevailing wind shows us a man who was able to act without sentimentality. He was not the only one to turn on Cromwell but he was assiduous in prosecuting the demands of the king. Much of the deposition prepared by Wriothesley for Cromwell's trial was, to put no fine point on it, unhelpful to Cromwell and to our eyes today was designed to prove his treason. He also ignored Thomas Cromwell's requests to explain himself to the king and to all intents abandoned the drowning man.

The line to be taken was that Henry was misled into the marriage with Anne of Cleves and it was all Cromwell's doing. Ambassadors on the spot sent glowing reports about Anne's character and personality and Cromwell had kept Henry informed every step along the way, but all was ignored in favour of this new interpretation. It has to be said that Wriothesley himself had been very much involved in the policy that led to the marriage but was clearly anxious to distance himself from it. Wriothesley's hand is all over these documents. He was also sent, along with Earl of Suffolk and William Fitzwilliam (at the time Earl of Southampton), to meet with the queen herself and persuade her to agree to the divorce. Anne showed herself to be politically astute. In return for a house in Lewes, a household staff and an annual income of £4,000 she agreed to the divorce and the adoption of a quiet life out of sight and out of mind. She died in 1557.

There is not much to admire about Wriothesley's behaviour at this point, and we are not revisiting this alone from the viewpoint of 21st century sensibilities. His behaviour attracted comment in his day:

> "And throw his benefactor to the wolves at a nod from the king"[40]

This is a poem about Bishop Gardiner, anonymously written and presented as a first person monologue by the Bishop himself.

> "The next way I thought was to find one out
> That Cromwell trusted and of his counsell here;
> As God would have it such one I found
> My secret friend and old acquaintance.[41]

Might the implied figure here be Wriothesley himself? Knowing the long-established association between Gardiner and Wriothesley and that they had become reconciled after the spat about the Parliament of 1539 it is not unreasonable to see Wriothesley acting as Gardiner's spy.

And Wriothesley himself is on record as an advocate of ruthless behaviour:

> "Spare no man when the tyme shall com, but be thyne own ffrend and thyne own executor.[42]

Self preservation is a strong instinct and no man can seriously be blamed for taking that option. Sir Thomas More could elect martyrdom on a point of principle but there was no point of principle here. Thomas Cromwell had lost the favour of a king who wanted rid of him. Wriothesley, as a man closely associated with Cromwell for a decade, was at risk, and in the aftermath some of Cromwell's former associates were indeed sent to the tower. Wriothesley appears to have been successful in demonstrating his loyalty (as well as his worth as an administrator) to the king. There was no questioning his competence and value to the monarchy.

Wriothesley at no time sprang to the defence of his former master and benefactor. This does not strike us at this distance in time as admirable. Cromwell himself was not afraid of defending and supporting Wolsey after his fall from grace, but Cromwell was a different man and in many ways a greater man. The saying 'discretion is the better part of valour' is particularly appropriate for occasions such as these. Nothing was to be gained from objecting to a king who had moved into a tyrannical phase of his rule and it was sensible to bring self-preservation to the forefront of thinking. Wriothesley was not the only one; all Cromwell's former colleagues and protégés kept their heads below the parapet.

The divorce proceeded in July 1540.

A few months later both Sadler and Wriothesley, as former protégés of the great man, found themselves exposed, and indeed, in January 1541, both men found themselves in the Tower. Sadler may have been more at risk as he had been in Cromwell's household since chidhood. The French ambassador, Marillac, wrote to King Francis on 25 January to report that 'chief Secretary Wriothesley, who rose by Cromwell's means, is on the verge of descending more quickly than he came upon, for he has already been examined upon some ticklish articles.'[43] We do not know what the accusations were nor the names of the accusers. Sir Thomas Wriothesley at any rate had friends amongst some in the anti-Cromwell faction, so although this must have been a worrying time, the incarceration was short-lived and both men were released to resume their duties. He was certainly performing his secretarial duties in February and in January he was appointed Constable of the castle at Southampton. Neither action by the king suggests that he was in the tower for long or had lost royal favour. Sadler was equally fortunate. Both men were highly competent administrators and essential for the proper functioning of the state; this reality probably outweighed any minor jealousies thatr might have seen them removed from office.

The role of Principal Secretary changed after Sadler and Wriothesley assumed their roles. Thomas Cromwell had made the office supremely powerful during his decade. There was almost no aspect of government that did not pass through the office, but his successors lacked that power and in that strange English way a new organisation emerged to complement and reinforce the work of the office. It was called the Privy Council and it first met in August 1540.

Some sort of King's Council had always been part of English government from the time of the Saxon *Witanagemot*. Later, the 13th century Parliament had emerged as a force in national decision-making. Henry VIII was not the only English monarch with autocratic tendencies and wherever possible preferred to circumvent Parliament, and while he had a man with the political and administrative skills of Thomas Cromwell, he could depend on the office of Principal Secretary to get things done. Neither Sir Ralph Sadler nor Sir Thomas Wriothesley could rise to the political effectiveness of Thomas Cromwell and the Privy Council emerged as a way of endorsing some of Henry's policies without resorting to Parliament.

It is difficult to draw modern parallels because the size and scope of government in Tudor times was tiny by comparison with government today, but the Principal Secretary has some affinity with a modern head of the Civil Service, with the Privy Council acting as a cabinet of ministers. The Principal Secretary emerged as the chief administrative officer of the crown, assisted by four clerks of the signet and various junior secretaries to help in the drafting of documents.

Before too much time passed Wriothesley emerged as the pre-eminent secretary who was rarely not in attendance on the king. Sadler, on the other hand, was often sent on ambassadorial missions, and after 1541 was almost permanently based in Edinburgh to deal with Scottish matters. Wriothesley spent his time in meetings with the king and the Privy Council and preparing letters from the king. He typically attended over 200 such meetings a year. He had unique access to the king and often quite influential people would run by an idea or proposal with Wriothesley before making commitment.

Henry now entered the final autocratic phase of his reign. Up to this point he had depended heavily on the advice of powerful counsellors like Wolsey and Cromwell but now he was his own man. No matter what Wriothesley or any of his colleagues thought, Henry's word was always going to be final, and their sensitivity to this reality often coloured or tempered the advice that was put forward.

Within those limits Wriothesley emerged as the most influential figure. The ambassador to Charles V, Holy Roman Emperor, Eustace Chapuys, met often with Wriothesley and reported to the emperor that 'secretary Vristley, as I have often written, is the man who enjoys most credit with the king and almost governs everything here.'[44] And with that influence went unsolicited rewards. 'A gracious present to secretary Virustley would not be amiss. I fancy that a gift of that kind would be well employed, and would be beneficial for the issue of the affair at hand and the emperor's service.'[45] Both the French and Imperial ambassadors include Wriothesley in their correspondence and because these documents have been preserved we have an insight into some of his work. We can assume with some confidence that on the domestic front he was handling requests on a daily basis; but those baronial records and correspondence do not survive.

Sir Thomas Wriothesley, as we have seen, was instrumental in facilitating Henry's divorce from Anne of Cleves. He had already proved his skill in delicate negotiations some years earlier when he persuaded the intractable Princess Mary to accept the Act of Supremacy. This job may have been easier and was competently done. Nobody except for Cromwell lost their head and one must assume the Wriothesley was eloquent in persuading Anne that she could live a comfortable and peaceful life in the country, far from the intrigues of court. Anne was in effect pensioned off and Henry was free to pursue his infatuation with the very young and rather foolish Catherine Howard. Once this wayward girl got into trouble, Wriothesley was called upon once again to deal with the crisis. He had already proved his skill in delicate negotiations in dealing with the intractable Princess Mary, some years earlier. The consequences for Catherine and the Howard family were less happy.

The witless Catherine had been planted by her cynical and ambitious uncle, the Duke of Norfolk, in Queen Anne's household to attract the kings attention and bring Norfolk back to the centre of power. The plan worked. Henry was somewhat disaffected by the choice of his fourth queen and his roving eye fell upon Catherine as the plotters had intended. This gave him the incentive to rid himself of Anne and, as a bonus for Norfolk and Gardiner, they eliminated Cromwell and stemmed the trend towards Protestantism. Henry married Catherine Howard on the 29th July 1540, only 19 days after the marriage with Anne of Cleves was annulled and the very day that Cromwell lost his head. For Norfolk and Gardiner the symbolism was intentional.

The eventual flaw in the plan lay in Catherine's personality. She was a full-blooded girl who did not have an unblemished past. This of course was kept secret prior to the marriage and might have remained so if she had been able to play the part she had been schooled for. Unfortunately, because her sexual needs were not being fulfilled in the marital bed with the ageing king she looked elsewhere among some of the young men of the court, certainly while Henry was away on his progress to York in June 1541, and she became less discreet too on other occasions. With the connivance of her ladies-in-waiting she arranged to meet a gentleman called Thomas Culpepper at secret venues. There were other men. Henry Manox, her keyboard instructor was heard to boast that he had taken her maidenhead, and a man called Francis Dereham, who had previously been intimate with her, was appointed as her private secretary.

This could not remain secret for long. John Lascelles, one of Howard's enemies, went to Cranmer with stories of the queen's indiscretions. Cranmer investigated and felt he had to report to the king.

Naturally enough Henry's first reaction was to doubt the evidence. He insisted that Cranmer investigate fully before laying the evidence before him. Manox and Dereham were interrogated and admitted to their carnal knowledge of the queen. At first Henry was relieved that there was yet no evidence that she had transgressed after marriage, but after her ladies were questioned the Culpepper affair was exposed. There was too much to ignore.

Wriothesley took charge of the investigation at this point (November 1541) and set about examining all the witnesses. The case was made very quickly - and there was a lot of evidence - and by 10 November the case against the queen was complete.

On 13 November Wriothesley went to Hampton Court to lay the charges before the queen and at the same time dismissed her household. In December he questioned the Duchess of Norfolk. At the same time he seized a considerable sum of money (500 marks and £1,000 in silver plate) on behalf of the crown.

Henry fell into a great rage at a secret meeting of the council in

December and swore that he would kill his wife himself. In time he calmed down and wept. There were no winners. Henry had been made to look a fool, The Duke of Norfolk lost power and influence. Dereham was subjected to the full brutal treatment of drawing, hanging and quartering. Culpepper, as a gentleman, was allowed execution by beheading. Lady Rochford, who had connived at Catherine's adultery, also lost her head. Maxon, because his affair pre-dated the marriage escaped punishment, and the poor unfortunate girl who had been used as a political pawn had her short life terminated.

Wriothesley prepared all the documents that proved her misbehaviour and treason and Catherine was sent for execution on 13 February 1542. Many of the Howard family had their possessions sequestered, although in most cases their property was later returned. The Duke and Duchess of Norfolk, who were instrumental in setting up this girl for her eventual fall, were pardoned by the king in August 1542, although Norfolk was never to come to the centre of power again. In fact he was once more under suspicion when his son the Earl of Surrey was involved in a plot against Henry. Surrey lost his life and the Duke was imprisoned in the tower. It is likely that he would also have been executed but for Henry VIII dying in January 1547.

On April 21st 1544 Sir Thomas Audley, seriously ill and near death, resigned as Lord Chancellor. He was a competent lawyer, and, more pertinent in the perilous world of Henrician court politics, was not politically ambitious. He was therefore able to occupy the position he took upon the execution of Sir Thomas More in 1531 and hold it. The real political power in those years lay with Thomas Cromwell who as Principal Secretary and Lord Privy Seal was the real heir to Cardinal Wolsey. Henry looked around for a replacement and his eye alighted on Sir Thomas Wriothesley.

The post of Lord Chancellor had traditionally been filled by senior churchmen, but in Tudor times men with legal training, such as Sir Thomas More and Sir Thomas Audley, had assumed the role. As far as we know, Sir Thomas Wriothesley had no training in legal matters, although he may well have picked up sufficient knowledge through his years at court. In this respect he was an odd choice; however, he was sufficiently trusted by Henry and sufficiently proven as a court official to be given the role. A few days later he was made Baron Wriothesley of Titchfield. He was now at the pinnacle of his court career. A year later on 23 April 1545 he was made a Knight of the Garter.

Lord Titchfield became only the third layman to hold the office. His predecessors, More and Audley were both respected lawyers and, as noted, brought their legal inclinations to the position, although neither enjoyed the power and prestige than the last churchman to hold the office, Cardinal Wolsey. More's celebrated, but short career, is well known, but his successor, Audley, carefully survived for 13 years without getting himself embroiled in controversy. He was a very rich man when he died shortly after retirement.

Wriothesley's instincts were to concentrate on the financial and administrative aspects of the Chancellorship rather than the legal, however, these legal commitments were not negligible. The two previous incumbents had, over 15 years, made the Chancery court pre-eminent in dealing with land disputes. The Lord Chancellor was also president of the Court of the Star Chamber.

The politics of the 1540s, in the last years of Henry VIII, now an old king, had changed from the 1530s. Whereas the evangelicals and the conservatives could find common cause in the need to reform the old medieval church, the conservatives no longer wished to take those reforms any further. Up to this point Wriothesley had been able to advance his career in a more or less neutral position, able to work alongside Lutherans and staunch Catholics alike. Now, men like John Howard, the Duke of Norfolk, Stephen Gardiner, bishop of Winchester and Edmund Bonner, bishop of London, felt that the reforms had gone far enough, perhaps too far. They were opposed to any further change and, ideally, would like to have been able to turn the clock back. Wriothesley was certainly in sympathy with this group.

Despite his revolutionary act in making himself the head of the Church in England, the old king had little sympathy with Lutheranism and was of a similar mindset to the conservatives. In this respect Baron Titchfield was perfectly in tune with his master. However, Henry VIII was nearing the end of his life, and the reformers had their eye on the succession. Everyone had to tread very carefully; there were aspects of Henry's personality in these later years which were irrational and erratic. Gardiner, for example, thought he was safe in investigating the beliefs of members of the privy chamber in July 1543. He proceeded with an indictment against Anthony Denny, an evangelical certainly, but also a favourite of Henry. Henry erupted in a rage and it was

Gardiner who found himself under a cloud. Further inquiries in this year, of which Wriothesley may have been a part, looked into the beliefs of Thomas Cranmer, archbishop of Canterbury. Henry, however, was a great admirer of Cranmer, even though he did not share the reformer's beliefs, and he scotched the enquiry by putting the archbishop in charge of it.

Stephen Gardiner was now treading on thin ice. Gardiner's enemies at court, Hertford, Dudley and Paget, were themselves examining the dogma of the conservatives, possibly with Henry's approval, in parallel with Gardiner's examination of them for heresy. The reformers succeeded in passing an Act in 1544 to restrict 'secret and untrue accusations' made against people who might be charged under the Act of Six Articles.[46]

6

THE CONSERVATIVE RESISTANCE

Secretary Vristley, who as I have often written, is the man who enjoys most credit with the king and almost governs everything here. – Eustace Chapuys

The English Reformation was never as complete or revolutionary as it had been in some parts of Europe. In many respects the hierarchy of the church had been maintained with its head, the Pope, being replaced by the English King. The liturgy and the translation of the Bible into the vernacular were more adventurous reforms that were hard fought (and for many people lethal) battles that in time resulted in the uneasy compromises of the Elizabethan reign. Many, including Wriothesley, were sympathetic to the old rites and dogmas and were becoming increasingly unsettled by the move to change from the reformers. The leading figures in this counter reformation were Stephen Gardiner, Bishop of Winchester, and Thomas Howard, Duke of Norfolk.

Gardiner's relationship with Wriothesley, as has already been described, went back a long way. He had been Wriothesley's tutor at Cambridge and was probably his sponsor in the first years of his court career. His nephew, Germaine, was a half brother to Wriothesley's wife Jane, so they were connected at various levels. After Wriothesley's rise to wealth and power the two men had become, each in his own right, powerful landowners in Hampshire. For most of their lives they appear to have got on well together. We have noted the one moment of strain in 1539 when Wriothesley became a candidate for Parliament in Hampshire against Gardiner's own candidate, but it appears that the rancour caused by this affront to Gardiner was quelled shortly after.

They remained close for the rest of Wriothesley's life.

Wriothesley's early humanist education may not have had such a deep impact as one might have thought. He was receptive to some of these new ideas but he was not in the final event willing to overthrow his core religious beliefs. In this context he has more in common with Sir Thomas More, a leading humanist of his time, who was also unwilling to deviate from his dogmatic beliefs about the role of the church. Thomas Cromwell, by contrast, had become much more revolutionary in this thinking.

Under Cromwell's tutelage Wriothesley was not at all unwilling to efficiently execute the dissolution of the monasteries, and indeed there was obvious self interest in this, but he is also on record as being keen to reform some of the old medieval practices and abuses of the church. He personally supervised the destruction of the bones and relics of St Swithun at Winchester for example and was plainly not uncomfortable with ridding the church of these examples of "idolatry". So in the 1530s he can be regarded as an efficient, even enthusiastic, executor of reform, but by 1540 some warning signals must have told him that the reforms could go too far and totally disrupt the realm. He was not necessarily wrong.

But in revolutionary times the pendulum tends to swing on a wide arc. The reformers wanted to press for more and as they did so the conservative faction shifted further to the right in reaction. Thus Bishop Bonner of London, once active in the reforming party turned into a zealous prosecutor of heresy and consigned many to be burned at the stake. Stephen Gardiner, who had once welcomed the translation of the Bible into English, was now dead set against the use of any language but Latin. After Henry's death the reforming party held sway for six years, but after the death of the young King Edward, the reactionary party gained power and tried to turn back the clock with deplorable consequences. Only with the accession of Elizabeth were matters brought to a level of uncertain calm.

The 1540s marked Wriothesley's years of greatest power and prosperity. They often showed him at his best as an efficient administrator of the Crown's affairs, but his efforts to restrain the trend towards Protestantism occasionally brought out the worst aspects of his personality.

A few years earlier, on 17 June 1539 Cromwell staged a pageant on the river Thames. Two barges rowed up and down the river between Westminster Bridge and the King's Bridge; one was the King's barge and the other was intended to represent the Pope's barge. The papal barge was filled with actors dressed as the Pope and his Cardinals. After some manoeuvring the two barges fired guns at each other and as the boats came together, the papal barge was boarded and the 'pope' and his cardinals were thrown overboard. The spectators massed on both banks cheered and roared their approval and delight. The message that everyone absorbed, by intention in this work of propaganda, was that Henry was the supreme authority over the Church in England. That much was clear. The king was head of the church in England and few had any quarrel with that idea.

Doctrinal matters were not that simple. Henry was not a true convert to Protestant reforms. He accepted some of the religious views of reformers he admired and trusted, like Thomas Cromwell and Thomas Cranmer, but he was never out of sympathy with the more conservative view of Stephen Gardiner, bishop of Winchester and Thomas Howard, Duke of Norfolk. In the last decade of his life Henry failed to adhere to a consistent line and in consequence there were two warring factions, who, depending on whether or not which group had the king's arbitrary support, held sway at one time or another. There were a number of casualties as the king blundered through his final decade.

Sir Thomas Wriothesley, who had proved himself adept at sitting on the fence, now had to choose sides. There was no longer any middle ground and he threw his lot in with his old friend Stephen Gardiner and the conservative faction. His own inclination and belief overrode his earlier caution. He was no longer a middling administrator but a man who held real power and he believed he could exercise that power to influence government policy.

In the same month as Cromwell's display on the river in 1540 the Act known as the 'Six Articles', but more formally 'An Act Abolishing Diversity in Opinion' was passed into law. Its main thrust was to affirm the belief that the consecrated bread and wine of the mass was indeed the body and blood of Christ. It represented a victory for the conservatives led by Gardiner and a defeat for reformers such as Cromwell and Cranmer. The absolute affirmation of priestly celibacy meant that Cranmer had to send his wife to Germany for her safety. Even so, Cromwell believed it to be a temporary delay. He did not live long enough to discover that it held for the remainder of Henry's reign

The first major heresy trial brought a man called John Lambert, who was also known as John Nicholson, to a show trial before the king himself on 16 November 1538. Pressure from the conservatives led the king to take action. Lambert was a prominent figure. He was a fellow of Queens College, Cambridge and had been chaplain to the English community in Antwerp. After a brief spell in prison in 1532 for his beliefs, he set up a school in London. At the centre of Lambert's heresy was his denial that the body and blood of Christ were actually present in the partaking of consecrated bread and wine at Holy Communion. This was a step too far for many and was anathema to the hard line conservatives. Henry's role at the trial was to present himself as the sole and just arbiter of all matters of faith. Lambert was questioned but refused to deny his belief. He was even given the opportunity at the end of the trial to recant and avoid death. He stubbornly refused and on 22 November was slowly burned to death at the stake.

The drive against heretics gathered pace in 1540. After Cromwell was beheaded on 28 July 1540, three reformers and three papists were executed two days later. The reformers, William Jerome, Robert Barnes and Thomas Garret were well known supporters of Cromwell. They were arrested and after interrogation admitted their indiscretion and signed a document that contracted that they would not make such indiscretions in the future. At Easter they were required to preach along orthodox lines at St Mary's Church in Spitalfield. That should have been enough, but Bishop Gardiner was unsatisfied and had the men re-arrested. Understanding their fate, they withdrew their recantations and faced up to their end. They were dragged on hurdles through the streets to their place of execution. Barnes challenged the authorities and asked the crowd if 'they had been led into any errors by his preaching'. All were silent. He then went on to proclaim his loyalty to the king.

> I have been reported a preacher of sedition and disobedience to the king's majesty. But here, I say to thee we are all bound by the law of God to obey your prince with all humility, not only for fear, but for conscience.[47]

At the same time three Papists, who had been in prison for some time, were dragged out and summarily executed. Some have suggested that this deadly charade was enacted to provide a public perception of balance, and this may be partly so, but Geoffrey Elton believed that it may have been more to do with what these men knew about the activities of Norfolk and Gardiner.[48] Gardiner was understood to have been the chief instigator of their prosecution and execution.

> Most men said it was for preaching against the doctrine of Stephen Gardiner ... who chiefly procured their death. God and he knoweth, but a great pity it was that such learned men should be so cast away without examination, neither knowing which was laid to their charge, nor ever called to answer.[49]

The watching crowd remained silent as the fires were lit to burn them to death. This was not a popular execution and the execution of the three papists who had denied the royal supremacy, did not provide to the crowd the intended balance for the injustice done to the Protestants.

The purge continued the following year and extended to quite ordinary and harmless people. One boy, an orphan of fifteen years called Richard Mekins was put on trial at the Guildhall. Two witnesses reported that he had denied the corporeal presence of Christ at the sacrament. It must have been apparent to the jury that the boy really did not understand what he was saying and the foreman brought in a verdict of not guilty as the case had not been proved. At this Edmund Bonner, Bishop of London, once a reformer of sorts but now an arch reactionary, fell into a great rage, according to the historian Edward Hall, and browbeat the jury into reconsidering their verdict. The jury, suitably cowed, delivered the wanted verdict and the poor boy was executed at Smithfield on 30 July 1541. Another young man, John Collins, had shot an arrow against a wooden statue of Christ because he believed it to be idolatrous. He had been in prison since 1538 but in the heightened atmosphere of 1541 he was dragged out of prison and burnt to death for heresy.

Wriothesley and his in-law Sir Anthony Browne aligned themselves with the standard bearers for the old orthodoxy, the Duke of Norfolk and the Bishop of Winchester. With Cromwell gone, the leaders of the reformers were Sir Edward Seymour, Earl of Hertford, Charles Brandon, Duke of Suffolk and Thomas Cranmer, Archbishop of Canterbury.

Cranmer was once more a target in 1545 when the conservatives thought they had detected heresies in a primer the archbishop had published that summer. Henry was told and agreed to Cranmer's arrest at the Privy Council meeting the following day. Henry once more made moves to protect the archbishop who was summoned to the place that evening to be warned. Cranmer naïvely believed that if he were arrested his innocence would protect him but the king was more savvy, knowing that once he was in prison his enemies would make sure that he never came out alive. He gave the archbishop his ring which 'they well know I will use for no other purpose but to call matters from the Council into my own hands to be ordered and determined.'[50]

On the following day Cranmer was accused of 'infecting the whole realm with heresy' as expected, but forewarned he was able to tell the council that the matter was out of their hands, and he produced the ring to show that the king was serious. Henry then affirmed his full confidence in Cranmer and delivered a not-so-veiled threat to those councillors who sought to overthrow him. Almost immediately those who were calling for his head a few moments before, and this group certainly included Wriothesley, were anxious to prove that they did not have any dark intentions.

So why this charade? Henry knew that he had factions within his council and had to contend with them. There is also a suspicion that he was willing to keep his councillors on edge, not knowing which way the wind was blowing. He had agreed to the archbishop's arrest the day before and then this elaborate charade had left them all humiliated.

Sir Thomas More, during his brief tenure on the Chancellorship, was no slouch when it came to pursuing heretics. In fact he was rather more keen on this than his predecessors or successors. In his three years as Chancellor in succession to Cardinal Wolsey he suppressed and burned many books deemed to be heretical and sent several men to the stake for their beliefs. More has enjoyed a good posthumous reputation, partly due to his principled stance against Henry VIII's break with Rome and partly because of the enduring fame of his literary work, *Utopia*, an ideal society which he had imagined in 1515. Yet a close reading of *Utopia*, shows us an ascetic society where conformity to the beliefs of that society was the only possible choice. Once More achieved positions of power, his pursuit of Utopia, became an uncomfortable reality. Indeed, the move towards Lutheran reforms pushed by Thomas Cromwell and Anne Boleyn, may have been easier to bring into play because of More's uncompromising stance on the role of the Church.

The removal of Cromwell in 1540 emboldened the conservatives to return to More's orthodoxy. Wriothesley also saw this as an important function of his watch and instituted periodic purges to root out heretics. He may have been a decade too late; the new evangelical ideas had taken strong root in England and many people in high places had taken the new faith on board, including many at court. And therein lay the rub for conservatives like Wriothesley, Gardiner and Sir Richard Rich; they were fighting a reactionary war against eventual dominance of the new creed. It was much like the North Americans Indians resisting the influx of Europeans; the numbers of European immigrants kept rising at a faster rate than the native population. These new ideas offered personal salvation and direct contact with the word of God printed in their native tongue. It was seductive. Salvation was within reach of ordinary people as faith replaced the medieval concept of "good works." It had been easy for the rich to endow a chapel or a monastery or a hospital and therefore guarantee an easy path to heaven, but the humble peasant could do no better than help to repair the church door, which could not count for much. As we know, such new ideas were not decided in Wriothesley's time and would take many martyrs, emigration and an eventual civil war to lay the issue of religious choice or conformity to rest. But Wriothesley was still living at a time when governments thought they could stamp out heresy. It was at this point that he appears to have lost control of himself.

Anne Askew (or Ascough) was the daughter of a middle-ranking Lincolnshire gentleman. She had enthusiastically taken on the practice of "gospelling", that is reading the gospel in English to groups of interested listeners. This was an outcome of another government policy which banned the sale and ownership of Bibles in translation. But you could not be prosecuted for listening to the book being read. Not for the first time and on many occasions since the effect of such a ban was to guarantee more widespread exposure.

More worryingly to Wriothesley perhaps was that she was not insignificant and had court connections. One of her brothers was a member of the Gentlemen Pensioners. A spy was employed to keep an eye on her activities and she was arrested and tried by Edmund Bonner, bishop of London. He sent her back to the Midlands; out of sight out of mind.

When Gardiner returned from his foreign mission in March 1546 he pressed for a more thorough pursuit of heretics. He arrested and examined Dr Edward Crome, a popular preacher of the day. Crome was then interrogated by Wriothesley and in the course of his examination revealed a number of important names with whom he had had contact. The hunt was on and before long Bonner had found four men and one woman guilty. He sought the King's permission to make an example of them but Henry advised caution. Two of these men who had repented were set free and the others consigned to be burned at the stake, but Henry insisted that the commission be dissolved.

The conservative faction were not to be deterred. They then developed a plan to discredit Henry's last queen, a forthright and intelligent lady who had grasped the message of the evangelicals and was not shy of discussing such matters. Catherine Parr, Henry's sixth wife, was educated in the humanist tradition. She was much taken with the protestant reforms and read widely and even held classes with her ladies. When Henry was infirm she took it upon herself to discuss matters of religion with her husband. On one such occasion when Stephen Gardiner was present Henry remarked, perhaps jokingly, that it had come to something when a man was taught by his wife. Gardiner, suitably scandalised, commented on the inappropriateness of such activity by women and sought, and received, permission from Henry to investigate her.

With the king's permission Gardiner, Rich and Wriothesley were now in full cry, but they did not approach the queen directly, thinking it more politic to question the ladies of the court to see what they could dig up. Apparently at this point Wriothesley suggested they bring Anne Askew back into the frame. She had by this time been examined a second time and sentenced to burning at the stake, but on 29 June she was taken to the Tower to be examined by Wriothesley and Rich. She was questioned for hours but she would not speak, thus exasperating her interrogators. Wriothesley summoned the Lieutenant of the Tower, Sir Anthony Knyvet, to prepare the rack. The rack was a gruesome instrument of torture. Arms and legs were chained at either end of the rack and by means of pulleys and a ratchet the chains could be gradually shortened and induce excruciating pain in the joints of the body.

Knyvet did as instructed and she was tied to the rack. He was not however prepared to do more than "pinch her", in other words give her a light tug to scare her. He would not countenance racking her and ordered his man to set her free. Wriothesley and Rich would have none of it and instructed Knyvet to do as he was told. Knyvet, who may well have ordered and witnessed some brutal treatment of prisoners in the past had his scruples in this instance. It was firstly illegal to rack a woman in Tudor times, moreover it was in the eyes of most people immoral to rack a woman, especially a gentlewoman. He would not budge and was sure that he was in the right.

What happened next was truly astonishing and must forever colour our opinion of Wriothesley. Seeing that they would not get Knyvet to do or order the racking Wriothesley and Rich decided to do the dirty work themselves. They took off their gowns and stepped up to the apparatus to rack this unfortunate woman. Sir Anthony Knyvet, a soldier who had seen more than one battle and probably some of the atrocities of war was appalled and he immediately left the room and the tower wishing to have no part of this act of barbarity.

The two lords continued with their grim work and eventually Anne Askew fainted. She steadfastly refused to incriminate any other person throughout the whole sordid process. Tudor opinion was quite shocked. She had been tried and condemned to the stake, so the law had taken its course and she should have been entitled to have no injury done to her body before the sentence was carried out. The actions of Wriothesly and Rich were against the law, although Wriothesley lamely tried to argue that it was his duty to search out and destroy those who offended against the realm.[51]

It was, in the end, a pointless piece of savagery. Two men, in the highest offices of the land who should have been above such activities demeaned themselves and their cause. One can only assume that Anne Askew's stubbornness drove them beyond reason.

At the time, neither Wriothesley nor Rich suffered. Henry was not particularly interested in the detail of what happened to Anne Askew. She was a heretic. She burned, and that was that. The conservative faction still had their propaganda coup in the burning at the stake and were mostly untroubled by her treatment. Posterity has come to a different judgement and Wriothesley's actions cannot be explained away. It will remain as a permanent stain on a remarkable career.

Undeterred the plotters continued to proceed against the real target, Queen Catherine Parr. They believed that they had the king's approval.

When the queen learned of this she immediately sought out Henry and apologised to him. Her only intention in discussing religious matters with him was to entertain him and take his mind off his physical pain and not to instruct him. Henry accepted this.

What followed next was farcical. Baron Titchfield had been previously instructed by Henry to arrest the Queen in her privy garden one afternoon. Accordingly, Wriothesley appeared with a guard of 40 men to arrest her, unaware of the king's change of mind. Instead he met Henry's fiercest hostility rather than acquiescence and he went on his knees to try to plead the agreed arrangements. Henry called him an arrant knave and a fool and asked if they had nothing better to do than try to discover information about a lady who surpassed them all in virtue? "Avaunt my sight!" he thundered and turned his back on Wriothesley, all smiles to the queen.

Whether this actually happened or not is a matter for some contention. The story is only told in Foxe's *Book of Martyrs* and there is not the slightest hint in other sources. The fact of a single source is by itself no reason to doubt it fully, but it does give us reason to question it. It is plausible that Gardiner would distrust Catherine Parr, and Wriothesley was certainly on a rampage against heretics. Would they have dared to proceed against the queen unless they felt that they had Henry's support? Unlikely. In some ways the story does fit with what we know of Henry's personality during this period. He was certainly erratic in his dealings with people and the idea that one day he might be displeased with the queen and the next day supportive is not implausible. If the story is true Wriothesley must have spent an anxious night or two worrying for his future.

George Blagge was a favourite of Henry and was gentleman of the privy chamber and had little political significance. He was overheard making some facetious comment about the Mass after listening to a sermon preached by the previously mentioned Edward Crome. Blagge was questioned about the sermon. He responded with some unwise remarks which were then reported to Wriothesley. Wriothesley moved with some speed. Blagge was arrested, interrogated and sentenced on the basis of hearsay evidence to burning as a heretic.

That might have been the end for the unfortunate Blagge but one of his friends reported the matter to Henry who took immediate action. Wriothelsley was summoned before him to explain. Notwithstanding that the king felt it was an affront to his dignity. Regardless of the outcome of the trial, Wriothesley was ordered to write in his own hand a pardon for Blagge.

Unsurprisingly, George Blagge held no love for his former persecutor and has this to say when he heard news of his death:

"The dogge is dead, the Sowle is gone to hell."

None of this sits too comfortably with the Wriothesley whose career we have been following. In his early and middle years he was bright, hard working and competent and had hardly put a foot wrong in negotiating the intrigues at court. He seemed to able to turn his hand to whatever task he was set and to accomplish it efficiently. He was also careful. He survived the fall of Wolsey and also, when he was much more senior, the downfall of Cromwell. But we might detect a change once he achieved the top job. He became, like his predecessor Sir Thomas More, a little too zealous for comfort, a little too impressed by his own dignity. The case of Anne Askew is a good example of this.

The persecutions continued for a while but this may have been the peak for the conservatives during Henry's reign. The reformers were soon back in charge of the council and the conservatives would have to wait another six years until Henry's Catholic daughter Mary came to the throne before they could continue their vengeful course. Wriothesley did not live long enough to see the day.

Wriothesley's life had been bound to Stephen Gardiner from the time he went to Trinity Hall as a teenager. Gardiner's career was stellar; he became the immensely wealthy bishop of Winchester and was a prominent figure in government. He now made a mistake, a misjudgement perhaps. In November 1546 the king wished to exchange some land with the bishop. It was a deal which was in the king's interest so that certain estates could be consolidated, but Gardiner did not see that it was in his own interest and refused to enter into negotiations. He discussed the matter with Paget and Wriothesley, who both advised him to go along with the king's wishes, but the bishop felt that he should stand firm. The volatile Henry was enraged and a subsequent grovelling apology from Gardiner would not mollify him. Gardiner's presence at Council was no longer welcome and Henry deleted his name from the executors of his will.

At about the same time the conservatives suffered another blow. Henry Howard, the Earl of Surrey, was the eldest son of the Duke of Norfolk. He was born in 1517. He had many talents, not least of which was his ability to write poetry of a very high quality. Yet like many clever men he was flawed. The Howards were a parvenu family in the 14th century, who by Tudor times they had convinced themselves that they were a natural aristocracy and in their own minds superior to everyone else. Henry Howard carried this attitude to an extreme. He held all of the "new men" in contempt and this would have been his attitude to men like Paget and Wriothesley who could not boast an aristocratic pedigree.

He was temperamentally unsuited to getting along with people who he did not regard as his peers or friends. He was arrogant and hot-headed. In 1536 he struck Edward Seymour after Seymour suggested that he was sympathetic to the 'Pilgrimage of Grace' rebels in the north of England. For this offence he was imprisoned at Windsor Castle for two weeks. In 1542 he challenged Sir John Legh, a member of the royal household, to a duel and was subsequently imprisoned in the Fleet. He was only granted his freedom after pledging 10,000 marks as surety against his future good behaviour. This did not last, and in February 1543 he led a group of his friends in firing pebbles from crossbows at a number of targets, mostly windows of churches and a number of big houses. They followed this up by getting into a boat on the Thames and used the same crossbow to fire stones at prostitutes on Bankside.

The Privy Council could not ignore this irresponsible and unseemly behaviour and on 1 April he was commanded to appear before them. He attempted to justify his actions by claiming that his fire was directed against papists and corrupt criminals, but the Council would have none of it, and he found himself once more in the Fleet prison.

His father, the Duke of Norfolk, arranged to have him freed a month later and he was sent off to the low countries to fight with the Spanish. He seems to have found a useful outlet for his violent energy and his career was not undistinguished, and in 1545 he was given command of Boulogne. Unfortunately for his future prospects, his impetuosity was his undoing. On 7 January 1546 he attacked a French force of 3,000 foot soldiers and 600 cavalry at St Etienne, and his rashness led to heavy defeat. On 21 March he was relieved of his command by Edward Seymour, the man he had assaulted a decade earlier. Seymour was now the Earl of Hertford.

Surrey's anger and hatred became even more intense. Although Paget advised him to seek to serve the king in some military capacity and gain experience, he stormed off to his home in June 1546 full of hatred for his perceived enemies. The Seymours were not fools, and they pre-empted any action by Surrey in launching a move to push him, and his father, from power. Richard Southwell, a Norfolk man, was brought before the Privy Council on 2 December to tell them that he had information about Surrey that 'touched his fidelity to the king.' This elliptical remark was then expanded by Wriothesley to a full scale charge of treason.

Surrey was arrested and taken to Wriothesley's house in Holborn for interrogation. His father, the Duke, was arrested and placed in the Tower. By the time the matter came to trial a number of accusations had been compiled. It was said that they planned to murder all of the Privy Councillors when they assumed power. They planned to seize control of the young Prince Edward and they were said to have placed emphasis on their own royal bloodlines. Even though most of the charges were fancifully created, the overall impression, that they lusted for power, remained. Crucially, Henry had turned against them and the outcome of the trial was inevitable. Surrey was executed on 19 January 1547.

Wriothesley was not slow to turn against his former allies and to use his legal skill to bring about the wishes of the king. From today's perspective the outcome off the trial looks like judicial murder, but Surrey's career of hot-headed action and his arrogant behaviour left him with few or no supporters. It is quite possible that Wriothesley believed in the potential of a murderous coup. In a letter written to the President of the Flemish Council dated 17 December 1546 he wrote 'that it was pitiable that persons of such high and noble lineage should have undertaken so shameful a businesses to join the seizure of the government of the king by sinister means . . .(and) intended to kill the council while they alone obtained complete control over the prince.'[52]

There is little doubt that Surrey had scattered a trail of unwise remarks about the monarchy and it was not a difficult matter for Wriothesley to amass sufficient evidence to make a case against him. Southwell, the key witness, was himself a proto-catholic and a seemingly unlikely source for material against the unwise earl. His motivation is unknown, but it is not beyond reasonable speculation to assume that the arrogant earl had upset or insulted him at some point. In any case, at the very end of Henry's reign, the Seymour faction were very much in the ascendant and it must have been clear to all but the most obtuse that the new regime would be for reform rather than a return to the past. Wriothesley certainly understood this, although he seems to have forgotten this prudence in a rash moment.

Two days later, a bill for the attainder of the Duke of Norfolk and the earl of Surrey was passed. All their estates were now forfeit. Norfolk continued to be imprisoned in the Tower and was actually due to be executed on the day of Henry's death. He was lucky; in the rush to deal with things on that day the sentence was never carried out. After the accession of Edward VI no one was much minded to do anything and Norfolk, no longer the power he once was, could safely be left to live out his remaining days.

The isolation of bishop Gardiner and the fall of the house of Howard left Wriothesley without natural allies on the Council and because he unwisely challenged the power of the Seymours, he was quickly on the outside.

Stephen Gardiner remained intractable. When Cranmer proposed a book of homilies Gardiner protested to the Protector. 'I can admit no innovations.'[53] He set himself in direct opposition and in exasperation the council imprisoned him for a few months at the end of 1547. After his release January 1548 he acquiesced to the point of not actively obstructing reforms but would not press any of them and he continued to be a thorn in the side of the reformers. After sermon preached on 29 June he was confined to the Tower, where he remained for the rest of Edward's reign. Thus Wriothesley was deprived of two of his strongest allies.

7

THE WILDERNESS YEARS

He was evermore too good for us all. - Thomas Cranmer, speaking about Henry VIII.

The old king was dying. That must have been evident throughout 1546, although nobody would have had the nerve to openly say as much. Henry's last decade had been marred by erratic and despotic judgements. Surviving councillors, able and dedicated men, knew that their position was secured only by the whim of the king and took every precaution to avoid royal wrath. Nothing could be gained, and everything lost, by stating the obvious, that the health of Henry VIII was in terminal decline.

He had been ill with various indispositions quite frequently during 1546 and he had become grossly overweight. Movement of the most limited kind caused considerable pain, and as a formerly active man, his incapacity caused him great frustration. Despite these handicaps the old determination was still driving him and in the summer he resolved to go hunting. A special ramp was constructed which enabled him to get into a saddle and the game was driven in front of him so that he could have a shot. He may not have had sufficient strength to draw the bow effectively and a kill was most likely stage managed by his courtiers. The activity exhausted him and in September he had to retire to Windsor Castle to recover. Nobody was brave enough to confront the truth. Lord Wriothesley wrote on 17 September that 'he only had a cold, and was cured.'[54]

His condition deteriorated throughout the rest of the year and he really only had a few moments when he could function properly, yet in the paranoid and fearful atmosphere of those last days nobody could do other than pretend that the old king was on the road to recovery. In truth he had done better that his grandfather, Edward IV, whom he much resembled in physicality, appetite and temperament. Edward lived only 40 years; Henry had at least got to the age of 55.

Lord Wriothesley had spent his entire career in court service, rising steadily through the ranks until he was appointed Chancellor in 1544. As described in earlier chapters, he had, along the way, served Cardinal Wolsey and Thomas Cromwell and been at the centre of some of the more dramatic political activities of Henry's reign. Like several other court insiders, he had been in the right place at the right time when the monasteries were dissolved in the late 1530s. In the space of very few years he acquired the old Minster and Hyde Abbey in Winchester, Beaulieu Abbey, Quarr Abbey on the Isle of Wight and Titchfield Abbey, which he converted into a great country house. Each of these properties came with large estates, mostly in Hampshire, and by 1538 he was, next to the bishop of Winchester, the largest landowner in the county.

At the end of 1546 he could reflect that he had spent his entire career in the service of Henry VIII and kept his head on his shoulders. Nor had he spent much time in prison or laboured under disgrace like, for example, his friend and mentor Stephen Gardiner. He was the consummate court official, always willing to carry out the wishes of his master and doing so effectively.

On January 31st 1547 Lord Chancellor Wriothesley, his eyes full with tears, announced to Parliament the death of King Henry VIII two days earlier. The sorrow was probably genuine. He had been a dutiful and faithful servant to Henry throughout his reign and it had been the only reign he had known. But there must have been an element of apprehension in his mind. The king he had served so loyally was no longer there to protect him against his enemies, and those enemies were present in the same room.

The main person to watch was Edward Seymour, uncle to the new king. He was the Earl of Hertford, shortly to become Duke of Somerset and a protagonist for the evangelical Christian faith. Wriothesley was no fool, and he had been watching as Seymour had worked to increase his support in Council and push aside the conservative faction. Bishop Gardiner, in one of his intemperate moods had got himself banished from court by Henry. The Duke of Norfolk was imprisoned in the tower under sentence of treason and Wriothesley was almost alone to represent conservative opinion, and, as he was to discover in the meetings that followed, he was the lone dissenting voice. While he was open to reform in his role as a state employee, Wriothesley was a devout Roman Catholic, who could stomach the changes under Henry VIII which were more a matter of governance than doctrine. The Protestant zeal of Seymour must have created great disquiet in his soul.

Immediately after the death of Henry VIII was announced, Edward VI was publicly proclaimed king. Soon after his privy councillors got together to tidy up the affairs of the last reign. It was customary to reward the faithful servants of the last king, but in the last months of Henry's life, apart from what was written in the will, none of the rewards the councillors were seeking, apparently, had been committed to writing. It was a difficult moment, but, to everyone's relief, Sir William Paget, Chief Secretary to the king since 1543, revealed that he had a photographic memory. He recalled that all of Henry's good intentions had been written down in a small book which Henry had slipped into a pocket of his nightshirt. For unaccountable reasons the book had gone missing and could be nowhere found. Paget then began to recall each of Henry's last bequests. Sir Edward Seymour, Earl of Hertford, was to be made Duke of Somerset and Earl Marshall. John Dudley, Viscount Lisle, was to be raised to the earldom of Warwick and become Great Chamberlain, William Parr, brother to his last wife, was to become Marquess of Northampton, John Russell would be made Earl of Bedford, Sir William Paulet, Lord St John, became Earl of Wiltshire, and Lord Wriothesley, Baron Titchfield, became Earl of Southampton.

Paget also recalled that there had been discussion about the estates of the Duke of Norfolk, who was at the time in a cell in the Tower under attainder for treason. His estates were forfeit to the crown but the king had not forgotten the need to reward his loyal servants; therefore some lands in Hampshire and Sussex were reserved for distribution. Edward Seymour received lands worth £800 a year and a further £300 a year 'from the next bishop's land that shall fall void', presumably with half an eye on land from the bishop of Winchester, who was also likely to be tried. Both Lisle and Wriothesley were to receive revenues of £300 a year and Edward Seymour's brother, Thomas, received land worth £500 per annum and some of the other players were similarly rewarded.

Paget was able to declare to the assembled council that all being 'remembered on his deathbed, that he had promised great things to diverse men, he willed in his testament that whatsoever should in any wise appear to his Council to have been promised by him, the same should be performed.'[55]

William Herbert, who had only recently been appointed as a Gentleman of the Privy Chamber, stepped forward to point out that Paget had missed out one name from the list - Paget himself. Herbert attested that he had himself raised the matter with the dying king, and the king agreed that he must be helped. It was therefore agreed that Paget should receive lands worth 400 marks a year.

Nobody raised an objection and Hertford, now in a most powerful position, spoke for all his colleagues when he announced that the bountiful gifts 'had been determined by our late sovereign lord and partly for the conservation of our own honesty and specially for the honour and surety of our sovereign lord that now is, we take upon us the degrees of honour and enter into the charge of attendance and service in the great and weighty affairs of Edward VI.'[56]

There were no dissenting voices.

Thus, in an extraordinary piece of political opportunism, all of the members of the king's household rewarded themselves. The 1st Earl of Southampton had already been awarded £500 in Henry's will and this extra £300 cemented his wealth. From now on, his house at Titchfield would be the country seat of the earls of Southampton, at least for the succeeding three generations. It is a remarkable story. Wriothesley, whose only claim to dignity when he was born was that he was the grandson of a knight, had started as a minor court official and risen to the exalted position of Lord Chancellor. It could be said of him that 'he rose without trace' because, for all his accomplishments, he rates little in the history books. The names of some of his contemporaries, Cardinal Wolsey, Sir Thomas More and Thomas Cromwell, have attracted much more attention, as have the chancellors of the 15th century, such as Cardinal Beaufort and William of Wykeham. He left no public legacies, such as a college, but he did establish a considerable fortune, which was to some degree depleted by his erratic son and grandson.

Wriothesley was lucky. He came of age and into government at a time when there were openings for men of his background. The traditional routes to power, through the military or the church had become less favoured. Clever, well educated men could fill essential positions in government without ever entering the jousting lists or committing themselves to holy orders. New currents of thinking in the new humanist age required men capable of more flexible thinking and the reigns of the Tudors saw to it that these new men filled those essential roles. The old aristocracy and several senior bishops lost power during this century and new men like John Russell, William Paget, Thomas Wriothesley and William Cecil founded dynasties which were to become part of the ruling fabric of future England.

It is an irony that at this point Wriothesley made the first serious mistake in a long political career where he had hardly put a foot wrong - he challenged the almost dictatorial powers that Seymour was gathering for himself. Wriothesley, as already noted, was a conservative in matters of religion and Catholic to the core. It should be remembered that Henry's Act of Supremacy merely transferred the headship of the church in England from the Pope to the King. On the ground little else changed and conservatives like Gardiner and Wriothesley could live with that. The radical moves by the Protestants under the boy king were more difficult to accept and during the six years of his reign there was no chance of a counter revolution.

The new council would need an executive head and two new offices were created - Lord Protector of the Realm and Governor of the King's Person. The executors, and there were sixteen of them, agreed that Edward Seymour should fill both roles with Wriothesley being the lone demurring voice. He was not necessarily wrong; the long minority of Henry VI was guaranteed by dividing key roles amongst the king's uncles. Humphrey, duke of Gloucester, was placed in charge of the kingdom in England and John, duke of Bedford, managed the disputed kingdom of France. Crucially, the role of Governor of the King's Person was separated from these other functions and handed to Thomas Beaufort. Combining the two roles under one person was regarded as potentially dangerous, as indeed it turned out when Richard, duke of Gloucester launched his coup in 1483. Wiser heads might have agreed with the earl of Southampton, but at this time they kept their counsel.

Seymour quickly strengthened his position. The Council of 16 was expanded to 26, all appointed by the Protector. Southampton objected to the legality of this but his objections were ignored. Somerset retaliated by accusing the Chancellor of legal malpractice. Southampton, in order to make sure he attended all council meetings, had off-loaded some of his chancery work by delegating the work to other lawyers. It was a practical measure, but this, Somerset claimed, was illegal and he set up a commission to look into the matter. The commission, headed by Sir Richard Rich, whose entire career had been characterised by a willingness to bend to the will of whomever held power, upheld the Protector's complaint and Southampton was stripped of the office of Lord Chancellor, confined to his London house and fined the huge sum of £4,000. The restriction to London was designed to keep him from returning to Hampshire and collaborating with Bishop Gardiner, no supporter of the new regime, possibly by raising an army.

Wriothesley and Seymour, now the Duke of Somerset, could not be more different. Somerset was a soldier and a reformer; Wriothesley was a courtier, diplomat and a conservative. Somerset tended to rule by decree, Southampton preferred more politic ways of getting things done. There was really not much hope of rapprochement between the two.

Southampton was initially extremely angry at his treatment and to some extent confirmed Somerset's charge that he was unruly and untrustworthy. However he did calm down and return to the level headedness that had served him so well throughout his career. Once he had taken stock of the situation he could see that Seymour would quickly use up any reserves of goodwill. Seymour began to act like Henry VIII but of course he was not Henry. He did not have Henry's political intelligence nor did he have the legitimacy of the throne behind him and his increasingly despotic behaviour was bound to alienate his supporters. It was only a matter of time.

The Earl of Southampton decided to wait. In the meantime he acted civilly towards Somerset and began to court the friendship of John Dudley, the new Earl of Warwick, then the second most powerful man in the kingdom. In a show of humility he offered to exchange houses with Warwick. Ely Place was an appropriate residence for a Lord Chancellor but not for a mere earl so at the end of 1547 Warwick moved into Ely Place and Southampton into Lincoln Place. His good behaviour paid off. His fine was remitted and he was allowed to travel to his estates.

Further political rehabilitation came a year later. Thomas Seymour, the Protector's younger brother embarked on a coup of his own and tried to recruit malcontents to his cause. Southampton was approached but he was too smart to get embroiled in such a scheme. Wriothesley reported the interview to the Protector and this act of loyalty got him restored to the Council.

Thomas Seymour filled the role of the troublesome younger brother to the powerful protector. He had been appointed Baron Sudely and made Lord High Admiral, but he seems to have been consumed by jealousy of his elder brother and neglected his duties and made trouble. He first married Henry's widow, Catherine Parr but she died giving birth to her first child. He pursued the Princess Mary and was rejected. He then resumed his pursuit of Elizabeth, who was certainly flattered by his interest in February 1547, when she was only 13 years old. This time she politely rejected his proposal by letter, but after his marriage to Catherine Parr he shared the same household as Elizabeth and Catherine. Testimonies given in 1549 by Kate Ashley, Elizabeth's governess and Thomas Parry, her cofferer, describe very inappropriate behaviour by Seymour with the 14 year old girl, how he would visit her and tickle her while in bed and generally act in a playful manner. On 11 June 1548 Catherine Parr came across her husband with Elizabeth in his arms. Elizabeth was sent to live with Sir Anthony Denny and his wife the following day.

The irrepressible Thomas believed that he should share the duties of Protector with his brother and he lobbied to that purpose, most intensely while his Edward was in the north fighting the Scots. He devised a scheme to marry Jane Grey, daughter of the Marquess of Dorset, to her cousin King Edward. He tried to recruit Wriothesley, again without success and had similar disappointments from other members of the council. Lord Dudley felt that he had had enough and on 17 January 1549 issued a warrant, signed also by Wriothesley, authorising the arrest of Thomas Seymour. He was then conveyed to the Tower.

Southampton misread the situation. He thought this gave him the opportunity to do the very thing for which he had condemned Thomas Seymour and embark upon a coup of his own. In this case he teamed up with the Earl of Arundel, and while Warwick was in eastern England dealing with a revolt and other council members were absent, Southampton and Arundel and their followers seized the Tower. The catholic coup was sudden, unexpected and seemingly complete. Somerset was held a a prisoner. However Warwick returned to London and was not willing to fall in line. When he and the whole council were present at Ely Place, Southampton led off by reading the charges against Somerset. Warwick would have none of it. He placed his hand upon his sword and challenged Southampton, 'My lord, you seek his blood and he that seeketh his blood would have mine also.' This action caused consternation amongst the council and few were ready for a violent confrontation. Most quietly backed away from the Somerset attainder and Southampton found himself stranded.

Wriothesleys final fall from power is another illustration of the volatility of Tudor political life. In November 1549 it appeared the Wriothesley was once more in an influential position. He was supported by the Earl of Arundel and the Southwell brothers, who had been instrumental in the fall of Norfolk but were themselves religious conservatives. Somerset was losing power as a consequence of his general mismanagement of the social unrest of 1548 and 1549. In October 1549 a unified council began proceedings against the Protector. After the fall of Somerset, Wriothesley and Arundel were two of the six peers entrusted with the king's safety. He seemed to be in a strong position. Even one of his opponents, John Ponet, a Protestant reformer, was compelled to observe that:

> Wriothesley that before was banished the court, is lodged with his wife and son next to the king. Every man repaireth to Wriothesley, honoreth Wriothesley, sueth into Wrioythesley.[57]

At the end of the month there was to have been a meeting with the Imperial Ambassador, Van der Delft, together with Arundel, Warwick and Southampton, to discuss English religious orthodoxy. Wriothesley was anxious to roll back some of the reforms under Henry. Arundel was supportive and Warwick seemingly so. In the event, the meeting never happened as Warwick developed a political illness. Wriothesley went ahead with the meeting on his own but little could be achieved. It seems that Wriothesley did have a serious illness at the time which kept him from Council meetings. Warwick, however, claiming to have a 'rheum' arranged for meetings to take place in his house at Ely Place, where presumably he could shape opinion. Van der Delft observed:

> The Earl of Southampton is very ill and in danger of death. If he were to fail us now I should fear matters might never be righted, for he is still in good hopes of accomplishing this,

and a good part of the council is now well disposed, but would go astray and follow the rest without him, for there is not a man among them of sound enough judgement to conduct opposition. So if the Earl of Southampton does not recover, and the earl of Warwick remains stiff in his opinion, we shall see terrible confusion and destruction in this realm.[58]

The Earl of Southampton's illness was genuine, but the Earl of Warwick's sickness was feigned, and with Wriothesley out of the way the Earl of Warwick convened a council meeting without Southampton and Arundel. That perennial political weathervane, Sir Richard Rich, left Wriothesley's camp to join Warwick, as did others. The Earl of Southampton was now isolated.

He did however sufficiently recover his strength by mid December to continue his interrogation of the Duke of Somerset. Somerset insisted that he had done nothing without the advice, counsel and consent of the earl of Warwick.[59] Wriothesley pounced on this as it implicated his new enemy Warwick with his old enemy Edward Seymour. He and Arundel were of one mind and they saw their opportunity to restore the old catholic faith and rid themselves of the reformers. They appear to have confided in Lord St. John, a conservative supporter, but he nevertheless warned Warwick, who had time to prepare.

At the next council meeting Warwick was ready. His own followers were easy to persuade, but he must also have worked behind the scenes to persuade those in the middle of the road and turncoats like Sir Richard Rich that he was the man to support. So when Wriothesley made his accusation, not only was he met with a robust defence, but also did he discover an almost complete lack of support amongst his fellow councillors. He must have assumed that the rightness of his case meant that he would be supported, but he made a fundamental political error of not guaranteeing that support prior to the meeting. He must have been profoundly shocked. And this time his career was certainly finished.

Two of Wriothesley's former supporters, St John and Russell had gone over to Warwick's side. One of Wriothesley's great, great granddaughters was to marry a Russell in the 17th century and her share of the great Southampton estate established the Russell fortune. At the same time Arundel and Southampton were placed under house arrest. He was now thoroughly in eclipse.

He could have been sent to the Tower and accused of treason. Both Gardiner and Norfolk were still in custody. But nothing was done and it can only be assumed that this was due to his poor health. He was literally a spent force and it was hardly worth the effort to go after him.

For him it was the end. On January 14th he was dismissed from court and once more placed under house arrest. He was now a broken man. For over 20 years he had worked diligently to rise to the very top of the political ladder. He had also made himself a very wealthy man. Nevertheless, he had burned his political bridges and could see no way back. Once again his highly strung temperament induced an illness or weakening of his health. It was believed that he was close to death. Van der Velde, the Flemish ambassador, wrote: "it is supposed that he cannot last two days longer."[60] This was premature. A week later he was showing signs of recovery, but he was not in good spirits. His world had collapsed and there were signs that he had lost the will to live.

Desiring as I am to be under the earth rather than upon it.[61]

He lingered for a few months and on July 30th he died.

Yet he was only 45. He could reasonably expect another 15 years of life and there was nothing in his lifestyle that suggested he was dissolute in his living habits. We do find reports of a periodic fever which would lay him low for a time. One writer has suggested that it was quartan fever and it does appear to have affected him at times of stress. Perhaps he contracted it one more time and at the lowest point in his life he had no strength to fight it.

> My lord Wriothesley, seeing all his heart was opened against him ... And (thinking) this act could never be forgotten, and (because) his ambitious mind could take no (lower) place, he killed himself with sorrow in so much as he said he would not live in such misery"[62]

It was rumoured that he was poisoned or took poison, not wishing to live with the shame. It is also possible that he willed himself to death or had no appetite for living. Perhaps we should accept that the Wriothesley males in this period were prone to living relatively short intense lives. William Wriothesley died at the age of 40, Thomas at 45, and, in the next generation, Henry died at 36.

In 1547 he had sat at the pinnacle of power, having risen from a modest background. He had transformed himself into one of the largest landowners in Hampshire and was richly rewarded with titles. His cousin, Charles Wriothesley, made this record:

> Memorandum: the 30 of July Sir Thomas Wrythesly, Lord Wryothesly, Earle of Southampton, and knight of the garter, and one of the executors of King Henry the VIII, departed out of this transitory life at his place in Holborn. He has bene long sicke.[63]

The following day the young King Edward made this perfunctory note: 'the Earl of Southampton died.'[64] Some were less charitable about his passing. The day after his death Richard Skidmore, or Scudamore wrote in a letter: 'yesternight God hath called to his mercy the Erle of Southampton, for which I gave to God most high thankes.'[65]

A funeral service was held at St Andrew's Church in Holborn and there he was buried. Bishop Hooper preached a sermon. A few weeks later his remains were re-interred at Titchfield and years later the body of his wife joined him. At the end of his son's life a great family monument was erected in the church. It has to be said that there was no sense at the time of a great man passing. No public grief has been recorded, and apart from members of his immediate family and perhaps a few friends his death was a footnote. He had quickly fallen from power in 1547 and in the last three years had become politically weakened, outfoxed by more devious politicians. Had he been a more physically resilient man and survived to the next reign, like his mentor Stephen Gardiner, he would almost certainly have played a prominent role in Queen Mary's reign.

However, the political and religious current had turned and was flowing in the direction of Protestant reform. Even Mary's reign could not resist the flow and her short and unhappy reign was trumped by her more politically adept younger sister.

Thus the death of Henry VIII cemented the fortune of the Wriothesley dynasty. His descendants were not merely wealthy; they had title and status and were part of the governing class.

8

THE FOUNDER OF A DYNASTY

31 July 1550: The earl of Southampton died. – Chronicle and Papers of Edward VI.

The judgements of posterity have not always been kind to Sir Thomas Wriothesley. A F Pollard, writing at the end of the 19th century, scarcely finds a good word to say about him:

> It is difficult to trace in Southampton's career any motive beyond that of self-aggrandisement. Trained in the Machiavellian school of Cromwell, he was without the definite aims and resolute will that to some extent redeemed his master's lack of principle. He won and retained Henry VIII's favour by his readiness in lending his abilities to the king's most nefarious designs, thereby inspiring an almost universal distrust. The theological conservatism with which he has always been credited was tempered by a strict regard to his own interests.[66]

That said, he did not differ at all from Henry's doctrinal position. Henry was a traditional catholic and not a Lutheran reformer. The reform of the English church largely came about through Henry's willingness to put his personal and political interests ahead of anything else. He used the services of men like Cranmer and Cromwell because they were able to effect the change he wanted, not because they had Lutheran inclinations. Men like Sir Thomas More and William Wareham, Archbishop of Canterbury, fell from power because they held firmly to principles that were contrary to the king's interest. Wriothesley was elastic in such matters and kept his head on his shoulders.

Historical assessments of both Cromwell and Wriothesley are often seen through a present-day lens. Wriothesley might agree with the charge of self-aggrandisement but would be puzzled that the charge was made at all. Every ambitious Tudor politician took the opportunities when they presented themselves to improve their social and financial position. This had been conventional practice from time immemorial and no Tudor person would have expected otherwise. John Thynne (1515-1580) had no influence in national politics in his day and was steward to Edward Seymour, Duke of Somerset. He nevertheless used his position to become a wealthy man and establish the dynasty which extends to today's Marquess of Bath. Court and judicial officials were often not paid a salary out of tax revenue but usually granted a sinecure that would provide some form of basic income. Further emoluments derived from gifts, grants and pensions from the people they were dealing with. Rewards depended very much on the value to the petitioner.

Wriothesley grew up in a court family who had been heralds for some generations and he knew very well, perhaps better than most, how the system worked. He was from his earliest working days in positions where gifts were made in order to get the attention of his masters, be it Wolsey or Cromwell and there was even a system in place where a percentage of the gift was paid to either Wolsey or Cromwell. Today we would regard this as a corrupt system of government but bear in mind that English government was a few centuries away from a system where officials were adequately and fairly compensated out of tax revenue and belonged to the concept of a neutral civil service. Many of the regular taxes which we now take for granted were yet to be invented and most taxation was a sporadic affair, only assessed when the crown had urgent need.

As a government official he was doing what his father, grandfather, uncles and cousins did as well as his contemporaries and colleagues. The difference perhaps between Thomas Wriothesley and his relatives and colleagues is that he took the opportunities where they came and became spectacularly rich in a short space of time, although probably not quite as wealthy as his former masters, Thomas Wolsey and Thomas Cromwell. In this regard he was lucky in being in the right place at the right time.

However, one cannot take away his talent. He was bright and hard working and seemed to bring competence to every task he was required to undertake, but his especial forte appears to have been finance. When he became Lord Chancellor in 1544 he augmented the position, hitherto purely legal, into an office for managing the financial affairs of the state. And in this he is considered to have done a very good job of regulating financial management. We see also during the years when he was Secretary to Henry that petitioners came to him for funds. He appears to have been in charge of managing the costs of Henry's northern expedition in 1542 without any formal assignment to do so. We can note that early in his career he worked for the cofferer Edward Peckham and was certainly grounded in these matters.

I am left with the suspicion that Wriothesley was a highly strung individual who for the most part was able to keep this under control. In all the years working for Wolsey, Peckham and Cromwell he proved himself an effective and competent deputy. Yet when he found himself at the top as Lord Chancellor he began to show signs of weakness. His treatment of Anne Askew, for example, can only be adequately explained by the fact that he himself felt under pressure. As we have seen there was no positive outcome to the torture of Anne Askew and the events show that on this occasion he lost control of his temper, possibly in exasperation and probably because he felt he was under pressure to get results. He also appears to have misinterpreted the mood after Henry's death and tried to lead the Conservative faction against Seymour. But without the support of Norfolk, who was in prison, and Gardiner, who was absent in disgrace from court, he was ineffective and isolated, finding himself as a leader with no followers.

He does appear to have regained his normal composure and circumspection after this setback, and did work to rehabilitate himself but again he got ahead of himself and tried to lead a coup against Somerset. He had counted on the support of the Earl of Warwick but this was a spectacular misjudgement which finished him at the early age of 45.

Southampton had again overestimated his leadership skills and it is this trace of impetuosity in his character (a characteristic that was dominant in his son and grandson) that proved his undoing. His rise through the court ranks had been steady and largely unblemished. But upon his elevation to one of the top jobs his practical caution seems to have escaped him and he may have fancied himself as the leader of the conservative cause. This was a talent beyond his natural gifts. Had he continued like his predecessor, Sir Thomas Audley he might well have retained his position and perhaps prolonged his own life. As it is the streak of impetuosity, which he must have governed throughout most of his career, took control, with unfortunate results.

He built up a considerable fortune before his death. He transformed himself into one of Hampshire's largest landowners and left a very large amount of money to his widow and heir. When he entered government service in 1524 as a junior clerk he could only boast of a family with good connections, but no real money to speak of. Sixteen years later he had transformed himself into a great landowner. This was remarkable.

His son and heir, as is often the case, squandered a lot of it when he came into his majority, but even so there was sufficient left to maintain the 3rd and 4th earls in the state the family had now achieved.

There had been examples in other centuries: Peter des Roches, in the 13th century who rose from modest beginnings to become Bishop of Winchester. Likewise William of Wykeham in the 15th century. William de la Pole, a Hull merchant, became a power in the land in the 14th century. The Tudor period created more opportunities and the Spencers, Russells, Cecils, Thynnes, Sandys as well as the Wriothesleys discovered new avenues to wealth.

When the second earl succeeded his father in 1550 he was a multi-millionaire by today's measure.

THE
UNHAPPY EARL

PART 2

The Earls of Southampton

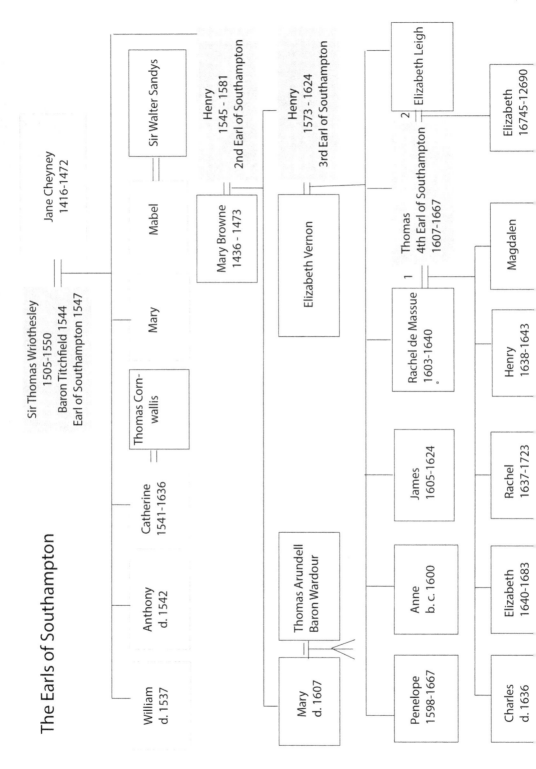

1

A SHELTERED LIFE

*to the Countess of Southampton requiring her, in the Queen's Highness'
name, without further delay or protract of time, notwithstanding her
former excuses, to take order that the Earl, her son, may be here at the
Court before Candlemass Eve next coming. - Letter sent December
1564*

The second earl, Henry, could hardly have had much memory of
his father and was raised by a mother who never remarried and went to
some lengths to insulate her son from outside influences. She appears
to have resisted any summons to court before 1564 and brought up her
son in a highly-protected environment. There were to be consequences.

No-one has recorded the feelings or state of mind of Countess Jane
at the relatively early death of her husband at the age of 45. She was
herself about 40 years old with three surviving daughters and a five year
old son. She was a very rich woman and her 'widow's third' gave her
financial independence. Without doubt she would have been an very
attractive prospect for men who would be quick to take the opportunity
to enrich themselves but she appears to have brushed off any marriage
proposals and set about devoting her life to her son. This was entirely
laudable, but in retrospect may not have been in the best interests of her
only surviving son who grew up without a father figure.

On the death of Thomas Wriothesley the earldom passed to his
son Henry who had yet to reach his fifth birthday anniversary. In the
custom of the day the wardship of the minor passed to the crown to be
administered by the Master of the Wards. He in turn sold the wardship
to the highest bidder, in this instance Sir William Herbert. The dowager
Countess of Southampton had sufficient resources of her own to buy

back the wardship from Sir William and proceeded from that point to manage the upbringing of the child.

The practice of wardship of a minor, whereby the ward was able to profit from the revenue of the estate, had its origin in feudal times. William I made grants of land to his followers on condition of knightly service in return. This arrangement enabled the king to call on a military force at any time without maintaining a standing army, and by the time of Henry II the system had been codified to specify a precise number of knights from each tenant. Where minors were concerned, since they could not bear arms into battle, the king, reasonably sought compensation for this loss of service, and income from the ward's estate could be used to hire mercenaries. Over time the original purpose was forgotten and the practice of wardship was used as a source of crown revenue. By the 16th century the practice had become quite corrupt; the crown would sell the wardship for ready cash and the owner of the wardship would profit from it.

A potential side benefit for the ward was that the new master was also obliged to take care of the boy or girl's education. This could be something of a lottery, depending much on whether this duty was conscientiously undertaken, but at the very least the youngster would be exposed to influences outside the immediate family. As it was the second earl never had this opportunity and was from the beginning under the dominant tutelage of his mother.

Jane, Countess of Southampton, was a devout follower of the Roman church. Her husband, although religiously conservative himself, had been more circumspect about his own religious leanings at the court of Henry VIII. Jane Southampton was under no such pressure and made sure that the boy's catholic education was absolute. Within three years, after the death of Edward and the accession of Mary, her commitment to the old church could be open. Five years later, after Elizabeth came to the throne and the Protestants were once more in the ascendant, it became more difficult to be overt in practice, but Elizabeth and her ministers were willing to tolerate private catholicism, provided that it would not jeopardise the state. Thus, the Countess and her friends were never under pressure to renounce their faith and most likely dreamed of a day when orthodoxy would return.

Countess Jane seems to have been successful in keeping the young Henry away from Protestant influences by bringing him up at

Dogmersfield and Titchfield far away from the pernicious influences of the London court. The boy, with only one parent, was exposed to a world view through his mother's prism. She appears to have been a possessive woman. Not only did she manage to keep the boy away from court but she apparently opposed his marriage to Mary Browne, the thirteen year old daughter of Viscount Montagu of Cowdray Park. This ought to have been highly acceptable as the Brownes were also committed catholics, but perhaps this matriarch had become too possessive. The father of Anthony Browne, Viscount Montagu, was Sir Anthony Browne, a descendant of the great Nevill family through his mother, and several other distinguished lines. He was also the half-brother of William FitzWilliam, who held positions of prominence at the court of Henry VIII and not incidentally was the first holder of the title Earl of Southampton. Fitzwilliam died childless in 1542 and left his very extensive estates, including Cowdray, to Sir Anthony Browne. The fact that Sir Thomas Wriothesley, a fellow conservative and associate of FitzWilliam, took the title of Earl of Southampton in 1547 is perhaps not coincidental. One must suspect that Countess Jane was unwilling to let go. Nevertheless, the 2nd. earl was of age and did not need his mother's permission and they married on 19 February 1566.

> 'Tuesday, 19 February 1566, the marriage was solemnised at London in my lord Montagu's house at his advice, without the consent of my Lady his mother.'[67]

Henry was far too young when his father died to be conscious of the lurch to Protestantism and as he grew in awareness Roman Catholicism was orthodox for five years under the reign of Mary. At her death the young earl was almost a teenager and his character and religious beliefs were fully formed. He was not to deviate from his passionate catholicism for the remainder of his life.

In retrospect, this sheltered life did him no favours. The summons to appear at court in 1564, cited at the head of this chapter, suggests that the countess had been stalling for some time. At the age of 19 his mind was made up, but his beliefs and character and his lack of experience of the political world of accommodation left him ill-prepared for the role that his position demanded of him. Elizabeth and her government took a moderate position and, where possible, steered clear of absolutism. While the country was officially protestant, adherence to the old faith was tolerated provided it did not lead to instability. Most of the peerage were catholic but her pragmatic policy was aided by the fact that many catholics did not want to go back to the turmoil of Mary's years.

The young earl inherited his father's intensity, but whereas Thomas was able to govern his temper through his political and careerist instincts, his son lacked that moderating influence. The story of Thomas Wriothesley, as described in the first section, showed him to be conservative in his religious beliefs, but he had been schooled by humanists and was thus able to work alongside Lutherans, such as Cromwell and Audley, as well as conservatives like Stephen Gardiner, and maintain professional relationships on all sides. Young Henry, who probably had no memory of his father, was entirely subject to his mother's influence, which in religious matters was pure and unadulterated by political considerations. There were no balancing influences on his upbringing to make him a more temperate adult.

In 1566, the year of his marriage and majority, he came fully into his estates and was immediately a rich young man. His wealth and status would have naturally made him eligible for a place at court and some office in government but he proved unequal to such expectations. Southampton was quickly marked as something of a hothead. It appears that Cecil arranged for the Queen to be hosted by Southampton at Titchfield during the summer of 1569. This did not come to pass because other, more seditious activities were taking place at Titchfield. The Earls of Sussex and Southampton, together with his brother-in-law, Viscount Montagu, met at Place House to discuss how they could support a proposed marriage between the Duke of Norfolk and Mary Queen of Scots. This proposed union was not without support - even Leicester was in favour - and Sussex and Southampton were not out of tune with a large body of opinion. Norfolk was a Protestant and such a union had potential to rersolve the succession issue with a 37 year-old childless and unmarried queen. However, when she learned of the proposal Elizabeth vetoed the proposed marriage.

1569 was a dangerous year. England north of the Humber only had fertile land in the vale of Yorkanf on the eastern coast and was at an economic disadvantage to the prosperous south. The population held tenaciously to their feudal lordships and to the catholic faith. So a rebellion in October 1569 led by the northern earls of Northumberland and Westmorelandwas serious the Earl of Sussex was sent north to suppress it and within a few months the uprising fizzled out.

Left to their own devices and in the belief that the northern uprising would lead to the regime change they desired, Southampton and Montagu consulted with the Spanish ambassador and with his encouragement decided to support the Duke of Alba, who was engaged in suppressing the Dutch protestants in the Netherlands. It was a fiasco. They set sail for Flanders but the winds were against them and they were forced back to England. By this time the word of their activity was out and once they had landed on English shores they were quickly escorted to the Tower.

Good will was still in plentiful supply. In February 1570 Henry Radclyffe, Earl of Sussex and himself married to one of the catholic Howards, wrote to Sir William Cecil to intervene with the young earl, "that he may be rather charitably won than severely corrected." The Queen and Cecil were prepared to tolerate Montagu and Southampton if they were willing to behave themselves in future. Montagu chose to be loyal. He was made Lord Lieutenant of Sussex and allowed to keep his religion. He never made trouble again and even, when an old man, came to Tilbury in 1588 to defend the crown against the Armada. Southampton, although let off leniently, was not the compromising type. Within a few months he was in trouble again.

In May 1570 he arranged to meet in London with John Leslie, the Bishop of Ross (an agent for Mary Queen of Scots) to seek advice about whether he should continue to serve his queen. In this very month John Felton had pinned to the door of the Bishop of London's house the Bull of Pius V excommunicating the queen. The authorities were on red alert and the earl's attempt to meet with John Leslie took him into very dangerous territory. They agreed to meet across the river on Lambeth marsh, a seemingly obscure place, but they were being watched and were arrested. The two men claimed that they were merely enquiring about the health of Mary, Queen of Scots, at that time under guard at Tutbury Castle but it was a weak and transparent lie.

Once more the Privy Council gave Southampton the benefit of the doubt and in the Summer he was allowed to move out of the Tower to live under house arrest in Surrey. They must have regarded Southampton as a political lightweight, an impulsive hothead with little judgement and no following. He could be, and was, kept under house arrest, as much to keep him from further foolishness rather than constrain a dangerous man. His custodian, Sir William More of

Guildford, was instructed to persuade Southampton to take part in household devotions using the book of Common prayer. If he did so, they could then interpret this gesture as conformity with the Church of England. After some resistance Southampton agreed to participate and in November was allowed to go free.

However, his meeting with the Bishop of Ross would come back to bite him. In September 1571, Walsingham's spies uncovered the Ridolfi Plot, which was to raise a catholic army under the leadership of the Duke of Norfolk, and, with the assistance of a Spanish invasion force, overthrow Elizabeth and put Mary Queen of Scots on the throne. Roberto Ridolfi was a Florentine banker with strong connections to the ruling classes and able to travel freely across Europe. He was appointed as an agent by Pope Pius V who was himself dedicated to the overthrow of Elizabeth's government. As with many of these plots the imaginings of the plotters was fanciful. It largely depended on an uprising within the country against Elizabeth and although they might depend on some catholic families like the Wriothesleys and the Brownes, it is far from clear that the majority of the country would wish her overthrow. It secondly depended on an invading force of 10,000 men led by the Duke of Alba, who still had his hands full in the Netherlands. The prospects of this were by no means certain. And finally, Thomas Howard, the duke of Norfolk, was himself a Protestant motivated more by personal ambition than ideology. It was less than certain that many catholics would be willing to risk their lives for a venture with such precarious outcomes.

The Bishop of Ross, John Leslie, as confessor to Mary, Queen of Scots, one of the central characters in this scheme and was arrested and charged. He then, to use a more modern phrase, began to sing like a canary, and amongst other things recounted the substance of his meeting with Southampton. The earl had of course questioned whether he could in conscience show loyalty to Elizabeth. The Privy Council could no longer pass over this treason as the folly of a young hothead and in October 1571 he was arrested and sent to the Tower of London, where he was to languish for 18 months.

After a long period of incarceration he appeared to see the error of his ways and on 14 February 1573 he wrote to the Privy Council to assure them that he was "careful and studious to leave no means undone by all humble and therewith faithful submission and attestation of loyal obedience, to recover her Majesties good grace, opinion and favour towards me".[68]

These were the right words and together with submissions from friends and supporters the Privy Council accepted his contrition and released him once more to the more tolerable custody of William More on 1 May 1573, and later on 14 July to his father-in-law at Cowdray.

The day of 6 October 1573 was a rare moment in the joyless life of the second earl; his countess gave birth to a son. He had an heir to his title and some assurance that the Wriothesley line would continue. He wrote an excited letter to his friend William More of Loseley:

> Yet I have thought to impart unto you such comfort as God hath sent me after all my longe troubles, which is that this present morning, at iii of clock, my wife was d(elivere)d of a goodly boy (God bless him!) the which, although it was not without great peril to them both for the present, yet now, I thank God, both are in good state.[69]

It is possible that the birth was premature. There are hints of risk at the time of birth in this letter, and, unless the child was conceived during a visit by the Countess to her husband in the Tower some months earlier, it is a matter of record that the earl was not released from the Tower before 1 May 1573. There is also the possibility that this child may not have been the first boy. One reference mentions that he was the second son, and if naming conventions were observed, i.e. naming the first son after the paternal grandfather, we might expect a Thomas. At any rate, this one was named after his father, Henry. At this stage in his life one might be forgiven for thinking that the young earl had sorted himself out. He had come to recognise his duty to his monarch and he now had an heir.

The birth occurred at Cowdray, the house of Viscount Montagu at Midhurst in Sussex, where his mother had been living during her confinement and while her stubborn husband was still under house arrest at Loseley Hall. The new boy came into a family with one older sister, Mary. The first born, Jane, appears not to have survived infancy. Although we know next to nothing about how he was brought up, one can conjecture that it was normal enough for a well-to-do Elizabethan family. The second earl was beginning to get some signs of favour from the court and was active in some estate business. His relations with his wife had not yet broken down so it is possible that the boy spent some of his character forming years in a conventional family unit.

One thing we can surmise is that he was brought up in the Roman Catholic faith. His parents were committed catholics - his father stubbornly so - and the absence of any record of a christening would suggest that he was covertly baptised by a house priest.

The infant Henry may have stayed at Cowdray for some time. In the Autumn the earl was summoned to court, presumably to confirm that he really had repented of his subversive folly, for in a letter dated 1 November 1573 it is evident that he and his wife were travelling to London together with his father-in-law Anthony Browne and Jane his wife. It would appear too that the Southamptons returned to Cowdray and stayed there well into 1574, possibly only moving to Titchfield when the boy was a year old. This was perhaps the only tranquil period of his parents marriage, although he was too young to notice one way or another.

The dowager countess, baptised as Jane Cheyney and the widow of Thomas Wriothesley, the 1st earl of Southampton died in the year following the birth of her grandson, Henry, on 15 September 1574. She had been a widow for 24 years and by law entitled to one third of the income from her deceased husband's estates and was therefore a rich woman. She had chosen not to re-marry and appears to have lived in considerable style and comfort. Her will made bequests in considerable detail of all the jewellery she had acquired. At her death the one-third of the estate's income reverted to the control of the earl. This windfall may have prompted him to embark of his great Dogmersfield project.

2

A DIFFICULT MARRIAGE

It may be that my Lord will unrip old matters, repented and long forgotten since. If he do, he may well blame me of folly, but never justly condemn me of fault. – Countess Mary to her faher.

While the earl was testing the tolerance of the authorities he was in the early years of his marriage to Mary Browne, a daughter of Anthony Browne and his first wife Jane Radcliffe, herself a daughter of the earl of Sussex. Mary never knew her mother as she died in the year of her birth, 1552, most likely after giving birth at the age of 20. Four years later her father married Magdalen Dacre from a prominent northern family. The Brownes and the Dacres were strongly Roman Catholic and Magdalen reinforced the religious leanings of the two families.

Her marriage then to Henry Wriothesley brought satisfaction to both families as neither of them deviated from their commitment to the old faith.

The marriage itself proved difficult. His teenage bride, Mary Browne, was pregnant at least three times in the first years of the marriage in between her husband's times in custody. There were two daughters and a son. There may also have been another son but the issue stopped after Henry. Once in her twenties the countess was able to stand up to her difficult, obstinate, wilful, and often bad-tempered husband. One mught imagine that after the birth of a healthy son she felt that she had fulfilled her duty and may no longer have been willing to share a bed with her husband. There were rows and perhaps not as many reconciliations as there should have been.

Her son Henry would have been an insensitive boy in 1577 if he had not noticed that all was not well with his parents. Both were self-willed and self-centred and both had personalities that preferred collision to giving way. The earl, as we have seen, was a proud and stiff-necked man who did not know how to compromise or even find common ground. His wife never saw herself as anything other than the aggrieved party. Matters came to a head in 1577 when the earl suspected her of having an affair with a man named Donesame and forbade her to have anything more to do with him. Later, in 1580, there was a breach, or reported breach of this order and the earl erupted with rage. However by this time he was no longer on speaking terms with his wife and communicated with her through an intermediary, usually his steward Thomas Dymoke, whom apparently the Countess could not stand.

An almost blow-by-blow account of this ruction survives in a letter written by the Countess to her father, dated 21 March 1580. Some caution must be exercised here because she only gives her side of the story, but enough can be divined from what else we know about the earl's character for us to piece together the likely course of events.

At the time of the letter the Countess had been banished from the earl's "board and presence" and was living in one of the Hampshire houses separate from her husband. Access to her son was also restricted in that visitors had to seek permission from the earl first. The major charge, that of adultery with Donesame, was a serious one, and she answered it thus:

> And as for the matter charged of Dogmersfield & Donesame his coming thither, he shall never prove it as he would, except he win some to perjure themselves about it. For by my truth, in my life, did I never see him in that house. Neither I assure your Lordship since I was by my Lord forbidden his company, did I ever come in it. Desire I did to speak with him I confess, & I told yow why and I wished that the cause with my meaning were uttered by the party himself upon his conscience (if he have any) wherefore I coveted to speak with him. And then (I trust) I should be acquitted of greater evil, then overmuch folly, for desiring or doing that, which, being by my enemies mistaken, doth breed this my slander and danger. [70]

It is difficult enough even in contemporary marital disputes to determine the right and wrong of either side, and at a distance of over 400 years and with so little information, impossible to determine who is telling the truth. We do know that the earl was a difficult personality and quite as likely to see offence where none was intended, or to magnify some slight to his honour. Was the countess entirely innocent, or was there a fire behind this little whiff of smoke? A piece of pedestrian rhyme by a poet by the name of John Phillip, *An Epitaph on the death of the Right honorable and vertuous Lord Henry Risley, Noble Earle of Southampton* includes these lines:

> In wedlock he observed, the vow that he had made:
>
> In breach of troth through lewd lust, he ne would seem to wade.[71]

Phillip could not claim to know the actual truth but he would have been aware of the gossip of the day and what we may take from these lines is that the gossip concluded that the Countess had behaved inappropriately. This is not to say that common gossip knew the truth. The Countess maintained strong denial at the time and even after the death of her husband.

The consequences were catastrophic for the marriage and must have had some impact on the son. His father's extreme reaction must have indelibly imprinted on the young Henry's mind. As a young boy of 8 he would have difficulty in understanding the sin of adultery and one may be sure that it was not explained by his father in a reasonable or sympathetic way. The countess was never allowed to see her son during the lifetime of the father and unsurprisingly he was never close to his mother. We can suggest that his early rejection of marriage may have had their roots in this experience.

There was also a cooling off of relations between the Montagus and the Southamptons, whether because of this dispute or an earlier cause. The countess's letter to her father suggests that there had been an earlier quarrel between Southampton and the Brownes. We are not on sure ground here but it is plausible. There was also a letter many years later suggesting that Charles Paget, son of Thomas Wriothesley's old colleague, may have contributed to the rift.

> I will overpass his youthful crimes, as the unquietness he caused betwixt the late Earl of Southampton and his wife yet living.[72]

Father Parsons, a Jesuit, writing many years after made this observation:

> One thing also increased the difficulties of the Catholics at this time, which was the falling out between the Earle of

Southampton and the Lord Montacute about the Earle's wife.[73]

How this was resolved, if indeed it was, we do not know because there is no further report of the matter and in any case the earl's unhappy life was to come to an end the following year. All that can be added is that she may have had a reasonable explanation for her meeting with Donesame but was traduced by gossip-mongers who had the ear of the earl.

This story tells us is that the earl was an insecure and jealous type and probably susceptible to the idea of anything said against his wife as being proof of her possible infidelity. It is likely that the countess may have harmlessly flirted with this man called Donesame (who figures in no other documents and is never heard of again) and there was no more to it than this other than the earl's initial overreaction.

Unfortunately for his own emotional well-being the young boy Henry was forced to take sides. His father banished his mother in 1579 and it appears that for the last two year's of the second earl's life he would not allow his wife to see her son. She did try to use the boy as an intermediary by writing a letter to the earl to be delivered by her son and although the six year old boy took the letter to his father the earl refused to read it. After this the boy was entirely under his father's influence and unsurprisingly in the circumstances took his side. His mother wrote in a later letter, "he was never kind to me" and we might trace the young Henry Wriothesley's own difficulties with women as a young man to these early experiences.[74]

Mary's unfortunate experience of marriage put her off re-marrying for a long time. She wrote to the Earl of Leicester resolving not to 'put self in the lyke condicion.'[75] Indeed, this comparatively young woman (she was barely 30) did not enter matrimony again until 1594, when she married Sir Thomas Heneage on 2 May 1594. Heneage was by this time an old man, over 60 years old, and indeed he was to die the following year. In October 1594 her son would come fully into his inheritance and she may have been motivated by concerns for her own financial security. Heneage was a Privy Councillor and was well-connected at court. He had been the holder of many offices of state and had himself built up substantial estates. This marriage was his second and his first wife had died in 1593.

It would seem however that the new couple genuinely liked each other and she did care for him in the last year of his life, when he was not a well man. His estate passed to his only daughter from his first marriage and the countess was entitled to her widow's third of the income from Heneage's estate. However he died with heavy debts, which his widow had to pay off over time.

Her choice for a third marriage was William Hervey, a Kentish gentleman who may not have been much older than her son. His date of birth is unrecorded but he was known to be at the court of Queen Elizabeth in 1587 and he distinguished himself on the lord admiral's flagship during the defence against the Spanish Armada in 1599, so we might estimate his birth date at between 1567 and 1570, and therefore only five years older than the third earl at the most. This may have been the reason behind the earl's hostility towards the marriage. He was never on close terms with his mother and on this occasion he made his opposition clear. Eventually the two married in secret, sometime around 1598. Hervey was a capable man and he had served with distinction in several naval engagements. This was Hervey's first marriage and he was marrying a woman old enough to be his mother. No doubt there was some opportunism here; the marriage to a dowager countess had career advantages and indeed he was made keeper of St Andrew's Castle in Hampshire, a post that brought him £19 3s. 4d. a year. Of course there were no children. Mary died in 1607 and he married a younger woman the following year. She bore three sons and four daughters. Hervey had a good career and became a baron in both Ireland and England. He died in 1642.

3

LAST DAYS AT DOGMERSFIELD

He was not known in the streets by guarded liveries, but by gold chains, not by painted butterflies ever running as if some monster pursued them, but by tall goodly fellows. – Gervais Markham.

For a while Southampton ceased to paddle in dangerous waters and his Queen and the Privy Council might have contented themselves with the opinion that, at the age of 30, the earl was prepared to settle down and attend to his estates. He was given some offices to encourage him in his loyalty; he was appointed to the Commission for the Peace for Hampshire and was later employed to survey the coastal defences. In 1579 he was appointed to a commission for the eradication of piracy. These were not large offices of state but they were signals to the earl that if he conformed he might expect better. It appeared that the earl did stay out of political trouble during these years and instead of fruitless plotting, he set about spending some of his father's inheritance. Thomas Wriothesley had been a careful manager of money and by this means had built a significant fortune. His son inherited the land and income but was inclined to live beyond his means. In 1624 a man called Gervase Markham, a contemporary of the third earl, published a book called *Honour in its Perfection.* The book itself is of little worth, amounting to a panegyric to impress the earls of Oxford and Southampton and Essex. Whether or not it did anything to further Markham's career I do not know. He wrote this:

> After this noble prince succeeded his son (i.e. The son of Thomas Wriothesley, 1st Earl of Southampton) Henry Earle of Southampton, a man of no lesser virtue, promise and wisdom. . . . . .his muster roll never consisted of four lackeys and a coachman, but of a whole troupe of at least a hundred well-

mounted gentlemen and yeomen. He was not known in the streets by guarded liveries, but by gold chains, not by painted butterflies ever running as if some monster pursued them, but by tall goodly fellows.[76]

Even allowing for exaggeration and the fact that Gervase Markham was not there to observe for himself, this strikes the reader as enormously expensive, possibly ruinously so. It suggests a triumph of show over substance. His father had been able to acquire enough money to make a large number of property purchases in the 1530s and with new revenue coming in the 1540s there is no doubt that the Wriothesleys were leading members of the nouveau riche. However, keeping a large number of men as retainers in livery would have been very expensive and one suspects that had the second earl lived longer he would have been in serious debt before too many years passed. Even allowing for some overstatement of numbers by Markham, this sort of thing represented a high cost. He was, when all said and done, maintaining Beaulieu, Titchfield, Southampton House, a house in Southampton itself called Bull Hall, a house in London, and to these he added the new project at Dogmersfield, and another residence at Itchell.

We know very little about this project except that it was unfinished at his death and even at his own estimate in his will the work might take up to ten years to complete. This appears to hint at a grand design, possibly one that was very expensive and as I have noted the executors must have abandoned or placed the project on hold. There is no evidence that his son or grandson showed any interest in resuming work at Dogmersfield.

There was a medieval bishop's palace on the site, owned and occupied by the bishops of Bath and Wells since the 12th century at least. At the Conquest it was a royal manor, which was later granted to Ralph Flambard, bishop of Durham. It fell back into royal hands during the time of Henry I, who then granted it to the Bishop of Bath and Wells. There were subsequent disputes about the rights to the manor but Henry II appeared to settle the matter in favour of the bishop. In 1205 King John ordered wine to be sent to Dogmersfield, 'to be placed in the house of the Bishop of Bath'[77] and in 1207 confirmed the bishop's right to the manor. The manor had a good hunting park and was favoured by the bishops, some of whom died there, until the 1530s when Henry VIII took possession.[78]

Some indication of the quality of the residence might be inferred from its choice by Henry VII as a meeting place for Arthur, Prince of Wales and his intended wife, Catherine of Aragon. Catherine had landed in Plymouth on 2 October 1501. It then took 33 days of travel over difficult roads for the young princess to reach Dogmersfield and it seemed proper for the king and her intended husband to make the effort to meet her part way. Ten days later she was able to enter London in the great pageant organised by earl Henry's great grandfather, as recounted in the opening chapter.

Henry VIII at first leased the manor to Oliver Wallop for 21 years in 1542, but on his death, Edward VI granted it to Thomas Wriothesley, 1st earl of Southampton. It is unlikely that the earl did much with his new property in the last three years of his life and there would have been no interest in developing the manor during the minority of the second earl. However, once released from prison the second earl seems to have adopted Dogmersfield as his special project. Almost nothing is known of the medieval bishop's palace. Henry Wriothesley's project must have planned a complete rebuilding of the medieval palace, probably to compete with his father's transformation of Titchfield. The earl was still a young man and with a career at court closed off to him needed some outlet for his energy. In this context the Dogmersfoeld project would give him purpose.

Almost nothing is known about the second earl's plans. Since he anticipated ten years of building we may assume that the project was ambitious, and from 1577 to 1581 he must have devoted himself to it.. The third earl had interests of his own and together with his financial difficulties may have completely ignored Dogmersfield. The 4th earl, when he came to straighten out the affairs of the earldom, sold the estate in 1629 to Edward Dickenson. This then passed to William Godson, descending to a female heiress, Martha, who married Ellis St John. They began to build a new house in 1728 which was enlarged throughout the 18th century.

The Elizabethan manor house, started by the 2nd earl was thus completely obliterated and no drawings survive to tell us what it might have been like.

The second earl appears to us as a man more committed to show than substance. As the owner of several properties, each of which would require staff, and, if we believe Markham, somewhat addicted to attendance by a retinue of liveried servants, he stands in some contrast to his high-achieving father.. It is tempting to observe, that once the rigid commitment to Roman Catholicism had been denied him, there was no substance to the man. He contented himself to showy displays of his own perceived magnificence.

Possibly the strain of these domestic difficulties may have unhinged the earl from the sensible conformist path he had chosen in 1574 because once again dangerous seditious plots were abroad and Southampton was once more implicated. This time the Jesuit, Edmond Campion, at the centre of yet another plot had been in touch with Southampton through his steward Thomas Dymoke in August of 1581. There is another report that he had been imprisoned on 16 January 1581, although we do not know for how long.

On the 4 October 1581 the unhappy earl gave up on his short and furious life. He was only in his 36th year. The cause of his death is not recorded although A. L. Rowse describes him as consumptive. It is possible that a bout of pneumonia brought down a body that had already been weakened by the stress of his marriage and his inability to steer clear of seditious activities, and if it was not pneumonia then it was something else. One might note that he was now the third generation of Wrythe/Wriothesleys to die prematurely. William Wrythe, his grandfather, died in 1513, probably in his thirties and his father the first earl only made it to 45. We know almost nothing about William Wrythe but our knowledge of the first earl gives us a highly strung, intense character who was subject to periods of illness, probably at the end of long periods of sustained hard work and it appears that his son Henry, although nowhere near as busy, was also subject to wearing himself thin because of his extreme temperament. At any rate, for the second time, the earldom fell into the inheritance of a minor.

He died at Itchell House, a few miles away from Dogmersfield, apparently with his son and daughter in attendance and he was buried in Titchfield Church on 30 November 1581. It is not known why six weeks elapsed before he was buried, but perhaps delays were caused by disputes about the will.

The second earl did have time to construct an elaborate will, which was dated 24 June 1581. He was unreconciled to his wife and it contained some vindictive provisions against her. His daughter Mary was given a legacy, but only on the condition that she never be in the same house as his widowed mother. The countess was legally entitled to enjoy a one third share of the estate for her lifetime, so there is nothing the earl could do to countermand that, but in the first will she received nothing more. As he sunk closer to his death the earl adopted a more forgiving tone and added a written codicil to the will. In place of the house at Dogmersfield he offered an annuity of £80 and further, to show the world the he died 'in a spirit of perfect charity' he offered her a bequest of £500. Dymoke did extremely well out of the will. He was given a legacy of £40 and a further legacy of £200. A further £40 a year was granted 'to be attendant dayly about the person of my sonn'. Dymoke got Whitely House and presumably the farmland around it, and when the third earl came of age he was to get Bromwich Farm on a 21 year lease - again adjacent to Titchfield. Dymoke was also one of the executors of the will.[79]

The Countess was not moved by any of this. All of their communication for the past years had been through intermediaries and the earl was obviously too stiff-necked to humble himself through a face-to-face attempt at reconciliation. She immediately set about contesting the will. She wrote to the Earl of Leicester, who was a cousin and then at the height of power and influence. He agreed to assist, but wanted assurance that the new earl was not going to turn out to be a committed papist. She replied that it was not her fault if her son refused to hear the Anglican service because she had not been allowed to see him for two years.

The first result of Leicester's intervention was that the young Lady Mary was restored to her mother's care where she apparently remained until she married. Her next victory was that Thomas Dymoke whom she detested as a man "void of ether wit, ability or honesty" agreed that while he would keep the benefits conferred upon him he would, in effect, step down as executor and stay out of the affairs of her son. He was relieved of his role as administrator of the estate in favour of Edward Gage.

There remains some curiosity about Thomas Dymoke. He was obviously a steward for the earl at Titchfield but he appears to have proved his ability and his functions extended beyond Titchfield. In his will the earl is fulsome in his praise of Dymoke as a man worthy of his trust. He received legacies of £240 and an income of £40 a year, quite substantial sums that would allow Dymoke to live in some comfort.

We can infer that the man was competent and an excellent servant to the earl, helping him manage his complex affairs, which he may not have had the temperament to cope with. Equally plainly the Countess detested the man, but this may be coloured by the fact that he acted as a messenger for her estranged husband. It is curious however that Dymoke has left little trace on Titchfield. The parish registers start in 1589, less than a decade after the earl's death but there is no sign of a Dimmock in any of the variant spellings. Thomas Dymoke was still alive in 1594 and living at Whitely Lodge as he was a participant in the Danvers' affair. After this he disappears without trace. There is no record of his burial in the Titchfield Parish Register, which begins in 1589, nor is there any evidence of wife or children. He may have given his name to Dimmock's Moor near to Whitely Farm. He may have been buried at the nearer church of St Bartholemew at Botley, but there the extant register only starts in 1679, so his end may remain a mystery.

The final extravagance of this will was the expensive tomb which rests today in the parish church of Titchfield. There was to have been two - one for his father and mother and another for himself. He demonstrated a lack of realism. He authorised £1,000 for tombs to his father and himself, an enormous sum. The entire Titchfield Abbey estate was purchased for a sum not far in excess of that amount of money. A further £1,000 was to be spent on his funeral. In addition, he bequeathed £2,000 to his daughter Mary, with the rather spiteful condition that she could not live with her mother.

Bear in mind that the annual income from the land and property he inherited was in the region of £1,300 a year,[80] so in effect he was willing away three years' income in his last desperate moments. It was too ambitious. Once the executors had opportunity to examine the earl's income and debts they wisely decided that both families could be accommodated in a single monument. In addition he charged his executors with the completion of Dogmersfield which he estimated might take up to ten years. Here again the executors concentrated their minds on the possible rather than the fanciful and may have done enough to make the house habitable as it was, without commissioning further expansion. The earl did indicate in his will that the interior walls at Dogmersfield had been plastered, a sign perhaps that a good part of the planned complex was near completion.

The earl pronounced himself in perfect health four months before his early death but one suspects that he must have had some premonition of his early demise. With the exception of his mean-spirited clauses directed towards his wife he showed himself to be generous. Too generous in the opinion of A L Rowse who felt that it was "extravagant with a touch of fantasy about it." [81] His bequests included 100 marks to be distributed in alms at his funeral, £200 to be distributed to the poor on his estates and £3 each to every almshouse in London and Hampshire. These were not small sums of money. £1,000 was to be spent on the two tombs already mentioned and to make substantial improvements to the parish church at Titchfield.

4

THE MONUMENT

Also two faire Monuments there to be made, the one for my Lorde my Father (whose bodye I wqulde have thether to be broughte and there buried), and my Ladye my Mother; the other for mee, with portraitures of white alabaster or such lyke uppon the said Monuments. - from the will of Henry Wriothesley, 2nd earl of Southampton.

This may be an ungracious remark, but the second earl may have made a greater contribution to his family in death than he did during his short and furious life. He had the time to prepare a will and ready his soul before he finally expired at Itchell on 4 October 1581 and he gave explicit instructions about the tomb which was to be erected in St Peter's Church in Titchfield.

> " I bequeth my body to be buried in the chapel of the parish church of Titchell, co. Southampton, where my mother lies interred; which chapel I will and direct to be newe altered and fynished by my executors within five years after my decease, in form following, that is to say,—Newe side windowes of stone to be made, the roof plaistered withe pendaunts being sett-full of my Armes, and all the walls plaistered lyke my howse at Dogmers Feilde, and the same faire paved and divided with yron gratte from the' church. Also two faire Monuments there to be made, the one for my Lorde my Father (whose bodye I wqulde have thether to be broughte and there buried), and my Ladye my Mother; the other for mee, with portraitures of white alabaster or such lyke uppon the said Monuments; and I will to be bestowed thereuppon one Thousande poundes by my foresaide Executors. And I will suche Funerall charges and obsequies to be donrie and bestowed uppon my saide buriall

as shall seeme meete and convenient to my executors for myne estate and degree, Soe'that the same exceede not a Thousand poundes. And I will to be given 100 marks (£66 13s. 4d.) at the time of my burial in charitable Almes according to the executors' discretion. Also to the needy poor within my several lordships the sum of, £200 to pray for the good estate of my soul, the souls of my ancestors and all Christian souls. Also (for the same purpose) £3 to every Alms-house in the City of London and County of Southampton."

This was the bequest of a very rich man. The £1,000 committed to the monument could be extrapolated to a sum upwards of £3,000,000 today and indeed the cost of his funeral, conducted by Garter, King of Arms was £138 6s. 4d. was itself over £500,000 in today's equivalent. The College of Heralds, with which the Wriothesley family were closely connected would have been happy to honour one of their own, but their services came at a price. The detailed cost of this funeral has been preserved among papers written by Robert Glover, Somerset Herald.[82]

The details of the construction of the monument seem to have been assumed by the second earl's father-in-law, Viscount Montagu of Cowdray. This can only be inferred. The tomb at Cowdray, probably constructed at the same time, so much resembles the Titchfield monument that one must conclude that they were both created in the same workshop. The Montagu monument was originally placed in a south side chapel at Midhurst, as is the one at Titchfield, and was free standing with four obelisks at each corner, again, as at Titchfield. Other than the differences in the figures themselves, the original monument at Midhurst, as apparent from old drawings bears a remarkable resemblance to the Titchfield tomb. The integrity of this monument was not maintained. In 1851 it was moved from Midhurst church to Easebourne, but in order for it to be accommodated in this smaller space the obelisks were removed.

Whatever the truth behind the strained relations between husband and wife, it would appear that Anthony Browne was determined to see to it that his former son-in-law was recognised with appropriate dignity.

It is quite probable that work on the tomb did not begin immediately after the death of the second earl. The will was proved at the Provincial Court of Canterbury on 7 February 1582 and it is most likely that the executors had many matters to attend to before they addressed the construction of the tomb. It was certainly not completed at the time of the marriage of the second earl's daughter in 1585.[83] We can also say that it was probably completed by 1592, when Viscount Montagu died, as his tomb was completed before his death.

The figure lying on the top altar table is the wife of Thomas Wriothesley, Countess Jane, given pride of place on the monument. She was effectively, the only parent the second earl had known, as his father died when he was five years old and he can therefore have had little memory of him. It is an established fact that the Countess' piety and dedication to the Roman Catholic faith had an enormous influence on her headstrong son. She also, lying in state after death, wears a coronet to signify her status.

To her right and left on the lower altar tables are her husband and only surviving son. The first earl is dressed in robes befitting a statesman, but the second earl is dressed in armour. He apparently had military pretensions, although there is no record of his being involved in any military activity, unless one can count the abortive fiasco where he, together with his father in law, tried to join a Spanish fleet in 1569.

Kneeling in prayer below the 1st earl are represented two of his four surviving daughters. Katherine married Thomas Cornwallis of East Horseley and Mabel married Sir Walter Sandys. Two others, not represented, were Mary, married Sir Richard Lister of Southampton and Elizabeth married Thomas Ratcliffe who later became earl of Sussex.

The second earl had only one son and daughter: Mary, who married Sir Thomas Arundel and Henry, who succeeded his father as 3rd earl Both are carved in relief in kneeling positions.

The tomb is impressive and boldly makes its intended statement. The Wriothesleys were to a degree a parvenu family and with the exception of the unsubstantiated claim that the Dunstanvilles had a bloodline that came from Henry I, their lineage was modest. The Brownes, on the other hand, could claim descent from such illustrious 14th and 15th century families as the de la Pole, Holland, FitzAlan, Neville and Montagu families. No doubt the second earl, for all his bitterness against his wife, did not wish to see this lineage brushed over for his posterity. Or perhaps, since Viscount Montagu may have had a direct hand in the design of the tomb, the quarterings on the shield painted on the tomb make no attempt to hide the Browne lineage.

While I would not go so far as the acerbic A L Rowse and describe the earls life as "useless", it is a fair judgement that he did not live up to the potential of his position. Sometimes the shadow of a father who achieves a great deal in a single lifetime can loom large over a son who may be expected to achieve as much and perhaps more, and in every age one never has to look far for examples. Since he was only six when his father died he never had the opportunity to know him other than as a child. His father's achievements would certainly have been advertised but there was nobody to school him as to how he might emulate his father. One unfortunate aspect of his upbringing was his mother's decision to isolate him from any insidious protestant influences. This meant that unlike his father who attended St Paul's School and Trinity Hall at Cambridge, where he might be able to compete and compare himself with other boys, he was educated at Titchfield by Catholic tutors whose dogma could be relied upon but whose learning might have been narrow. Swithun Wells, who was executed in 1591 for his sedition and extreme Popish sentiments, was a tutor to the second earl. He was a well-educated man but his narrow focus on Catholic doctrine limited the outlook of the young second earl. Thus the earl's education might have inclined him to absolute positions untempered by knowledge of the real world.

His father Thomas, as we have seen, was a highly strung character, often quick to temper; yet he was enough of a politician to know when to give way. Stubborn opposition often resolves nothing, and Wriothesley knew how to keep his head - in both senses. Had he lived longer, he might have been able to pass on this wisdom to his son, who appeared to be of similar temper. William Cecil lived to a great age and was able to school his son Robert in the arts of politics and statesmanship. Henry Wriothesley had no such model.

It was still the practice in Tudor times for members of the nobility to "take in" the sons of lesser gentry, partly for their own advancement, partly to provide companionship for their own children, and partly to build a sense of obligation and support amongst their followers. Lord Burghley's education of his wards, for example, amounted in practice to a school. While it is possible that a limited number of boys of his own age may have had access to the young earl, one is left with the impression that his early life was hermetically sealed against any possible pollution from protestantism. As a young adult he emerged with views verging on zealotry. He was part of that first generation born after the creation of the Church of England and those young people were open to the influences of Protestant theology, yet this young man aligned himelf with his mother's generation.

He would not have found himself much out of kilter with the older peers of the realm; there was still a majority among them of conservatives who adhered to the old faith. However the majority of that majority held views which were tempered by political realism. The world had changed and it would have been very difficult to undo the reformation under Henry VIII as the benighted reign of Mary had proved. Therefore, the wisest course was to maintain one's private faith while cleaving to public policy in the interests of state. It was the earl's tragedy that he did not have sufficient education or breadth of understanding to grasp this political reality.

There was a streak of blind stubbornness in his character, partly temperamental, but largely due to his upbringing, which we can probably characterise as that of a spoiled child. He was obviously used to getting his way and in the face of any resistance would obstinately stick to his own predetermined course rather than try to negotiate his way through the difficulties. This aspect of his character came to the fore in his dealings with the state over his meddling in various abortive catholic conspiracies and in his marriage which did, incidentally, some harm to the emotional development of his son. He was lucky in a way that Elizabeth and Cecil had wiser heads on their shoulders than he, and rather than reach for the executioner's axe, decided on a policy of chastisement and containment. They correctly judged him as a lightweight who might add to, but certainly would not lead, a conspiracy.

And it was as a lightweight that he was treated in public office. He was granted a few small public offices in Hampshire but nothing near as befitting as his status as an earl. His father and his son and grandson each held high offices of state at one time or another; the second earl came nowhere near such a brief.

Instead he appears to have occupied himself with the rebuilding of Dogmersfield in North Hampshire. Unlike his father, who had been able to husband sufficient resources to complete the Titchfield project in very short order, the Dogmersfield reconstruction may have been too ambitious. The earl had already developed an extravagant lifestyle but due to his religio-political activities had not put himself in a position where he could enlarge his income.

Had he lived longer and come to a more mature understanding of his role in Elizabethan society the story might have been different. He may have been awarded higher office and thus enjoyed greater income. He may have finished Dogmersfield and bequeathed a mansion of the size and magnificence of, say, Cowdray. As it was, none of these things happened and the wealth and position created by his father passed, somewhat depleted, to his only son Henry, who, at the age of 8 was to become the third earl.

THE
INDEPENDENT
EARL

PART 3

1

ANOTHER LONG MINORITY

When he died in 1581 it was discovered that his debts and legacies far exceeded his personal assets. - Lawrence Stone

Two Elizabethans have come down to us with their famed undimmed - Queen Elizabeth I and William Shakespeare, and there is a supporting cast of other Elizabethans such as Sir Walter Raleigh and Sir Francis Drake who for one reason or another have become household names. It is the young Southampton's association with William Shakespeare that makes his life of more interest than it might otherwise have been. The 3rd Earl of Southampton came of age around the same time that Shakespeare was beginning to make a name for himself in London and the youthful earl chose to act as his patron. Subsequently the earl moved on to matters of more contemporary consequence. He was a capable soldier, a patron of the arts, a patron of the settlement of Virginia, and a Privy Councillor. However it has to be said that without the Shakespeare association he would be a minor figure in history.

The young earl became Shakespeare's patron in 1593. The theatres had been closed down by the authorities and William Shakespeare the actor was effectively out of work. He had other poetic ambitions and set about proving himself by writing a poetic allegory in the contemporary fashion. He took from Ovid's *Metamorphoses*, a tale about Venus and Adonis, and using the same title fashioned a narrative poem that became a best seller. Henry Wriothesley sponsored the work and as a result the poem made the names of both men.

The youthful earl was only the third in a very new dynasty. We have seen how his grandfather Thomas Wriothesley created a fortune from his career as a court official and had steadily risen, without much controversy, to become Henry VIII's last chancellor. On Henry's death he was created Earl of Southampton. Earlier chapters have also described how his instinct for staying out of trouble deserted him on the accession of the boy king Edward VI and the reformers who were closest to the king quickly ousted the Earl of Southampton. Always a highly strung individual his nervous system failed after being out of office and he died in 1550 at the age of 45.

In 1581 the widowed countess immediately set about a legal struggle to secure her rights. Other interested parties stirred to secure the wardship. All of these manoeuvres may have passed over the head of the eight year old boy who was nonetheless the focus of all attention. Even so it took some time for the executors to arrive at proper assessment, which they recorded in a book called *The Sale of the Wards*. The yearly value of the widow's third, assigned to the countess, was £362 19s. 0¾d.; the lands assigned to the crown were valued at £370 16s. 8d.; and the land allowed to the minor earl was valued at £363 11s. 2¼d. The total income amounted to just over £1,000.

There are figures which assess the value of the Southampton estate, but, although they appear to be accurate, may be an undervaluation.[84] The true income, as Lawrence Stone suggests in his careful study, was often much higher.[85] The income of the estates after the death of the first earl in 1550 approached £3,000. On reaching his majority and after the death of his mother in 1574, the second earl may have enjoyed revenues as high as £6,000. So the figures put forward after 1581 must be considered a serious underassessment.

After the Inquisition Post Mortem reporting in June 1582 we are presented with this picture:

> The yearly value of the Earl of Southampton his Lands as well in possession as in reversion. The yearly value of the Countess of Southampton her revenue parcel of the Premises £362. 19s. 0¾d.
>
> The Lands descended to the now Earle in her Majesty's hands per Annum £370. 16s. 8½d.
>
> The Lands devised by the late Earl's last will to the Executors per Annum £363. 11s. 2¼d.
>
> Summa total. £1097. 6s. 6½d.
>
> The yearly revenue which the said Erle shall receive at his

full age Imprimis his Lands which are in her Majesty's hands because of his minority, and the lands which the Executors have by the device of the last Earl's will shall be out of lease at his full age to grant which will be yearly worth £4,000, over and above the said Countess' jointure being of the yearly value of £362. 19s. 0¾d.

Item, there will be made also by a great fine at the least £2,000. Item the Leases of Micheldever, Estratton and West Stratton, and of the Parsonage of Titchfield with the other leases will be yearly worth £400.

Sum of the said Earl's yearly Revenue £4,000, over and above the said Countess jointure being of the yearly rent of £362. 19s. 0¾d.

Item the Executors may not by the said Earl's will let or grant any copyhold or ferine, but the same must be at the disposition of the Erle at his full age.

Item that the said Erie shall have his houses well furnished, and stuffed with all manner of furniture, Armour and plate, and his grounds well stocked and stored with cattle, which the executors must perform, beside the great quantity of wood growing upon the said Earl's lands.

Lands and Leases which presently ought to be in the said Earl's possession The Manor of Itchell, purchased in the Earl's name, of the yearly value of £100.

Item the Leases of Estratton Westratton and Micheldever, and the parsonage of Titchfield of the yearly value of £300. summa £400.

Even if we accept this estimate at face value, the projected income of the third earl, when he came to majority in 1594, was still huge.

Accordingly, once the estate had been valued and divided into thirds, Lord Howard of Effingham was granted the wardship for the sum of £1,000. It was a good investment. Over the next 13 years he would be able to draw revenues of about £4,000 from one third of the estate. However, it does appear that Howard transferred the wardship to Lord Burghley, probably for a financial consideration, although there is no surviving documentation to attest to this. The arrangement was not unfavourable to the Earl of Southampton; he got probably the finest education available to a young man of his class at this time, and he made a lifelong friend of Robert Cecil, which probably saved him from following the earl of Essex to the executioner's block in 1599.

Burghley himself, a man of letters rather than a man of action, had noted the scandalous deficiency of education for wards when he became Master of the Wards in 1561 and set about doing something about it. As a general practice those who purchased wardships focused their attention on taking profit and minimising expenses, and one of the areas where they could safely cut back was the cost of tutors for their wards. Burghley therefore set up a school in his own house and hired some of the best tutors as instructors. He had, of course, a vested interest when his own children were young, but after they had grown, and when Southampton was in attendance, he continued to maintain the same high standards and to take a personal and active interest in his charges.

The Burghley household was firmly protestant. It was also a well-regulated and happy household, and this is worth mentioning. G P V Akrigg makes the interesting observation that Southampton was translated 'from a disorderly ill-managed household where an underling ruled, he passed to the machine-like good order of Cecil House.'[86] It could not but have had an effect on the bright and sensitive young boy. The Burghley marriage was a happy one. When he married Mildred Cooke she was already (unusually) an educated woman and they since both shared a love of learning and they got on well together, surely an eye-opener for Southampton who had only known quarrelling between his parents. One anonymous biographer, who had spent twenty four years in the Burghley household, left these admiring comments:

> His kindness most expressed to children; to whom there was never a man more loving nor tender hearted. . . . And how aptly and merrily, he would talk with them; and such pretty questions, and witty allurements, as much delighted himself, the children, & the hearers.[87]

While his parents were strong adherents to the Roman church the young earl was not hostile to Protestantism as an adult. The roots of it are to be found in Cecil House, but we might also take consideration of his adult friendship with Robert Devereaux, earl of Essex.

Southampton's estates did not escape the attention of the meticulous Lord Burghley. He initiated a quiet clear out of Roman Catholic tenants on the Southampton estates; the second earl's zealousness had ensured that only practitioners of his own faith were tenants. This policy was reversed by Lord Burghley. It was not practical or even sensible to remove everyone and I imagine that those who were willing to subscribe to the Book of Common Prayer were allowed to stay, while those who were obdurate were quietly asked to leave. One passage from the Beaulieu Account books may illustrate:[88]

> The names of the persons remaining there
> Mr John Chamberlain the eldest and his wife
> Mr John Chamberlain his son, and Elizabeth his wife
> Mrs Margaret Kingston, widow, aunt to Mr John Chamberlain the elder
> Elizabeth daughter to Mr John Chamberlain the elder,
> 4 women servants, 6 menservants
> The names of the persons lately departed
> Mr Thomas Gifford and Cycely his wife and Mary Lyon
> Mr Michael Chamberlain and Elizabeth his wife
> Another chambermaid with Mr Giford, Two men of Gifford's
> Mr Richard Chamberlain his servants, Ursula Trussell his maiden
> Elizabeth Hussey her kinswoman, Thomas Jennings and Nicholas Lockley.

The division appears to have cut across family lines with one branch of the Chamberlains willing to accept the new religious order and another branch taking their livelihood elsewhere. It is interesting to note that the servants, who may have had little choice in the matter, stayed with their respective families.

In 1585, at the age of 12, the young Southampton was sent to St John's College, Cambridge. This was a common enough age to begin University studies and they usually took their degrees at the age of 15. St John's, a newish college founded in 1511, was, by 1585, strongly Protestant and this may also have had an impact on Southampton's religious beliefs. One might detect Burghley's influence in the decision to send him there. At university he was taught rhetoric, logic, ethics, arithmetic, geometry, perspective, cosmography and also ancient and modern history, and it all had a theological dressing in the Protestant thinking of the day.

Two of Southampton's undergraduate essays apparently survive and illustrate a capable mind well able to handle ideas in written form at the age of 13.[89]

After taking his MA he entered Grays Inn, near to Southampton House, to complete his education. Legal education of some sort was a final step in the preparation of the young Southampton for his coming into his inheritance. As a landowner who would undoubtedly be involved in legal transactions of one kind or another, he would obviously benefit from some knowledge, even though he would be able to employ specialist lawyers to do the necessary work. It has to be said that many of the young gentlemen who enrolled at the Inns of Court had little interest in hard study and much more interest in following the urges of their young manhood. In this respect they were not dissimilar to the Oxbridge Universities of two or three generations ago, where young men of wealth and status had a jolly good time and paid little attention to their studies. Serious study was left to those of less exalted backgrounds who had to put more effort into making their way in the world. We don't know in which camp Southampton found himself, but it is more likely than not that the attractions of the good time group were hard to resist.

It is tempting to imagine that the third earl's first exposure to the theatre occurred on the evening of 16 January 1588 at Gray's Inn where an unspecified comedy was enacted. It was a thoroughly respectable occasion with the Earls of Warwick, Leicester and Ormond in attendance together with Lord Burghley and Lord Grey of Wilton. He still had to complete his studies at St John's.

It would have been here that he encountered the joys of the theatre. He was proposed by Lord Burghley to Gray's Inn on 29 February 1588.[90] On the following day, the first day of March, he was admitted to the inn. Only the night before a play by Thomas Hughes, the *Misfortunes of Arthur* had been performed. Play performances at the Inns of Court were not uncommon.

It seems almost certain that these young bloods were regulars at the theatres when they were open and regularly trooped off as a group to the theatres across the river or in the suburbs. It is quite possible that he met William Shakespeare during these excursions.[91]

The young earl emerges from the later years of his wardship as a highly intelligent and personable young man. Possibly his education in Burghley's school and at St Johns College Cambridge had developed a more rounded and more sociable personality than his rather moody father. Nevertheless there were still some traits of his father that were embedded in his personality, most particularly a certain stubbornness that set his face against more sensible behaviour. The first issue was that of marriage.

It was Burghley's intention, and indeed his right, to marry off his granddaughter Elizabeth de Vere to the young Southampton. Part of the arrangement that Burghley came to with Lord Howard of Effingham was that he would arrange the marriage of Southampton. This would in effect be the compensation for his trouble and expense in raising and educating the boy. They were close in age and of equivalent social standing, Elizabeth being the daughter of the Earl of Oxford. Despite the obvious self-interest for Lord Burghley it was, and would have been, judged a suitable match, not only in status, but also because it could bring additional wealth into the Wriothesley family. It is worth bearing in mind that the young earl inherited debts from his father and that he only had the income from one third of his estate to discharge them. This was not a matter for love but a matter for practical economics. The plan was sound. Most Elizabethans would have regarded this as a good match.

There was one problem - the young earl was not interested. When pressed, he took the line that he had no objection to this girl in particular, but he was not ready for marriage. Burghley persisted and enlisted the support of Southampton's mother and the ageing Viscount Montagu. his grandfather. Montagu discussed the matter with the young man and informed Burghley by letter that "this general answer that your Lordship was this last winter well pleased to yield unto him a further respite of one year to answer resolute in respect of his young years."[92] This proposed compromise most likely came from Lord Montagu; the young man was not inclined to budge.

Burghley was not the only entrant into this marriage market. Southampton was a very eligible young man and there is a surviving letter from Sir Thomas Stanhope from 15 July 1590 indicating that he was looking to marry his daughter to the young earl. He was offering a dowry of £3,000 and £300 a year 'for threescore years.'[93] One must assume that Burghley's offer was equally generous. However, Stanhope felt somewhat aggrieved that he had been left dangling without any proper response from the Earl of Southampton or his mother.

It has also been suggested that the Queen herself was brought in to advise the young man when she visited Titchfield at the end of August 1591. The queen's progress that Summer had taken her through Guildford and south to Cowdray for six days in August for some lavish entertainment. She then moved to Chichester, Portsmouth and then Titchfield 'for two standings for her Majesty.'[94] From thence to be entertained by the bishop of Winchester at 'Bishop's Walton', presumably the palace at Bishop's Waltham, and then northwards to London.

In this matter he showed the same stubborn streak that had so characterised his father' behaviour. He was against marriage and would not be moved. Again he stood firm. Not even the queen could persuade him and in this respect Southampton was the loser; the queen never held him in much regard for the rest of her life.

At one level this independence was admirable, and with the benefit of the twentieth century study of psychology, we can understand the damage done to him by the venomous breakdown of his parents' marriage. It would be hard for the young man to see much personal advantage in marriage. Eventually Burghley found a suitable husband for his grand daughter in William Stanley, the new earl of Derby and a grand ceremony was held with the queen in attendance on 26 January 1595. One must assume that the outcome was satisfactory for Elizabeth de Vere.

It was much less so for the 3rd earl of Southampton. There was a high price to pay for this intransigence. In the first instance Burghley exacted a fine of £5,000 against Southampton in 1594, as he was legally entitled to do. The source of this is some papers written by Father Garnett who informs us "the young Earl of Southampton, refusing the Lady Vere, payeth £5,000 of present payment."[95] Father Garnet was certainly in a position to hear something but the figure seems improbably large, extortionate even, and one which, one would have thought, bankrupted the Southampton estates. Fines for marrying without permission, or not, as in this case, were conventional and often large, but this one doesn't seem quite right. In the circumstances, with estates that were scarcely recovering from his father's extravagance and that the young earl was also committing to an expensive lifestyle, such a large fine may not have been supportable. In addition, his mother, as dowager, was entitled to one third of the revenues. The estate would be hard pressed to manage this without substantial borrowing, and this assumes there were lenders out there. The only comparable instance of a punitive fine of this nature was when Henry V slapped a 10,000 mark fine on the Earl of March in 1415 (£6,667) for marrying Anne Stafford without permission. Mortimer was far richer than the new earls of Southampton but even he had to borrow money to meet the fine, which even then was considered disproportionate, even though there were serious state security issues at stake. Even allowing for post-dissolution inflationary pressures on the Elizabethan economy the figure of £5,000 was probably an amount that was misheard or inflated or guessed at by Father Garnet. A fine of £1,000 may have been more plausible.

In mitigation it must be acknowledged that he was not the only young man to resist the idea of marriage at an early age. A decade later, William Herbert, heir to the earldom of Pembroke, took a similar stance, and it has been argued by some that the Sonnets 1-17 by William Shakespeare were addressed to Herbert and not, as others assume, to Henry Wriothesley. More on this subject in the next section.

Southampton therefore came into his inheritance with an immediate bill of huge proportions, whatever the actual figure. This could be overcome in time. Of more lasting damage was his reputation with the Queen, who noted the young man's stubborn streak with disfavour. Nowadays this sort of principled stance would win him high plaudits; in Elizabethan times such action was regarded as foolhardy.

Even so, the 3rd earl in 1593 was on the verge of a rich inheritance. During the twelve years of his minority the estates had been competently managed and the debts of the 2nd earl had been squared.

Henry Wriothesley was young, energetic and wanted to cut a figure in the world. Military service of some kind would have suited him well, particularly service under the bright star of the earl of Essex. There was indeed some prospect of this at the outset of 1591, when English foreign policy was leaning towards support of Henri IV of France against the catholic insurgency. There were some rumour that the earl of Essex would be sent over with a force and this may have prompted the impetuous Southampton to take matters into his own hands.

The Corporation of Southampton granted the earl the freedom of the town on 9 January 1591 and it was from Dieppe that he wrote to Essex in a letter dated 2 March. One guess is that he left Southampton port in January to be ready to be joined by the earl. This did not come to pass and he was ordered home in frustration. There must have been further frustration in the Summer when Essex was eventually sent over with a force of 3,000 men. The young earl was not one of them as his presence was required at Titchfield in September to entertain the queen.

There were other ways he could draw attention to himself. The Renaissance arrived later in England after its continental origins in Italy in the previous century, but by the second half of the century a young aristocrat was expected to demonstrate his intellectual credentials. men such as Sir Thomas Wyatt and the Earl of Surrey, became accomplished poets as well as statesmen, and young aristocrats of the next generation began to vie with one another to demonstrate their intellectual as well as physical accomplishments. The ideal for the age was held to be Sir Phillip Sidney, the soldier-poet. The Earl of Oxford, Edward de Vere, was a poet of some ability and he is now held by some to be the author of Shakespeare's plays. The claim of course is arguable, even preposterous, but the fact the de Vere wrote at all shows how important such accomplishments were for the Elizabethan aristocracy.

Another way of burnishing your intellectual credentials was to become a patron of the arts and young Southampton, with a decided interest in these matters, and coming into his majority, was a target for hopeful scribblers, including Shakespeare.

The Southampton earldom, despite his father's extravagance, was still a source of great wealth and the young 3rd earl was about to come into his fortune. It was also a propitious moment for another young man who had been born in a Warwickshire town in more modest circumstances, William Shakespeare.

2

ENTER SHAKESPEARE

Nothing that we know of Shakespeare's heredity points to a source for his talents. - Stanley Wells.

William, the son of John Shakespeare was baptised at the Church of Holy Trinity at Stratford upon Avon on Wednesday April 26th 1564. The Rector or the parish clerk of Holy Trinity duly recorded "Guilelmus filius Johannes Shakespeare." There is no mention of the mother but we know that John Shakespeare was married to Mary Arden. In any case, she would not have been present; baptism was a responsibility of the father and the godparents. We don't know the actual date of birth of the infant but we like to infer April 23rd, St George's Day. Why should it not be that the date of birth of England's greatest poet would coincide with the man who had been patron saint of the country since the time of the crusades? There is a pleasing symmetry to this.

In truth we cannot assert this as a reliable fact. It is reasonable to assume that a good Christian family in those times would hasten to baptise their child at the soonest date to protect its soul from original sin, but he could have been born at any time in the preceding week.

We have been lucky in some respects. Not all church records from that period in the 16th century survive, or perhaps were not recorded in the first instance. There is no baptismal record for Samuel Daniel, for example, a contemporary poet and historian whose background was at least as good as Shakespeare's and whose status as a poet was high during his lifetime. His inferred year of birth is 1562 and he died in 1619, and was thus an exact contemporary. But his place and date of birth have eluded researchers, although there is some slight evidence that he was born in the west country.

William's mother, baptised Mary Arden circa 1556, had already borne two children before her first son came along, but both, named Joan and Margaret, had died young. William was later joined by a younger brother, Gilbert in 1588 and by Joan in 1569. The family expanded with Anne, born in 1571, Richard in 1574 and Edmund in 1580.

William was the first child born to the Shakespeares to survive infancy. Even so, his survival must have been a close run thing. Barely three months after his birth there was an outbreak of plague in Stratford which claimed 237 lives over its course. William was either tough or lucky; perhaps his mother took him to the country at Wilmcote. The odds against survival for a newborn infant were not favourable. From the wealthy to the very poor, infant life was equally uncertain.

The Shakespeares were not obscure. Richard Shakespeare, William's grandfather, farmed in Snittersfield, some four miles north of the town and sustained a house in Stratford itself, a substantial property with a hall and seven rooms. His son John, born in 1529, was apprenticed to a glover in Stratford and inherited £38 17s 0d from his father. The sum appears paltry in today's money, but in the middle of the 16th century an annual income of £5 could provide for a family. By 1556, John Shakespeare was an established glover in the town. This was, however, not his sole activity. He farmed with his father at Snittersfield and at times with his brother in the village of Ingon. He was involved with the slaughtering of animals on the farm and this may have given rise to the rumour, reported by John Aubrey, that his father was a butcher. John Shakespeare had entrepreneurial talents and several times appears as a wool dealer. Later, he became a man of sufficient substance to buy property and lend money. Such activity tells us that he was a restless and ambitious man, a trait inevitably communicated to his eldest son.

John Shakespeare's trade was not an insignificant one. Gloves were tailored to the hand out of fine leather and could only be afforded by those of some means, and it appears, apart from some periods of financial difficulties, that John Shakespeare was reasonably well off. He was a member of the town council and had status in the community. He could afford to send his children to the local schools, and it was at the Grammar School that William got the foundation of his education. If William Shakespeare had never been tempted to go to London, nor had fallen in with a group of players and poets, and had he done no more than stay in Stratford upon Avon and followed his father into the glove making business, we might find that he, in common with everyone else, only existed through his baptismal record, his marriage, possibly through his children's baptisms and by his burial record. Only if he had found himself involved in a legal dispute would we find additional material about his life.

But he was who he was, and the remarkable legacy of his plays and poems was accompanied by contemporary reports, some lawsuits, the acquisition of some modest wealth as a man of the theatre, a few portraits, contributing as full a picture as we are likely to find of anyone who lived during that period. What is missing from his life is a period of about seven years, from 1585 to 1592, where he has left no trace. It is his life as a young married man.

He is on record for 27 November 1582, when the episcopal registry of the diocese of Worcester made out a special marriage licence for William Shakespeare of Stratford and Anne Hathaway from Shottery. He was 18 years old and she around 26. Their first child Susanna was baptised on 26 May 1583. It requires no expertise in mathematics to compute that Anne was already pregnant at the time of marriage. Almost two years later, the parish register recorded the baptism of 'Hamnet and Judith son and daughter to William Shakespeare' on 2 February 1585. So far, so conventional. We do not know what William was doing, but it may be fair to assume that he was assisting his father in the glove maker's trade. It is quite possible too that his parents accommodated the young family in their house on Henley Street.

At some time after this, and certainly before 1592, William Shakespeare moved to London, where he became an actor. There is some evidence that he had ventured into writing plays, either in collaboration with others or independently and it was probably in this year that he was able to seek, and be granted, the patronage of the 3rd Earl of Southampton.

On the 18 April 1593 an entry was made at the Stationer's Register for a poem called *Venus and Adonis*. The printer was a man called Richard Field, whom Shakespeare knew from growing up in Stratford, and the dedication was to the 3rd. Earl of Southampton, couched in respectful language:

> To the Right Honourable Henry Wriothesley, Earl of Southampton, and Baron of Titchfield. Right Honourable,

I know not how I shall offend in dedicating my unpolished lines to your Lordship, nor how the world will censure me for choosing so strong a prop to support so weak a burden, only, if your Honour seem but pleased, I account myself highly praised, and vow to make advantage of all idle hours, till I have honoured you with some graver labour. But, if the first heir of my invention prove deformed, I shall be sorry it had so noble a god-father, and never after ear so barren a land, for fear it would yield me still so bad a harvest. I leave it to your Honourable survey, and your Honour to your heart's content; which I wish may always answer your own wish, and the world's hopeful expectation. Your Honour's in all duty.

and signed by the then unknown William Shakespeare.

The earl was barely 20 years old and the provincial wordsmith, struggling to establish himself in the world of letters was a day or two shy of his 29th birthday. The younger man was at the top of the Elizabethan social order and William Shakespeare was practically a nobody. If, like his exact contemporary Christopher Marlowe, he had tragically died in 1593 Shakespeare would be known for this poem and possibly, had they survived, an early play or two. We would not, it is fair to say, be rating him as one of the greatest writers of all time, although some scholars would note that *Venus and Adonis* was an exceptional poem, and may have regretted that Shakespeare did not live long enough to write more. As a playwright and man of the theatre, which is the source of his present fame, he would be dismissed. By extension, we would not be much interested in the third Earl of Southampton. Yet it is by this happy circumstance, a helping hand at a difficult time, that Shakespeare was set upon his path to future fame.

The poem was an immediate success. It marked out Shakespeare as a poet of rare talent and it brought kudos to the earl as a man who was able to identify a literary star.

The printed edition of the poem first became available in June 1593. It sold out very quickly and Field printed a second edition in 1594. He then sold the copyright to John Harrison who brought out a third edition in 1595. Demand did not abate and 16 known editions of the book were printed by 1640. Each printed volume was so much read and handled by so many readers that the few editions that survive today are in very poor condition. Shakespeare's story was sourced from Arthur

Golding's translation of Ovid's *Metamorphoses*. The tale describes the pursuit of the beautiful mortal Adonis by Venus, the goddess of love. He resists her advances at first, but eventually succumbs to her charms and they spend 24 hours in each other's company, which ends when Adonis insists on hunting a boar despite warnings of the danger by Venus. He is killed by the boar and the love story thus has a tragic end. The atmosphere throughout the poem is sexually charged and it was this characteristic, unusual for the time, made it a "best seller" if that term can be applied to books in that period.

It was fashionable at the time to mine Ovid for works that could be read in English. Michael Drayton wrote *Endymion and Phoebe*, Thomas Peend, *Hermaphroditus and Salamis*, George Chapman the *Banquet of (Common) Sense*, Thomas Lodge, *Scylla*, and Christopher Marlowe, *Hero and Leander*, which he left unfinished at his death. *Venus and Adonis* outranks them all in its telling of the tale, it's lyric fluency and Shakespeare's instinctive ability to generate real people from mythological material.

Today we celebrate Shakespeare for his plays and scarcely read his poems, but in 1593 the situation was reversed. Poetry was the highest literary aspiration; play writing was a journeyman's craft. In 1598, when Francis Meres compiled a survey of Shakespeare's work he placed *Venus and Adonis* at the head of that list. Plainly he believed that it was of more enduring importance than, say, *Romeo and Juliet*.

However, the patronage of *Venus and Adonis* could not have come out of the blue. The dedication written by Shakespeare carries with it an assurance that the two men did at least know each other.

In the early 1590s the young earl was a vibrant young man who was about to control a large fortune. He attached himself to roistering friends who were often the talk of the town. They gambled, drank, womanised, frequented playhouses and occasionally got into fights. One young woman described Southampton as "fanstastical"[96] implying that his behaviour was 'over the top.' That sharp observer of London life, Thomas Nashe, has left this account.

> For whereas the afternoon being the idlest time of the day, wherein men that are their own masters (as gentlemen of the Court, the Inns of Court, and the number of captains and soldiers about London) do wholly bestow themselves upon pleasure; and that pleasure they divide (how virtuously it skills

not) either into gaming, following of harlots, drinking, or seeing a play ...[97]

He may have encountered Shakespeare on one of his frequent visits to the theatre. In 1592 Shakespeare and his fellows faced some hardship because of recurrent outbreaks of the plague. The playhouses had been closed in June for this reason. A further outbreak in September brought an order that they should be closed until December. Lucrative as the theatre business was, it could not stand six months of closure. Touring was the only option.

The playhouses did get a reprieve in January 1593, but another flare-up caused them to be closed after only one month of operation. As things turned out they would not reopen until June 1594. This was a serious handicap to a newish theatre practitioner and emerging playwright. He could earn some sort of living by travelling on the road, and possibly he did just that.

Literary patronage was a desirable condition for publication. Men like Henry Howard, earl of Surrey. Sir Phillip Sidney or the Earl of Oxford could comfortably afford to have their own work printed, but conditions were changing. The printing press had only been in England for a century. Type was set by hand in galleys, inked with rollers and placed into the bed of the press. Paper (itself an expensive commodity) was fed into the press one sheet at a time. When sufficient sheets had been printed, they were cut, folded, sewn together and bound between the covers of the book. Although the ingenuity of printers had probably found ways to reduce the time and cost of making a book, there was no way such a product could be cheap. Fortunately, there was a growth in the numbers of literate people who could afford such luxuries. Writers were inventing ways of making a living with their pen. Writers like Robert Greene and Thomas Nashe discovered that the sale of pamphlets on various scurrilous topics could bring them some income. Those associated with the theatre could also earn money from their writing. Poets however, depended very much on the time-honoured practice of seeking a patron from among those who were wealthy and titled. The transaction worked both ways; the poet was published and had a few pounds in his purse to live on; the patron was able to burnish his or her intellectual credentials. The Earl of Southampton, already a bright and leading figure in 1592, was himself keen to underscore his Renaissance credentials. He was inevitably approached by several writers (Thomas

Nashe was certainly one of them) and it is not particularly surprising that William Shakespeare put himself forward.

Consider this example. In 1601, while the earl of Southampton was cooling his heels in the Tower of London for his part in the Essex plot, the poet Samuel Daniel published a poem addressed to the earl. The poet praised his steadfastness in the face of adversity and urged him to be resolute.

> The world had never taken so full note
> Of what thou art, hadst thou not been undone;
> And only thy affliction hath begot
> More fame, then thy best fortunes could have done; [98]

This was a sentiment shared by many who felt that Southampton had been caught up in a plot not of his making and had been rather severely treated. That is a discussion for a later chapter, but I quote this here to show that Southampton was still a magnet for poets seeking patronage. Samuel Daniel was a very good poet who was able to demonstrate a mastery of rhyme, rhythm and cadence. In his lifetime he was highly regarded, but unlike his Warwickshire contemporary he never transcended his age, and is today largely ignored. In his own time he did very well out of patronage and together with some court appointments during the reign of King James was able to make a very comfortable living.

Because William Shakespeare became *William Shakespeare* there has been a tendency to make more of the relationship than may have been the case. Nobody, to my knowledge, has tried to argue for a relationship between Samuel Daniel and the 3rd earl. They have assumed, rightly, that this was a business transaction. The poem was acknowledged and a sum of money was paid, much as one would pay a musician for entertainment.

In truth, we have very little evidence of money changing hands in matters of patronage. The writers may have written their dedication more in hope than expectation, but on the whole, we may take it that there was a convention that the poet should be rewarded with a gift of some sort. In the 18th century Leopold Mozart maintained a careful tabulation of all the gifts he received while presenting his precocious daughter and son in European courts. Frequently, these gifts were not in coin and it may be safe to assume that the Elizabethan system of patronage was equally whimsical. In fact during the whole of this period there is only a single record of a sum of money being paid to a writer, and this was £10 paid to Thomas Nashe by the Earl of Pembroke. A similar sum, if anything was paid at all, might be expected from the purse of the Earl of Southampton. Shakespeare would have been grateful. £10 would keep his family going during a difficult year. It would have been nowhere near the extravagant speculation of the figure of £1,000, put forward by Nicholas Rowe in the late 17th century.[99]

I have frequently read accounts that assume that Shakespeare and the young earl were close friends and some even suggest that the two men were lovers. In the 19th, and for much of the 20th centuries, this became a difficult subject for critics, particularly when interpreting the *Sonnets*. We live in a more open-minded age where such relationships are more easily accommodated within social mores. That said, there was a wide gulf in social status between the two men and it is fair to ask if it was possible for two men from very different stations in life to form close friendships. Both men in 1593 and 1594 would be very conscious of their social status. Southampton was a wealthy young man with a title and would see himself and be seen by others as a person of high degree. William Shakespeare was, if the term had any meaning in the 16th century, from the middle class. The Shakespeares owned no land to speak of although they were doing reasonably well by using their intelligence and know-how. John Shakespeare, although he did get into financial difficulties, was not a poor man. He had status in his community and could afford to have his children educated. Nevertheless, he was very distant in degree from the young aristocrat.

These relationships were well understood at the time. Edward Alleyn, whose origins were not dissimilar to Shakespeare's, if not more obscure. Alleyn's father came from the village of Willen, near Newport Pagnell in Buckinghamshire. There is no evidence that the Alleyns held any land although he must have had some resources as he moved to London and purchased an inn in Bishopsgate. Two of his sons, John and Edward, found their way into the theatre business. Edward became a star actor and later a theatre manager. He certainly outstripped Shakespeare in wealth and was able to found and endow Dulwich College on the manor he had purchased some years earlier. Alleyn cultivated good connections in the governments of the day and like Shakespeare was able to acquire a coat of arms. He aspired to a knighthood, but this eluded him and it is thought that his activities in the theatre tainted his reputation somewhat. Sir Francis Calton, who sold him the Dulwich manor, had some regrets about it after the sale and insinuated that due to Alleyn's origins as a player he was not worthy of the manor. Alleyn robustly defended himself of course, but the snobbish insult could not be eradicated.

And both Henry Wriothesley and William Shakespeare understood this. There was a social gulf that can only be understood as a master-servant relationship. The earl was willing to patronise the talented and ambitious poet; the poet was suitably grateful for the promotion. It is worth underscoring this point. In the years since 1945, English society has been rapidly transformed from one which was highly deferential to those in the so-called 'ruling class' into one where social distinctions are more fluid, but in the years before that, and certainly in the late 16th century, the station you were born into mattered a great deal.

Nevertheless, there is still a possibility that a close relationship developed between the young earl and Shakespeare, if only for a short time. The 3rd Earl of Southampton may or may not have had homosexual inclinations. There is some evidence, admittedly slight, to support such a contention. As a boy he was very much under his father's control and witnessed the breakdown of his parents marriage at an impressionable age. When he was offered a suitable bride he refused to marry, demonstrating the same inflexibility of his father. Thomas Nashe, who was at St John's College, Cambridge at the same time as Southampton, wrote a dedication in his *Pierce Pennilesse* in 1592 to that 'matchless image of Honor, and magnificent rewarder of vertue, Joves Eagle-borne Ganimed, thrice noble Amyntas.'[100] Some scholars have accepted that Amyntas is Southampton, but it is the reference to 'Ganymede' that should give us some hint. A ganymede was a term used for homosexuals in Elizabethan times.

Nashe was never one to be too careful about causing offence in his writings, and he may have been taking a risk. But perhaps no-one cared, least of all the earl of Southampton, and the remark was never contested.

An important clue came a few years later while Southampton was on active military service in Ireland. One writer sent this report to Sir Robert Cecil:

> I do marvell also what became of Piers Edmonds, called captain Pearse or Captain Edmonds, the earl of Essex man, born in

strand near me, one which has many rewards and preferments by the earl Essex, his villainy I have often complained of, he dwells in London, he was corporal general of the horse in Ireland under the earl of Soiuthampton, he ate and drank at his table and lay in his tent, the earl of Southampton gave him a horse, which Edmonds refused a 100 marks for him, the earl Southampton would cole[101] and hug him in his arms and play wantonly with him.[102]

There is considerable textual evidence to support the assumption that William Shakespeare was a homosexual at some point in his life. Many of the *Sonnets*, for a start, are homo-erotic. The love between Bassanio and Antonio in *The Merchant of Venice* is overt, and it does rather reinforce the notion that contemporaries of Shakespeare saw no inconsistency between homosexual preference and conventional marriage between a man and a woman. Castiglione, in his *Book of the Courtier,* translated into English in 1561, and very influential in the Elizabethan Age, had observed that the highest form of love could only exists between two men. Hamlet's outpourings of invective against his mother and Ophelia are as good evidence as any that Shakespeare had become disillusioned with women. It may be that his unfortunate affair with the 'dark lady' finished him with women, and we can also note that he fathered no children with his wife after 1585. We now have sufficient examples of married men who turn to homosexuality in later life to understand Shakespeare's transition.

Could there have been a homosexual relationship between the young earl and a man almost a decade his senior? The earl was a very good looking attractive man who clearly preferred the company of men to women at that time. William Shakespeare was a very witty man whose company could be readily enjoyed. Elements were there for the two men to fall in love with each other. A homosexual relationship between the earl and Shakespeare cannot be dismissed on the grounds of the gulf between their respective stations in society. As Alan H. Nelson has pointed out, "A homosexual relationship of an unequal sort is recorded between the Earl of Oxford, then in his late twenties, and the Italian choirboy who accompanied him on his return to London from Venice."[103]

It is hard to reach a conclusion. As described above, prevailing social mores in the past have coloured discussion and in recent decades, as we have taken a more liberal attitude towards homosexuality, people have stepped forward to claim Shakespeare as a gay icon. People are more complex than the labels that may be applied to them; something which Shakespeare intuitively understood and was able to reveal in his plays. A straightforward comparison of Marlowe's jew, Barabas, and Shakespeare's Shylock will illustrate how far Shakespeare was ahead of his gifted contemporary in creating nuanced portraits.

Close, passionate relationships between men did exist and may only have been short term. These affairs should also be understood in the context of 16th century status of men and women, which were very far from being equal. Marriage between a man and woman was intended for procreation, and, at the aristocratic level, subject to stringent control. Outside marriage, relationships between two men or a man and a woman were considered of little importance.

So it is entirely plausible that Henry Wriothesley and William Shakespeare embarked on an affair that brought no social risk to either party. Social status was not an issue for the earl as such a relationship had no bearing on his destiny as a member of the elite. The social gulf was important to neither man since they both knew that the relationship could never be cemented. We can therefore reasonably speculate the Shakespeare and the earl did have an affair that may have grown less intense after both men moved on with their lives in 1594.

3

A SHARED FAITH

which might be proposed in the first Parliament and National Council of England after God of his mercy shall restore the same to the Catholic faith. – Robert Parsons, Jesuit Priest.

If we are to look for correspondences between the lives of the earl and Shakespeare other than the literary, it must be that both men were raised in households committed to the old faith. Whether or not this has a bearing on the relationship between the two men is speculative, but it can be noted. The third earl was not as ardent as his father in defending the Roman Catholic faith and neither was Shakespeare a religious zealot.

In the 16th century people divided along Protestant and Roman Catholic lines and the struggle took another 150 years to play out. In the lifetime of the two men the issue was never fully settled. In the 1530s Henry VIII decided to challenge the primacy of the Papacy and part company with the Roman Catholic Church. The issue polarised opinion in his own country in a manner which is not at all dissimilar to the recent issue of leaving the European Union. There were those who embraced the new humanism that had been washing through Europe for thirty years and there were those who resolutely defended the status quo. Broadly speaking, the established aristocracy adhered to Rome while newer men such as Cromwell and Burghley were quick to understand the possibilities that the new thinking offered. Ordinary people, like the Shakespeares, had no effective voice and were compelled to swim with the prevailing government tide.

The Roman Catholic Church had dominated thought since it was first introduced to the island in the 7th century. By the 16th century it was rooted in every part of life, culture and government. The new humanist wave of thought, which had originated in the late 15th century was beginning to attract new adherents and it found its focus in several northern European countries around the idea that the word of God could be communicated directly from the Bible, rather than through the words of priests. The Papacy, which was at the head of the church, had become deeply corrupt over time and was under the control of a few powerful families. Popes were often venal men who protected their family interests and were frequently engaged in war.

As described in earlier chapters Henry VIII's dissolution of the monasteries in the 1530s was not universally unpopular. Some monasteries were visibly corrupt and all of them were sucking money out of the economy and putting little back. Henry's seizure of the assets and land of the monasteries was morally questionable but it certainly invigorated the English economy. Such reforms were tolerated by a majority, but the rejection of the Roman Catholic faith was, for many, a Rubicon that was not to be crossed. The first Earl of Southampton had actively participated in the dissolution and was one of the principal beneficiaries; however, he was conservative in matters of religion and was unwilling to go along with men whom he saw as radical reformers, such as Archbishop Cranmer. Faith was deeply embedded and reform was unwelcome in matters of dogma and ritual. Many families, like the Southamptons and the Shakespeares took this position.

The reforms during the six year reign of Edward VI were seen as too extreme by the conservatives and when Mary came to the throne in 1553 the suppression of the reformers was reactionary in equal measure. When Elizabeth succeeded her in 1558 she seemed to understand that the difficult act of keeping the two factions onside was a paramount responsibility. The reform movement was allowed to continue and the conservatives were given the option of continuing to practice their faith privately as long as they did nothing publicly to undermine the state. This was a compromise that the second earl was unable to come to terms with.

Many, including the Shakespeares, found it hard to adapt to these revolutionary changes. In the 16th century the traditions associated with Christian belief were sanctified by time, and were not to be changed one iota. The newer men understood that opening up the mysteries of Christianity to ordinary people by, for example, translating the Bible from Latin and Hebrew and Aramaic into the vernacular, would be a positive development. The conservatives regarded such innovations with horror. They felt that the word of God would be debased through its expression in the English language.

With 21st century hindsight we can see that England benefited economically from this revolution. Spain was at that time by far the richest kingdom in Europe and the Italian states and France were not far behind. A few centuries later it became apparent that the countries and states that opted for Protestantism had enjoyed better economic development. England did not make swift or even easy progress, but the foundations were laid in the 16th century. Elizabeth took a more pragmatic approach. Like her father and brother she claimed the right to be head of the church in England, but she avoided persecuting recusants if possible. If they were loyal to the state the she would turn a blind eye to Romish practises in their own chapels or in the privacy of their own homes. It was an intelligent policy. Practising Roman Catholics were kept in plain view and Elizabeth's network of spies was able to keep a close watch on any deviants who plotted against the state.

And there were several - not least of which were members of the Wriothesley family.

As described in Part 2, Sir Thomas Wriothesley's son Henry was a determined Roman Catholic, who pursued a course of action which brought him into direct conflict with the government. Since he died when his only surviving son, the third earl, was only eight years old, there was some hope for the third generation. While his mother remained a constant Catholic, he was educated in Lord Burghley's Protestant household and as he grew to adulthood he was much less a zealot than his father. This is not to say that all traces of allegiance to Rome were wiped away and he may well have been in sympathy with William Shakespeare, who also came from a Catholic family.

In the Spring of 1580 John Shakespeare was summoned to appear before the Queen's bench in Westminster. He did not turn up because there was little point in making the long and expensive journey to argue a case that he was bound to lose. We cannot be precise about the exact nature of the charge, but since his case coincided with that of about 200 other men and women from across the land, it must be supposed that he was charged with recusancy, that is, a refusal to attend church in compliance with the Act of Uniformity. The English state was under serious threat during these years, with the incumbent Pope determined to see that Elizabeth was replaced on the throne by a catholic monarch, and various efforts to undermine the English throne were undertaken in these years, not least the ever present claim by Mary Queen of Scots. Adherents to the old faith had taken to absenting themselves from church services, and while earlier acts of uniformity levied a fine of 1 shilling for absenteeism, the fine was considered a manageable, although it was not an insignificant fine. The 1580 Act raised this fine to £20. Saying or singing Mass was subject to a fine of 200 marks (£13 6s 8d). A few years later the stakes were raised higher and recusants who were repeat offenders could lose all their goods and one third of their land. Financial ruin was a serious price to pay for adherence to one's faith.

John Shakespeare was fined £40 on this occasion and this was a hefty fine in the 16th century. He paid up.

The Shakespeares were not alone in Stratford upon Avon in thier sympathies for the old religion and it seems that William Shakespeare's teacher at the Grammar School were also committed to the old faith. Revolutions such as these, which require men to surrender their souls are hard to accomplish, and it was not until the 18th century that the matter was in any way settled. 1580 was a very early date for wholesale conversion. Henry VIII's claim to be head of the church in England changed very little, but subsequent efforts by the protestants, holding power between 1547 and 1553 and returning to influence in 1558, moved England on a protestant path.

John Shakespeare was well aware of his exposed position as a recusant and took steps before 1580 to protect his livelihood and his property. In 1577 he suddenly left the town council. There appears to be no evidence that he was in a poor financial position and he retained the respect of his peers for many years to come. The reason for his abrupt resignation is not recorded but it can be reasonably inferred that his staunch catholicism was a factor. An ordinance drawn up by a commission set up by the Privy Council in 1576 determined that there should be inquiry into 'all singular, heretical, erroneous and offensive opinions.' And, 'to order, correct and reform any persons wilfully and obstinately absenting themselves from church and service.'[104] It would have been clear to John Shakespeare and his fellow aldermen that it was no longer possible to turn a blind eye to recusancy, and much as they may have sympathised with his beliefs would no longer be possible for the corporation to publicly acknowledge such a position.

The relative tolerance of the Elizabethan regime was giving way, under external pressure from the Papacy and other catholic nations, to a harder line. In the Autumn of 1577 John Whitgift was appointed Bishop of Worcester and he immediately turned his attention to Stratford to root out heresy. At this stage the council could claim to be entirely orthodox having no recusants in the corporation.

John Shakespeare knew he was at risk. On 12 November 1578 he sold 70 acres of land to Thomas Webbe, a nephew of Mary Arden on the understanding that after 21 years the property would revert to the Shakespeare family. Two days later in a similar transaction he mortgaged a house and 56 acres at Wilmcote to Edmund Lambert, a brother in law of Mary Arden, as security on a loan of £40, to be repaid in 1580. In this case Lambert defaulted and John Shakespeare had to sue him. These examples were part of complex pattern of transaction which were designed to prevent the government from seizing his property on charges of recusancy.

Much of Warwickshire at the time was strongly catholic in sympathy and where the nobility led, lesser mortals followed. The leading catholic gentry were the Catesbys, the Ardens and the Somervilles. The reformers were the rising families of the Lucys, Dudleys and Grevilles. Sir Thomas Lucy was assiduous in rooting out Catholics, and used his position as Justice of the Peace to pursue catholics, seek justice against them and not incidentally, enrich himself by acquiring their land. He was on two occasions a signatory on charges levelled against John Shakespeare. Sir Thomas was not well-regarded in the Shakespeare household.

One tale that occurred in two sources during the late 17th century was that William Shakespeare was caught poaching deer in Lucy's park and was summoned before the magistrate and whipped for it. It has been suggested that Shakespeare created the comic figure of Justice Shallow in the *Merry Wives of Windsor* as partial revenge for his ill treatment. The story, which has become legendary, has its attraction but founders when the facts are investigated. The park at Lucy's estate at

Charlecote was not created until many years later and deer were only introduced in the 18th century. The land in question had the status of free warren so William Shakespeare could not be convicted of a non-existent crime against non-existent deer.

There is little doubt as to where the Wriothesley family's religious sympathies lay. They were with Rome and the old religion. The mule headed second earl was and stubbornly fanatical in his adherence to Rome and was imprisoned until he was willing to mollify his position. He was also married to Mary Browne, from the Sussex family at Midhurst, who were equally committed to the Roman church. Countess Mary Browne Wriothesley was still alive at this date and not without influence.

These experiences of two men from very different segments of society illustrate what was happening in the last quarter of the 16th century. Their grandparents lived in a world where questions about the true faith did not really arise. Sir Thomas Wriothesley, the 1st Earl of Southampton was active in reform, but only of the management of the church. He believed that that his king could represent God on earth just as well as a venal Pope in Rome and as long as doctrinal matters were left as they were, he was content. He only became seriously worried when the reformers moved into power. The parents of William Shakespeare lived in a time of transition which they found uncomfortable and reacted as most conservatives would by holding tenaciously to what they knew. Their children held a better sense of the new direction and adapted accordingly.

It would be fair to repeat at this point, that although both men were brought up to be committed catholics, neither turned out to be as zealous as their parents.

4

1594

Beseeching you that in the matter you will not begin at the death of Mr. Long, but at the murder of one of Mr. Danvers' men, . . . derisions and foul abuses offred to my husband's chief officer and open scorns of him and his in saying they had knighted him with a glass of beer; last of all, letters addressed to my son Charles, of such form as the heart of a man indeed had rather die than endure. – Lady Danvers to Sir Robert Cecil.

1594 was a seminal year for both the earl and William Shakespeare. The earl achieved his majority and a government rationalisation of control of the players' companies had the unintended consequence of making William Shakespeare and his player colleagues prosperous men. Theatres were not popular with the City of London authorities as they attracted crowds which facilitated the work of pickpockets and prostitutes, but the court had an interest in maintaining professional players for the occasional entertainment of the queen and the aristocracy. Lord Hunsdon, who was Lord Chamberlain at the time, developed a plan to allow two regulated companies and William Shakespeare became a sharer in one of these. This duopoly lasted beyond Shakespeare's life. There were also other events of great significance to the two men.

The earl formally reached the age of 21 on 6 October 1594, and although there are indications that he was already acting as if he was fully in control of his affairs throughout the year, the date was of great legal significance. A celebration was planned for this anniversary.

However, two nights earlier a sensational event was to overshadow the celebrations.

Late in the night of 4 October 1594 the porter was wakened by a banging at the gatehouse door of Place House. Three men, who had clearly been riding a long distance, were demanding admission. Two of them were recognised as Sir Henry and Sir Charles Danvers, both good friends with the earl, and were admitted. The servants took away the hot and tired horses and one of them noticed that Sir Henry's saddle was covered in dried blood. Danvers' servant, John, was also fed and accommodated.

The brothers were admitted to the earl's presence where they explained what had happened. There had been a quarrel with an old adversary Sir Henry Long which led to an affray, during which Long had been killed. The two men were therefore fugitives from justice and needed help from their good friend. It was not denied and at first light they moved to Whiteley Lodge, the home of the Southampton's steward, Thomas Dymoke. This house, which later became Whitely farm house, was very much off the beaten track and no doubt Southampton hoped that they would be safer there than in the more public view of Place House at Titchfield.

There is a surprising amount of detail about the event and the aftermath mainly because Queen Elizabeth had no tolerance for this sort of behaviour and commissioned a full enquiry. Distilled to its essence, it appears that Sir Henry Long and his brother Sir Walter were at dinner with several other gentlemen at the Chamberlain's house in Corsham. The Danvers brothers burst in upon them with 17 or 18 other men with the intention of settling their long running feud with the Longs.

Corsham in Wiltshire is some 70 miles away from Titchfield and the three men must have ridden extremely hard to reach Titchfield in a day. One must assume that they changed horses several times along the way.

There is some suspicion that the Danvers brothers had planned this showdown and even that the Earl of Southampton had foreknowledge. As with all quarrels between neighbours that develop into feuds, there is no way to determine who cast the first stone. Recriminations were mutual with each side blaming the other. The last straw may have been, according to Lady Danvers, that the Longs had killed a Danvers man.

On Saturday morning the fugitives were holed up at Whiteley Lodge. This was politic. At his coming of age party many people would be coming to Place House to mark the occasion and it would be impossible therefore for the Danvers brothers to hide. Southampton did ride over on Monday to see his friends and on Tuesday they were escorted to the Bursledon ferry, where a boat took them down river to Calshot Castle on the New Forest shore. Dymoke accompanied them. There they remained as guests of the Deputy Keeper of the Castle until Friday when a message came from the earl that the authorities had picked up the trail. The castle was now a risky place to be, because if challenged, the keeper would have to yield his guests. They left hurriedly, 'in a great hurly burly' and appear to have returned to Whitely, at least temporarily. A boat was now ready to take the fugitives to France, arranged by a young Arthur Bromfield, who had just entered the earl's service and who would one day become his steward. Possibly the craft set out from Titchfield. Dymoke left four pieces of gold at Calshot Castle to be divided between the soldiers of the castle. Out of the country the brothers were now safe.

But the authorities were still looking.

Lawrence Grose was the sheriff of Southampton, and was one of those who raised the hue and cry against the Danvers brothers. He was on his way to Titchfield when he met some of the Earl of Southampton's servants at the Itchen Ferry. They threatened the sheriff in the hope of deterring his furtther oinvestigation.

> Whereupon the said Grose passinge on the Itching ferry with his wife, the Saturday following, one Florio, an Italian, and one Humphrey Drewell the saide earle of Southampton's servants, being in the saide passage Boate, threatened to cast him the saide Grose over board, and saide they would teach him to meddle with his fellowes, and many other threatening words.[105]

John Florio, who, according to his book *Second Fruits*, published in 1598, was some years in the service of the Earl of Southampton. He was not a passive intellectual and was evidently willing to be robust in defence of the honour or interests of his lord. He was willing, anxious even, to show that he could be of good service no matter what the contingency.

Frances Yates suggests that Burghley may have appointed Florio as an Italian tutor to his three young wards, Southampton, Rutland and Bedford, as early as 1589 and there is some internal evidence from his *First Fruits*, published in 1578, to support that thesis.[106]

John Florio was an interesting man and a writer of some prominence in Elizabethan and Jacobean times. He was born in London in 1553, and his Italian father, who was a former Franciscan reformed as a Protestant was then living in exile in England. When Mary came to the throne in 1555 he had to leave England and the family settled in Switzerland, where John was raised. As an adult, John made his way to England and was very successful in being adopted by a series of patrons, including the 3rd Earl of Southampton. Florio and Shakespeare certainly knew each other and Shaespeare introduced many Italianate words and phrases into his plays as direct borrowing from John Florio. This example does provide us with evidence that the earl was prepared to take literary men into his employ.

Meanwhile the earl excused himself from Titchfield and went up to London.

Once in France the two brothers were well-received by King Henri IV. They were out of the reach of the English authorities and in that sense were safe; however, they were young men anxious to take up their careers at court as there was no future in exile, All they could do was amuse themselves while friends at court negotiated terms for their return. Essex was a voice for the Danvers brothers; even so, it took time, three and a half years in fact, before they were permitted to return. They were assessed a fine of £2,000 and a further £1,500 was to be paid to Sir Walter Long, brother of the murdered man. Once paid, the Danvers brothers were pardoned on 30 June 1598 and allowed to return and take up their places in the Essex entourage.

It cannot be a coincidence that Shakespeare's play about feuding families, *Romeo and Juliet*, appeared the following year.

But let us turn back to another very significant event, earlier in the Spring of 1594. Shakespeare's acting career spanned two companies in his early years, Lord Strange's Men and the Earl of Pembroke's Men. He may also have worked briefly for the Earl of Sussex's Men. The long closures of 1592 and 1593 played havoc with the stability and profitability of these groups and the patronage became uncertain. Lord Strange died in April 1594 and it was not at all clear that his widow had the interest to continue the patronage. The Earl of Pembroke's men had fallen apart during the plague year.

Matters could have been left to drift but in 1594 there was one very important client who required player companies to be available for

Christmas entertainment - Queen Elizabeth. The Lord Chamberlain, Lord Hunsdon, who held this responsibility, took charge of the deteriorating situation. He licensed two acting companies, one under his own patronage, and the other under the patronage of his nephew Charles Howard. They became respectively the Lord Chamberlain's Men and the Lord Admiral's Men. This duopoly prevailed and the Lord Chamberlain's Men, which was re-named the King's Men after the accession of James I, survived until the theatres were closed in 1642.

The various men of the theatre at that time coalesced around two leading actors, Edward Alleyn and Richard Burbage. Alleyn used Phillip Henslowe's theatre, the *Rose* on the south bank, and Burbage led the actors who would perform in the Burbage theatres at Shoreditch. Shakespeare joined Burbage's company. The two companies divided the repertory between them. Alleyn's group held the rights to Marlowe's plays and Burbage's company were able to use the plays that Shakespeare had so far written, and had yet to write.

The key to Shakespeare's future prosperity was that he became a sharer in the new company. There were eight or possibly nine sharers in Burbage's company. They all became prosperous men. They owned the costumes and the rights to the plays. They hired men to play small parts while they themselves carried the major parts in the repertory. There are no precise figures for what Shakespeare and his fellow sharers put into the company in 1594 but it has been estimated at around £50 or £60. This was a great deal of money at that date. In 1597 Shakespeare was able to purchase New Place in Stratford, at the time the second largest house in the town, for £60, so that puts his investment into some perspective. Whether or not he had such a sum put by, or he was able to source the money from elsewhere, we do not know. We can speculate, but however he acquired the necessary money, by borrowing, savings or gift, he was certainly in a position, a mere three years after he became a sharer in the Lord Chamberlain's Men, to stump up £60 for a house in Stratford. The entertainment business, then as now, could be very lucrative for those who were successful in that field.

What must be clear is that from 1594 onwards he was fully occupied with the theatre, and would have little time to work for the Earl of Southampton in any capacity. John Florio remained attached to the earl, as he was dependent on patronage. Shakespeare had access to cash income from play production and while the theatres were open he prospered. Unsurprisingly, the connections with the earl start to wear a little thin. Shakespeare was busy. The earl grew into his high position in Elizabethan society, he married and has his estates to attend to. There appears to have been only one later connection, when a performance of *Richard II* was commissioned on the eve of the Essex rebellion in 1599, but it may be fair to observe that the brief chapter that brought the lives of both men together was pretty much closed at the end of 1594.

The year closed with revels at Gray's Inn in London, according to some accounts a riotous and disreputable affair. Southampton may have had some connection with the proceedings and it would appear that Shakespeare's early play the *Comedy of Errors* was performed at Gray's Inn at this time.

The *Comedy of Errors* is almost certainly an early play in language, style and stagecraft and it may be very early indeed. The American critic Harold Bloom favours this theory. We do know for certain that this was the actual play that was performed at Grays Inn on 28 December 1594 but the consensus is that it was written at an earlier date and pulled out rather hurriedly for performance on that evening.

The play is a straight knock off from a Plautus play called *The Menachmi*. It is pure farce. Two sets of identical twins became separated as a consequence of a shipwreck. One pair were slaves and the other pair men of quality. One set of twins were born to a merchant of Syracuse. They are both named Antipholus, but the shipwreck left one washed up in Ephesus. The slaves are named Dromio: one lives in Syracuse and the other in Ephesus. Antipholus of Syracuse comes to the town of Ephesus with his slave Dromio and this accident create the circumstances for the farcical complications that follow.

The customary revels had not been permitted for two years because of plague restrictions, so the students entered into the project with great zest. They built a stage in the hall and elected Henry Helmes as their 'Lord of Misrule" giving him the preposterous title of Henry, Prince of Purpoole, ArchDuke of Stapulia and Bernardia, Duke of High and Nether Holborn, Marquis of St Giles and Tottenham, Count Palatine of Bloomsbury and Clerkenwell." The evening descended into drunken and riotous behaviour and during the uproar the Templar's, who had ben invited, walked out. After they left a play "a comedy of errors like to Plautus his Menæchmi" was staged by players brought in for the purpose. Was this Shakespeare and his company? It seems that the whole evening was considered a disgrace to Gray's Inn.

The following day in an action which may have compounded the 'error' the students held a mock court. A "conjurer" was charged with causing the confusion by foisting "a company of base and common fellows to make up our disorders with a play of Errors and confusions" upon the evening.

Thus ended a momentous year. William Shakespeare became a sharer in the new company known as the Lord Chamberlain's Men. The company outlived Shakespeare and survived until 1642. The earl had come of age and was now in control of his own destiny.

My own conclusion is that there was little connection between Southampton and Shakespeare after 1594. Shakespeare's follow-up narrative poem, *The Rape of Lucrece* was entered in the Stationers Register on 9 May 1594. The earl was huge dedicatee of that poem, but after this Shakespeare was fully occupied with the theatre and wrote no more narrative poems. He was thus less dependent on patronage of any kind or indeed from any source.

The playwright and actor had a busy and fulfilling career and the earl was able to take his rightful place at the forefront of society. The lives of the two men were evolving in different ways. Although there are many who like to believe in a continued relationship between the two it seems more probable that regular contact would cease after this date.

5

THE ROISTERING YEARS

With my Lord Southampton on St George's Down at bowls, from 30 to 40 knights and gentlemen, where our meeting was then twice every week, Tuesdays and Thursdays, and we had an ordinary there, and cards, and tables. – Sir John Oglander.

In addition to the Danvers brothers, Southampton's young friends included Roger Manners, who became the 5th Earl of Rutland. Manners had also become one of Burghley's wards after the death of his own father in 1588. Together, they formed a group of rich, boisterous young men who put their surplus energy into drinking, gaming, wenching and the pursuit of adventure. They were naturally frequent attenders of the theatres. The old queen, in the last decade of her long life, did not approve, and Southampton's association with these young bloods did nothing to advance his court career. The queen was now at an age when she preferred serious and sensible young men like Robert Cecil; the roisterers no longer delighted her. Efforts were made to guide these youthful aristocrats, including the Earl of Southampton, onto a more conventional path, but to no end. He was not ready.

Burghley's efforts to marry his young ward came to nothing, as described on page 131. He showed no inclination to marry during these years and it has often been surmised that Shakespeare's sonnets, numbered 1 to 17 were written in this period to urge the young man to settle down. There are many doubts about this interpretation. Perhaps the explanation for his behaviour in these years is the most straightforward: he was a rich young man with much energy to burn and the concept of marriage, particularly after observing his parents' turbulent marriage, was a prospect that could wait. When marriage did come, it was unplanned.

In September 1595 Henry began to pay attention to one of the Queen's maids of honour, Elizabeth Vernon. She was born in the same year as Southampton, 1573, and had been recommended for the Queen's service by the Earl of Essex, who was a first cousin. Her father had died in 1591, leaving a son and four daughters.

Southampton's closeness with the Earl of Essex brought him into the same orbit as Elizabeth Vernon and before too long the gossips had material of interest. Rowland White mentioned in a letter to Sir Robert Sidney, "My Lord of Southampton doth with too much familiarity course the faire Mrs Vernon."[107]

Even so, the earl was still not yet ready for marriage, and for that matter, could not afford it either, with heavy fines outstanding, so while there are indications that he continued to show an interest in Elizabeth Vernon, nothing was to come of it, for now.

Young aristocrats had limited options: they could quietly and diligently manage their estates, they could pursue a political career at court, or they could seek military glory. In some cases they might enjoy all three. The first course was the least risky and the second required mastery of the art of compromise. The third offered adventure, excitement and the prospect of fame and for a young man of the earl's age and temperament the draw was irresistible. He was disappointed in this ambition; he was destined to wait.

In the spring of 1596 Elizabeth authorised an expedition to attack Cadiz. Lord Admiral Howard, an experienced campaigner, and the Earl of Essex were given charge of the venture. This should have been an opportunity for Southampton and he would certainly have been selected by Essex, but the Queen still did not regard him favourably and it appears that he was not allowed to go. On 13 April the Queen sent specific instructions to Essex that he was only to take those men who had licence to travel - Sussex, Rich, Herbert and Burgh. Southampton was not on the list.

He was compelled to cool his heels in frustration, anxious for preferment but continued to be ignored until the Spring of 1597, when it was reported that he was finally granted leave to go to sea. There were complex preparations and delays but eventually, on 11 August, Elizabeth gave permission for Essex to attack the port of Ferrol on the north west coast of Spain. Sir Walter Raleigh was to lead part of the fleet but the Earl of Essex was in overall command. Southampton was among his young lieutenants.

Some ships were damaged in a storm in the Bay of Biscay and had to be sent home. As a consequence Essex decided that his fleet was not strong enough to attack Ferrol and as they sailed down the coast where they learned that the Spanish fleet had sailed to the Azores to escort ships home from America. Sensing an opportunity, they set direction for the Azores, where they succeeded in taking three treasure ships, one of them seized by Southampton, who was knighted by Essex for his enterprise. The remainder of the Spanish fleet escaped to harbour in Terceira, where they were protected. Essex decided that he was not strong enough to attack the port and set course for home with their booty. They were pursued by Spanish warships but they outran them. They reached England in late October.

It has recently emerged that Essex's vainglorious diversion to the Azores may have triggered a second Spanish Armada to invade England.[108] The Spanish acquired intelligence about the Azores excursion and apparently decided that English defences at home would be weak and that this would be a perfect opportunity to invade. England was lucky. The fleet encountered heavy storms off the Scilly Isles and had to turn back. The invasion never happened and was unreported in English history. Nonetheless, it must be supposed that English intelligence knew about the second Armada and Elizabeth would certainly have taken the view that Essex's buccaneering had put the country at risk. The Azores expedition did nothing to assuage her feelings about Essex's recklessness, and by extension the Earl of Southampton, whom she already held in low regard.

If Southampton believed that his part in this broadly successful expedition would bring him into the royal sunlight, he was to be again disappointed. The political winds had changed at home and Essex's star was on the wane. Sir Robert Cecil had been appointed Chief Secretary to the Queen and was also made Chancellor of the Duchy of Lancaster, an office to which Essex aspired. Cecil was a supporter of Raleigh, the great rival at this time to Essex. The Queen was also displeased that Essex had knighted so many of his followers, including Southampton.

In January 1598 the earl might have looked forward to a bleak year. The Queen continued to be frosty towards him, his mother had been recently widowed for the second time and her second husband, Sir

Thomas Heneage owed £528 18s. 1d. to the Treasury, and he was still under a debt burden due to the fine to Lord Burghley.

A trivial incident brought Southampton once again into disfavour with the queen. He was playing a card game called Primmer in the Queen's presence chamber. The queen had retired for the night, and Southampton, Sir Walter Raleigh and a man named Parker continued playing. Ambrose Willoughby, an official, asked the men to stop the game as the Queen had gone to bed. Raleigh folded his cards, picked up his money and left, but Southampton took exception to the order and told Willoughby he would remember it. He did, and on another occasion, when they met in the garden, struck Willoughby and the two got into a scuffle before they were parted. The Queen, on hearing the story, took Willoughby's side and recorded a further black mark against Southampton.

Cecil must have decided that it were best for the young hothead to be out of the way. He was undertaking an embassy to France and procured a license for Southampton to accompany him. He was at this time actively courting Elizabeth Vernon and there was every expectation that they would marry. But not now! On February 2nd it was reported that "it is secretly said that my Lord of Southampton shall be married to his fair mistress" but "he asked for a little respite."[109]

Nevertheless, the earl was able to travel to Paris to meet up with his old friends, the Danvers brothers, who were spending fruitless time in exile after the murder of Henry Long in 1594. At this point the old friends planned a tour of Italy, but this adventure was interrupted by news from England that the two brothers would be pardoned as a result of an agreed settlement brokered with the Long family. This meant that the Danvers brothers had to return to England immediately.

Southampton was not far behind. His plan for a two year travel period was interrupted at the end of August by news that Elizabeth Vernon had had to leave court and take refuge in Essex House due to "an illness." The lady was pregnant.

There was only one way to put this right and at the beginning of September Southampton quietly returned to England, secretly married Elizabeth Vernon, and immediately returned to Paris. He had been noticed. The Queen was informed that he had 'privily' come to England and Cecil was instructed to deal with the matter. Cecil wrote a stiff letter to Southampton.

But I must now put this gall into my ink, that she knows you came over very lately, and returned very contemptuously; that you have also married one of her maids-of-honour, without her privity. For which, with other circumstances informed against you, I find her grievously offended, and she commands me to charge you expressly (all excuses set apart) to repair hither to London, and advertise your arrival, without coming to the Court, until her pleasure be known.[110]

It was a summons that he could not ignore and it was just as well. He was wagering large sums of money on games of tennis, and apparently lost 3,000 crowns to Marshal Biron, according to one report, and 18,000 in another.[111] The earl was compounding his misfortunes. He made another secret trip to England at the end of September, when he met with Essex and placed his new wife in confinement with Lady Penelope Rich, Essex's sister and the "Stella" of Sir Phillip Sidney's sonnet sequence. He came over unofficially, in early November, at the time his first daughter was born, and he was sent to the Fleet prison for two weeks. Form was satisfied and the Queen turned to more important matters.

At 25, the earl was now married to a powerless woman and they had a daughter. He was heavily in debt. He was out of favour at Court. What were his prospects?

He had little choice but to continue to hitch his wagon to the splendid engine of the Earl of Essex.

Robert Devereaux, Earl of Essex, was the stellar character of his time. He was tall and had a commanding personality. He was highly intelligent and like most of those young people who had been a ward of Lord Burghley was well educated. But he was not merely well-versed in the academic knowledge of the day, he was also an accomplished writer and could turn his hand to verse or prose with a facility which was often better than some of the professional writers of his time. He loved action and adventure and in the military engagements of the day won fame and approbation. The Queen liked him and took him on as one of her favourites, in some ways replacing his aging stepfather the Earl of Leicester. He was a most attractive man.

With these attributes it is not surprising that ambitious young men were drawn to this bright flame. He was a natural leader.

Yet for all his gifts Essex was flawed. Honours came easily to him and when things did not go his way he tended to behave petulantly. He became arrogant and was even at times offensive to the queen when she would not permit him to do as he wished. He was an aspirant to become the leading statesman of the realm, the only conceivable successor in his own mind to the venerable Lord Burghley. He possessed many of the gifts that would have served him well as a leader in the 16th century but he had no patience with the subtleties of politics and no understanding of any way but his way of doing things. One wonders if Shakespeare had him in mind when he created the character of Coriolanus.[112]

His victory at Cadiz in 1596 was justly applauded but while this was happening the hunchback Robert Cecil, the antithesis of the vigorous and handsome Essex, was stepping into his father's shoes. His preferment deeply rankled with the proud Essex who felt slighted and continued to be awkward. So when Ireland became an issue once again at the end of the century there were those on Council who were eager to push for Essex to lead the expedition. Ireland, as they well knew, had been a political graveyard for many in the past and an actual graveyard for some.

One night in 1598 the poet Edmund Spenser had to flee for his life from his home at Kilcoman Castle due to a general uprising by the Irish against the English. Spenser had first gone to Ireland in 1580 and while there wrote his most famous work of poetry, *The Faerie Queene*. He had prospered in Ireland but his hurried departure left him completely destitute - homeless, landless and without any source of income. He died on 13 January 1599. He was only 46 and Ben Jonson later wrote that he died "for want of bread."

The Irish problem began some years earlier when Turlough O'Neill handed over the chieftainship of Ulster to his cousin Hugh, Earl of Tyrone. The new O'Neill had been educated in England and was a very sophisticated man. The English would have considered him to be a safe pair of hands but he confounded all when he decided to embrace the Irish cause once he became "The O'Neill." Tyrone formed an alliance with the neighbouring O'Donnell clan and arranged for money to be sent from Spain, who were only too happy to destabilise Elizabeth's government. He bought good weapons and trained his Irish soldiers in contemporary warfare. Before long he had built up a formidable fighting machine and at the Battle of Yellow Ford 15 August 1598, he routed the English army. This success encouraged other clans in Ireland

and poor Spenser, living near Cork, became one of the casualties.

The English garrison in Ireland had been reduced to little more than the Pale around Dublin, and Elizabeth was faced with larger problems than the fate of Edmund Spenser. If Ireland was lost it would quickly become a base for King Phillip of Spain and that outcome would be serious. A call went out to the shires to raise a large force, and after some political wrangling, Essex was chosen to lead the invading army. He was not altogether enthusiastic. He had lost some of his lustre after the last Spanish expedition and he knew as well as anyone the perils of warfare in Ireland. Nevertheless he agreed.

Essex received his commission as viceroy and commander in chief in Ireland on 12 March and the expedition started from London on 27 March 1599. Southampton must have been overjoyed at the opportunity to finally achieve his youthful ambition of military service. He was first among Essex's array of young officers, which included the Earl of Rutland, Charles and Henry Danvers and Lord Grey. With the exception of Lord Grey the group were very much united by kinship and friendship and were very much the core of the Essex circle. They arrived, not without a difficult sea crossing, on 4 April. The intention of the expedition was to subdue the Earl of Tyrone's rebellion in Ulster. On 15 April Essex appointed Southampton as "Lord General of the Horse in Ireland." Sir Henry Danvers, Southampton's long-time friend was made "Lieutenant of the Horse: and the Earl of Rutland was appointed "Lieutenant General of the Infantry."

Essex's mission was to destroy the Tyrone uprising in the north but when he reached Dublin that Spring he was advised that there would not be enough forage for horses or food for the army in the north immediately after winter and he was counselled against such an expedition. He decided, probably correctly, to use his army to bring Leinster and Munster under control, and on 9 May he moved west to Athy, where the garrison was surrendered without contest. Southampton travelled north west to Maryborough with about 160 horse. There he was challenged by about 200 mounted Irishmen. He did lead a successful charge against the Irish and after the skirmish the Irish retreated.

Then a quarrel broke out between Southampton and Lord Grey of Wilton.

The ill feeling between the two had probably been festering for some time. Grey was certainly the more experienced soldier and resented the young Southampton being his superior officer. At Maryborough, Grey decided to freelance and led a charge against the retreating Irish despite orders not to engage. Southampton rightly reproved him and disciplined him by placing him under arrest overnight. Grey was incensed at what he saw as a humiliation and was ever after an enemy of Southampton. Grey was not the forgiving type nor would he meekly conform to Southampton's authority. At a battle at Fermoy on the return journey Grey led a charge of the vanguard cavalry against some rebels who were seemingly in retreat. Unfortunately this was a deliberate tactic by the Irish; once the vanguard had been drawn off, the main Irish force attacked the baggage train and it took fierce fighting, during which Sir Henry Danvers was injured in the face, for Essex to bring his forces safely through. Soon after, Grey returned to England and was able to give his version of events to the Queen.

He found a willing ear. The Queen had never had a high opinion of Southampton following his youthful rejection of Burghley's choice of wife and his subsequent impregnation of one of her maids of honour, and Grey's version of the incident was accepted without question. She sent a blistering letter to Essex making her feelings plain in a letter of July 19th.

> For the matter of Southampton, it is strange to us that his continuance or displacing should work so great an alteration either in yourself (valuing our commandments as you ought) or in the disposition of our army, where all the Commanders cannot be ignorant that we not only not allowed of your desire for him, but did expressly forbid it, and being such a one whose counsel can be of little, and experience of less use; yea such a one as, were he not lately fastened to yourself by an accident, wherein for our usage of ours we deserve thanks, you would have used many of your old lively arguments against him for any such ability or commandment; it is therefore strange to us, we knowing his worth by your report, and your own disposition from ourself in that point, will dare thus to value your own pleasing in things unnecessary, and think by your private arguments to carry for your own glory a matter wherein our pleasure to the contrary is made notorious. And where you say further that divers or the most of the voluntary

gentlemen are so discouraged thereby, as they begin to desire passports and prepare to return, we cannot as yet be persuaded that the love of our service, and the duty which they owe us, have not been as strong motives to these their travails and hazards as any affection to the Earl of Southampton or any other. If it prove otherwise (which we will not so much wrong ourselves as to suspect) we shall have the less cause either to acknowledge it or reward it.[113]

Essex had little choice but to comply with the command and remove Southampton from his position. It was a small victory for Grey, but Essex did not abandon his friend; he simply abolished the position of General of the Horse and allowed Southampton to continue with his duties. As a captain, Southampton continued to serve his leader and friend.

The campaign to subdue the two southern Irish provinces largely achieved its objective. The force moved west to Limerick and returned via Waterford and Wicklow to Dublin, arriving there on 2 July. Later that month there was a shorter expedition into Offaly.

While military tacticians might endorse Essex's sensible approach, the council in London, particularly those members hostile to Essex placed their own interpretation on events. The message that they chose to receive was that he was frivolously wasting his time on targets which in any case could have been dealt with by the resident garrison in the Pale of Dublin. The queen wrote angry letters to him in July condemning his inaction and withdrawing his licence to return, which had been included in the original indenture. Essex now felt that he had been exiled indefinitely, and was possibly in a similar position to Richard, Duke of York in 1450.

He was now in a difficult situation. With a small army of perhaps 3,000 - 4,000 at his disposal, a shortage of supplies and the prospect of facing a larger force in Ulster, his army council, all experienced officers, agreed that they had little hope of success. Nevertheless Essex set out with his force on 2 September. A few days later he met for a parley with Hugh o'Neill, Earl of Tyrone, and on 8 September they agreed to a truce to last for the winter. Essex then returned to Dublin with his army.

Essex had defied the queen but he hoped that he could justify his action, so he left Dublin and arrived in London on 28 September. He burst into Elizabeth's bedchamber before she had had a chance to dress to give her the news. This now elderly woman, without make-up, was much affronted by the intrusion and Essex was ordered to keep to his chamber while the council met. The following morning he was questioned by the council for three hours. It appears that he made a good case for himself, since the majority of the council favoured lenient treatment and release. The queen however was not to be appeased and he was committed to the custody of Sir Thomas Egerton.

During the Irish campaign Southampton has acquitted himself with some distinction, although this did nothing to mollify his queen's opinion of him. As matters turned out it was also his last opportunity until 1624 to engage in military adventure, as almost the whole of the reign of James I was a peaceable one.

Tyrone of course broke the truce and Essex's efforts came to nothing; nor did this do anything to improve the queen's temper and he remained a prisoner for almost a year and was also deprived of various offices. Eventually, on 26 August 1600, he gained his freedom. He was now a bitter man and his mind turned to plot and rebellion. Essex House became a gathering place for discontents whether they be puritan or papists. He called his close friends, Henry Wriothesley, Sir Charles Danvers, Sir Ferdinand Gorges and Sir John Davies to organise a plan. The plan was to seize the council and pressure the queen into following their agenda. Meetings were held in Southampton's London residence, Drury House.

In order to buoy up their confidence they commissioned a performance at the Globe Theatre of Shakespeare's *Richard II,* his play about the deposition of a king. By now the authorities were very much aware of the plot and the participants. Essex was summoned to council but refused to attend. There was now confusion and a failure of nerve. The original plot was discarded in favour of improvisation. Essex would come to London with 200 armed men and, with the expectation of strong popular support in London, would be able to press his case. In the event the citizens of London were surprised, amazed and uncomprehending. There was no popular support. This was not 1399, when a popular duke was seeking to claim his rightful inheritance from a tyrannical king. While Elizabeth might be old and tired, she was not unpopular enough for people to welcome deposition. The government put up barricades and Essex was forced to retreat by water and find his way back to his house outside the city walls. Government troops then surrounded the house and he was forced to surrender. He was arrested with others, including Southampton..

They were tried on 19 February 1601. Essex, Danvers, Blount, Cuff and Merck were sentenced to death but Southampton was surprisingly spared.

There appears to have been some residual sympathy for Southampton as perhaps illustrated in Robert Cecil's letter to George Carew in March:[114] "It remaineth now that I let you known what is like to become of the poor young Earl of Southampton, who, merely for the love of the Earl has been drawn into this action." It is likely that Cecil's intervention saved Southampton. He had been condemned to death along with the others but now he was merely left to languish in prison, a state of affairs that lasted until the queen's death.

There is a surviving portrait of Southampton in his chamber in the Tower. It is three quarter length. He is dressed in expensive clothes as one would expect of a man of his station. His face is long and growing a small beard, a young man's beard for he was only 27, but it is the face of a sadder, wiser man. By intention or not, the inclusion of Trixie the cat in the portrait suggests to us that he had little else for company during these years of confinement. His head was saved from the block but he was still in no position to take his place in society.

Shakespeare was learning too. His play of this period *Alls Well that Ends Well* presents us with a young count who is spoiled and immature. He will have his own way and has determined not to marry or carry the obligations that go with his rank. The king in the play chooses a bride for him but he will have none of it. Shakespeare has been able to draw upon his association with some of the great people of the land, particularly the earl and his friends and family over the previous seven years. Shakespeare was a quick study and has picked up a thing or two from those in a higher station in life. The aristocratic world he portrayed was now more flawed less glamorous and less awe-inspiring, than that created in his early history plays.[115]

The earl too had been chastened. Blinded by his own youth and vanity and by the star that was the Earl of Essex he probably, after a few years of incarceration, came to see that he needed to adapt to the world as it was rather than a world that was a reflection of his own image.

He may also have had a lot of time to reflect on a wasted decade.

His father had been an extravagant man and had been compelled to sell two manors to relieve his indebtedness, but from 1581 to 1594 the estate had been competently managed by trustees and was probably in a state of full recovery when the third earl came of age in October 1594. Money quickly slipped through his fingers and within a short time he was heavily in debt.

In 1595 two remaining manors in Devon were sold to Thomas Arundel of Wardour for £5,000. In 1596 he sold the manor of Faringdon Episcopi for £4,100 and in 1598, Robert Bold, who became the mayor of Portsmouth in 1613, scooped up Portsea and Copnor for £1,500.

The sale continued. Sir Thomas Fleming was able to buy North Stoneham for £5,000 in 1599 and in 1600 the earl parted with a manor in Long Sutton, Somerset for the sum of £4,900. At this same time he also sold Corhampton and Bighton in Hampshire, although in the two last cases there are no figures of record. Without including those two sales he raised the staggering sum of £20,500.

More money came into the coffers through the mechanism of offering very long leases for a large fine and very low rent. Micheldever was let in 1595 for the lives of three young children (thus at least 30 years) for a fine of £650. In 1599 he granted a 33 year lease on some pasture at Beaulieu and in 1600 he let the house, rectory and mills at Beaulieu for 60 years. The fine is not known, but one assumes it was a large one.

Even so, he was still carrying a debt burden of £8,000 in 1601.

In this decade he had depleted his inheritance by about one third. The very considerable land acquisitions accumulated by the 1st earl had been diminished and his annual income was probably reduced to about £2,000 a year. His mother, the dowager Countess, was still alive and drawing her entitlement of one-third. He allowed his wife an annual income of £312 and because of charges against outstanding loans it has been estimated that his actual disposable income in 1601, was £319.[116]

For a man of his standing this was a trifling amount of money. He had much to reflect upon during his incarceration.

6

A FRESH START

One wishes that the Earl of Southampton and some others were pardoned and at liberty. – John Manningham, March 1602.

He was in luck.

Time eventually caught up with the ageing queen. She died at about 2 a.m. on 24 March 1603, coincidentally, the very last day of the old calendar year. Lady Day, 25 March, the traditional beginning of a new year, was seen to carry good omens for a better future. The old queen's reign, for all of the glorification of the 'Elizabethan Age', had become tired and stale in her final decade: hence the impatience of the Earl of Essex and his young followers, one of whom was languishing in the Tower and who had great hopes for the accession of the king of Scotland.

He was not out of tune with the times. Sir Robert Cecil, the Howard family and many of the centrist English nobles supported the Stuart accession. In addition, James, waiting impatiently in Scotland, had been very much in sympathy with Essex and his followers. So one of James' first acts before leaving Scotland for Westminster, was to sign an order for the release of Southampton. Southampton was at last at liberty.

> 10th April 1603, I heard that the Earl of Southampton and Sir Henry Neville were set at large yesterday from the Tower.[117]

Those with sensitive political antennae quickly understood that the world had changed and sought to ingratiate themselves with Southampton. Sir Francis Bacon and Sir John Davis were quick to send letters of support.

Southampton rode up the great north road and on 25 April he met the new king at Burghley, where he was warmly welcomed.

Three days later, preparations for the lavish funeral of Queen Elizabeth had been completed and the cortege set out from the palace of Whitehall, where the dead queen had been lying in state, towards Westminster Abbey. Great sums of money had been spent on costly black cloth so that everyone could be suitably attired and the carriages and horses were draped in this symbolic colour. The coffin, with a life-size painted effigy of the queen on top, was carried on a wagon canopied in purple velvet. Over 1,000 mourners of various estates comprised the procession. Two men were not present: the future king James, whose presence was not politically appropriate, and the Earl of Southampton, who was enjoying his liberty at Burghley House. It would not have occurred to him, but it is worthy of observation that the earl's great great grandfather, John Writh, would have been a central organiser of these proceedings a century earlier. Now, Henry Wriothesley, 3rd earl of Southampton, was finally a figure in the government of the country his ancestors once worked to glorify.

Those who believed in the Wheel of Fortune would not have been surprised to see a reversal of the circumstances of Southampton and his erstwhile enemy Grey, At a meeting at Windsor in June Queen Anne enquired about the failure of the Essex rebellion. Southampton replied that once the Queen had been brought into the matter they had no choice but to yield. Had not the Queen been brought into it their enemies would not have dared to oppose them. Grey, who was present, contradicted Southampton, and once more the old quarrel between them flared up. Both were restrained overnight.

Grey's time in the sun was over. He became involved in the rather ill thought out plot of 1603. The motivation, which included both catholics and some puritans, was to achieve religious toleration, and the objective was to seize the new king and use him as political leverage for their ends. Ironically, the plan was not so different from the intent of Essex a few years earlier. Grey was one of the implicated, although it appears that he was only party to discussions in June before exempting himself. Nonetheless, he was tried and found guilty in November and sentenced to life imprisonment.

On 16 May the king granted Southampton a full pardon. This meant that he could resume the title of earl and that his lands would be restored to him. Even better, he was rewarded with the Captaincy of the Isle of Wight, worth 6,000 crowns a year. He was formally re-created Earl of Southampton and Baron Titchfield at a ceremony at Hampton Court on 21 July.

James was crowned king of England on 25 July 1603 but it was a necessarily small ceremony as an outbreak of plague had shut down all public events in London and Westminster. James compensated for this lack of public ceremonial in the following year by organising an extravagant coronation procession from the City of London to Westminster on 15 March 1604. It was the display of pageantry Londoners had come to expect. Seven triumphal arches had been constructed for the occasion and a display of a moving globe had been built above the Fleet River. Musicians had been recruited and actors delivered speeches at various stations along the route. The Earl of Southampton was in attendance, as was William Shakespeare, who appeared in scarlet livery alongside some of his fellow sharers in the King's Men. One of James' early actions was to take over the patronage of the Lord Chamberlain's Men, who were henceforth known as the King's Men. He sent them 4½ yards of scarlet cloth so that they could make their livery,

On 22 August there was even better news. Southampton was awarded the farm of sweet wines. This was a slight refinement on the old medieval practice of assigning tax gathering to a noble on behalf of the king. In previous practice money was gathered and an acceptable amount was paid to the treasury while the collector retained what he could. In this new model Southampton was granted the rights to levy import duties on sweet wine, and for this he paid an annual rent to the crown of £6,000. He could then make from the franchise what he could. The farm had been worth £2,500 a year to the earl of Essex and when Southampton later surrendered it to the Crown in 1611 he was given a pension of £2,000 a year in compensation, so one must assume that it was worth at least that amount.

The earl had bounced back. While Elizabeth was alive he was living in the Tower with a much reduced income as a consequence of his youthful extravagance, but by August of 1603 he was in a position to double his income! There was no longer any need to live a constrained and frugal life.

A year after Southampton's liberation the Countess was brought to bed to give birth to their second child. It was another daughter. Her precise date of birth is unknown but she was baptised in April 1604 in the Chapel at Whitehall. Queen Anne stood as a godparent and the baby was named Anne, in honour of her godmother. In the following year, on 1 March 1605 an heir to the earldom was born and he was baptised on 27 March. He was named James in honour of the king. On 10 March 1607, a second son joined the family. He was named Thomas after the founding earl.

Despite the apparent return to normalcy the times were still uncertain. The new king had spent his life in Scotland in fear of assassination and this did not change when he came down to Westminster. His fear was not without cause, as the early plots against him were uncovered. In 1604 Southampton himself was at the centre of one of these bouts of paranoia. On the basis of a rumour that there was a plot to kill the king, Southampton, Danvers and some others were suddenly arrested on orders of the council on 24 June 1604.

The Venetian ambassador made this note on July 6th, 1604:

> On Sunday night was arrested the Earl of Southampton, Baron Danvers and others, who were confined separately and examined, but all set at liberty yesterday morning. I have not heard the reason, probably the malignity of their enemies, of whom they have many,[118]

He was never able to get to the bottom of the matter:

> I have not found out the real reason. It is said that it was a charge of treason against Southampton that he meant to kill some Scots who are much about the King, charged by unknown enemies. Southampton went to the King and said that if he knew the name of his enemy he would challenge him, but it passed off with fair words.[119]

There was some speculation that James was jealous that Southampton was spending too much time with the queen but this seems highly unlikely. It is probable that the rumour was started by someone hostile to Southampton and was easily dismissed as such, and obviously James held no ill will towards Southampton at this stage as he made a grant to him on 25 July of some lands in Basildon and Dunmow in Essex.

Later that year, in November, a minister by the name of Nalton was sent to prison for "speaking lewd words against the Earl of Southampton."[120] It is not known what these lewd words were but it is probable that the minister was a Puritan who called Southampton a recusant. In these very uncertain times unconsidered words could fall on one side or the other.

The famous year 1605, when the plot by disaffected catholics to blow up the Houses of Parliament, was uncovered, must have caused Southampton some discomfort. There is no evidence that he was even tangentially involved in what became known as the 'Gunpowder Plot', but some of his Montagu cousins of Cowdray were certainly aware of the conspiracy. Nevertheless, none thought to send him a friendly warning and had the plot succeeded he would have been blown up with everyone else. Viscount Montagu may not have been directly involved, although he might have been aware that something was afoot. Almost certainly his grandmother, a member of the Catesby clan, who regularly entertained priests at her house at St Mary Ovaries, did have knowledge of the plot. Whether or not that was communicated to her grandson is unknown. Perhaps not. Southampton did dine with his mother two weeks before the event who, if she did know anything, most likely would have dropped a hint that he should stay away on the appointed day. It is more probable that she knew nothing. Even though the circle of conspirators was widening, the plotters would want to keep that number to a minimum, and the dowager countess had little political importance in 1605. Southampton, whatever his residual sympathies for his mother's religious beliefs might have been, was unlikely to involve himself in any rebellions after the chastening experience of 1600. Besides, he was in a favoured position at court with James. Montagu was placed under house arrest in London and later at Cowdray. Sometime in 1606 he was restored to freedom.

Southampton did, like his friend Rutland, steer clear of some more hot-headed adventures, but the old personality could not be changed. He was reported to have exchanged blows with the earl of Montgomery with tennis rackets in 1610 but there appear to have been no other incidents. He continued to gamble and he was well known in Hampshire for the splendour of his social life. Sir John Oglander in his old age reflected on the good old days when he was "with my Lord Southampton on St George's Down at bowls, from 30 to 40 knights and gentlemen, where our meeting was then twice every week, Tuesdays and Thursdays, and we had an ordinary there, and cards, and tables."[121]

There were more land sales in this period. Great Compton was sold for £2,000 and Romsey Extra for £450. He purchased Fairthorne Manor at Botley but then had to sell it in 1611. Four other Hampshire manors were sold at the same time. These sales were probably necessary to raise money for his daughters' marriage portions. He had to put up £4,000 to marry his eldest daughter Penelope to Lord Spencer. The marriage portion for his second daughter is unknown.

Royal favour translated into the largest part of Southampton's income between 1603 and 1621. In addition to the lucrative farm for sweet wines he held the Keepership of the New Forest, Vice Admiralty of Hampshire, Governorship of the Isle of Wight and James also granted him pensions and other sums for unknown reasons. Lawrence Stone has estimated that his Crown income during these years was £1,500 a year at a minimum and may have been as high as £4,000.[122] The income from his estates, as we have discussed, jogged along at about £2,000 a year. On balance, it can be said that he could afford to live very well on £6,000 a year. He could also afford to invest periodic sums of £500 and £1,000 in the Virginia company explorations. It is almost impossible to determine whether or not he got any return on that investment.

Since most of the estates were concentrated in Hampshire he was in no sense an absentee landlord. This relative closeness to his tenants may have deterred him from making any hard-headed business decisions about land use and rents. Custom and tradition ruled and copyhold leases were passed on from generation to generation with little change. Whereas landowners in other parts of the country were testing and implementing the more efficient policy of land enclosure, Southampton was content to retain the land arrangements he had inherited. He was probably very popular with his tenants.

Traditional practice was to lease land for a period, often 20 years or more for an initial fine and thereafter an annual rental. The rules might vary, but the generally accepted fine might represent between three and six years rent for a twenty-one year lease. Thus a rental of £48 per annum over 21 years might engender a fine of £248. A copyhold rent, where ancient rights flowed from father to son, was even more disadvantageous to the landlord. An annual rental of £2 for a lease of 99 years would bring in a fine of only £100. These arrangements were perfectly good in non-inflationary times but the early 17th century was subject to such pressures and the earl apparently showed little interest in modernising his practices.

7

A COLONIAL PIONEER

O brave new world! - Miranda, The Tempest.

One striking characteristic of the third earl was his intellectual interest in new ventures. The humdrum management of his estates did not excite him and he was content to leave matters to his stewards to carry on much as before. What did get his juices flowing was any prospect of a new and exciting venture. The exploration and settlement of the North American coast captured his imagination and he became a leading participant in the Virginia Company.

Bartholemew Gosnold was the son of a Suffolk family who could afford to send him to university and have him trained at the Middle Temple as a lawyer. What turned him to an interest in seafaring is unknown, but by 1602, at the age of 29, he was actively promoting the idea of colonising Virginia, as the coast of North America was then known. He sought backers and found a principal in the Earl of Southampton, then languishing in jail and with little to occupy his time lent his active support. Gosnold was able to set sail with 31 others from Falmouth in Cornwall in 1602. He travelled to the Azores and from there made landfall on 14 May 1602 on the coast of Maine.

The following day he sailed into a harbour at what is now Provincetown at the very end of a long finger of land stretching out from the coast, and he named it Cape Cod, because of the abundant fishing. A few days later he discovered an island which he named Martha's Vineyard after his daughter and the apparent abundance of wild grapes. By May 20th they discovered Cuttyhunk Island, which they decided to settle.

The settlement did not work. Relations between the new arrivals and the initially friendly natives grew hostile and the new immigrants were reluctant to stay. In the end all decided to return with the boat when it set out for England on 11 June 1602.

Nevertheless they returned with enthusiastic reports:

> 'This Main is the goodliest continent that ever we saw, promising more by far than we any way did expect. For it is replenished with fair fields, and in them fragrant flowers, also meadows, and hedge in with stately grove, being furnished also with pleasant brooks, and beautified with two main rivers (as we judge) may haply become good harbours and conduct us to hopers menus greedily do thirst after.[123]

Such discoveries excited great interest in England and there was no shortage of would be investors. Experience had taught them, particularly with Raleigh's failed efforts that more was required than simply planting settlers, and the whole business of founding new colonies was still highly experimental. No obvious solution had emerged in this first decade of the new century, yet investors, including the Earl of Southampton, were happy to front the money despite the obvious risk to the investment. Hope triumphed over experience, but the earl was a gambling man by instinct and in the long term his instincts would prove to be right. However, there was still much to learn about founding a colony in a distant land, and only later would it become apparent that the key to success was strong leadership among the new settlers. The discovery of this truth had to wait until the 1620s.

In 1609 a charter was given to the Virginia Company with full power to govern the colony. No fewer than 650 individuals and 56 city companies were anxious to subscribe. At the head of the list was Lord de la Warr, putting up £500, the Earl of Pembroke, who committed £400 and the Earl of Southampton who contributed £350. Lord de la Warr was to be the Governor, but he sent a deputy, Sir Thomas Gates in his place. Nine ships sailed from Plymouth carrying 600 colonists.

The voyage was not without incident. The fleet encountered a hurricane. The leading vessel, the *Sea Venture*, was washed up on the shore of Bermuda, where, without loss of life, the stranded mariners were able to survive the winter with a plentiful supply of food. The remainder of the fleet reached the mainland. The story, when it reached England, was to inspire *The Tempest*, one of Shakespeare's last plays.

One source was almost certainly a letter written by one of the survivors of the shipwreck, William Strachey. Strachey, who was born in 1572 lived in the Blackfriars area. He certainly knew Ben Jonson and it must be inferred that he also knew William Shakespeare. He wrote a long narrative in a letter to "a noble lady', most likely the wife of Sir Thomas Smith, a member of the Virginia Company. It is conceivable that Shakespeare by report or actual sight of the letter drew much material from the venture for his play. Strachey reported "that they can be no habitation for men, but rather given over to Devils and wicked Spirits"[124] Shakespeare's island is full of magic.

Once discovered, this island, later known as Bermuda, became a target for colonists and the Somers Island or Bermuda Company was established in 1615. Southampton was a founding investor.

The new Virginia settlement ran into the now familiar problem of lack of effective leadership. Lack of provision for the winter of 1609-10 meant that many starved and when Lord de la Warr arrived with 350 men in the Spring he found only 60 alive from the 500 or so that had landed the previous year.

> 'No man would acknowledge a superior nor could from this headless and unbridled multitude be anything expected but disorder and riot."[125]

A new subscription of £18,000 was called for in 1611 and three more ships were sent out. One of Southampton's men, Sir Thomas Dale, sailed with this expedition to try to restore order to the colony. The intriguing and exotic character of Pocahontas now had a role to play in the future of the Virginia Company. She was an Algonquin Indian and a daughter of the chief Powhatan. She had been used as a hostage and a diplomatic pawn during the various outbreaks of hostility between the settlers and the native population. During her captivity she had become fluent in English and Sir John Rolfe, one of those who had been stranded on Bermuda in 1609, became infatuated with her. They were married in 1614. The company directors in London saw this marriage as a useful opportunity to encourage investors to stick with the project, as interest was waning fast. Thousand of pounds had been invested, hundreds of lives lost and the returns had been minimal. Accordingly Rolfe and his wife, together with some Indians, were invited to London where Pocahontas became a sensation.

The company leaders resolved on a change of policy. All settlers would be granted 50 acres. This appeared to work and the new crop of tobacco was able to feed a growing habit in Europe. Finally a cash crop! The colony did not exactly thrive during this period but it did at last provide some return for the investors. The '50 acre' policy salvaged the enterprise.

The accidental discovery of the uninhabited Bermuda was also a bonus. The land was fertile and the climate salubrious, and the absence of a native population meant that the colonists could set about their business unimpeded by native interests.

Nevertheless the principal colony on the mainland in Virginia was struggling. In 1616 the company had no money left for administration and there were no more than 300 settlers.

Southampton not only had interest in the Virginia and Bermuda companies but also the East India Company, apparently for £500 and 'a brace of bucks yearly.' He was admitted in May 1609. The East India Company may have been less attractive to him as we don't hear much about Southampton's investment in the east, but his interest in North America continued to grow. In 1610 he put some money to support the explorer Henry Hudson and in 1612 he was one of those who incorporated the North West Passage Company. In 1614 he subscribed £100 to Edward Harlow's voyage to the New England coast. In sum, this illustrates a high level of interest in risky ventures.

There is not much evidence that anyone made any money out of the North American ventures. In 1619, the company leadership was reconstituted with Sir Edwin Sandys as the new leader. At this time the capital of the company had dwindled to £1,000. Sandys was the right kind of man, young energetic and forceful, but even he struggled against the dead weight of previous inexperience and mismanagement. He was also unacceptable to the king, who held a grudge because Sandys had opposed him on an issue in 1614, In consequence Southampton was nominated and acclaimed as the company leader, although behind this front Sandys was very active. Between August 1620 and February 1621 six ships were sent out. The *Bona Nova* carried 120 people, the *Elizabeth* 20 people, the *Mayflower* 100.[126] The *Supply* set sail from Bristol in September with 45 new colonists. The *Margaret* and the *John* left in December with 85 and in February carried 230. In the space of one calendar year Southampton and Sandys between them sent out 24 ships taking a total of 1,300 colonists.

And yet this year was remembered in history for a smaller expedition of three ships sailing from Southampton and Plymouth in September to land at Cape Cod in what was later to be called the state of Massachusetts. This voyage was successful because these colonists were highly disciplined and led by men who forced the settlers to conform and protect themselves against winter. They entered the history books as founding fathers of the New World while the earlier settlers of Virginia were still struggling to understand how they could effectively organise their new society.

The company now tried to concentrate on building revenue, and, as the habit was spreading, the plantation and export of tobacco was the most promising source. The Virginia company tried to negotiate a monopoly with the government and the Earl of Middlesex, then Lord Treasurer, seemed agreeable to the idea provided that revenue went to the crown. The company were minded to give up a share of 25% but the Lord Treasurer insisted on 33% and would not budge from that position. On 22 November 1622 a somewhat crestfallen Southampton had to report that this was the best the company could do. Unfortunately the company had already set up the administration for tobacco importing and had set the salaries of the official rather too high in expectation of reasonable profits. The impositions of the Crown left little margin for profit.

In March 1622 the Virginia colony came under attack by the Indians. 374 people were massacred, and the loss of equipment and stored food exposed the colony to another winter of starvation. A further 500 were lost in that winter. A census taken in 1624 recorded only 1,275 people - this out of 4,000 who had voyaged to Virginia since 1620. The company would in time come to prosperity but at the time of Southampton's death in 1624 he and his fellow investors had very little to show for their commitment.

The company was in any case in serious difficulty. Sandys reported that the company had spent £80,000 of public stock and there was £5,000 of debt. Various factions within the company fell to arguing and recrimination and the king decided to intervene. He appointed Sir William Jones to investigate the affairs of the two companies - the Virginia Company and the Bermuda Company. Effectively neither company could now operate. It was the end. The law courts ordered that the charter be vacated in April 1624. After 18 years and the expenditure of a great deal of money and considerable loss of life the failed venture was over.

Some felt that Middlesex's intransigence had led to the failure of the company and set out for revenge. He was impeached in the Lords for his mismanagement of the Treasury. He was condemned and spent some time in the Tower before being released on payment of an enormous fine.

There was some sort of legacy from this. Southampton held title to land in Virginia and Colonel William Byrd was able to buy these lands from the estate of the 4th earl, who did not share his father's interest in the New World. Southampton is now remembered by a county in Virginia and a town on the island of Bermuda.

8

AN EARLY INDUSTRIALIST

Now /The furnace and the bellows shall to work, /The great Sejanus crack, and piece by piece /Drop i'the founder's pit... – Ben Jonson, Sejanus.

The third earl's restless curiosity for the new and modern did not lie solely with exotic lands across the ocean. Closer to home he established an ironworks.

Roger Manners, Earl of Rutland and bosom friend of the 3rd Earl of Southampton took an interest in his family's acquisition of Rievaulx Abbey in North Yorkshire, principally because the land included medieval ironworks. Rutland developed these ironworks with some success and his friend, ever curious about new ventures decided to emulate this venture on the south coast.

He may have started on this project soon after his release from the Tower in 1603 because by 1605 there were already complaints about the demand for wood creating a fuel shortage. He established a furnace at Sowley on the Beaulieu estate and another at Funtley on the Meon. The Sowley furnace was able to access ironstone from Hengistbury Head and Hordle Cliffs. Both furnace locations had access to a large supply of wood and both could use the rivers for shipping. The Sowley furnace produced pig iron, which was then shipped to Funtley to be refined into wrought iron.

He was initially ambitious for the project and must have planned for expansion. When he leased the Botley Flour Mill in 1608 he inserted a clause that allowed him to cancel the lease should he decide to build an ironworks there instead. The option was never taken up and it must have become apparent to the earl that the potential profits were limited in what had become a crowded market. In 1622 he abandoned direct management and granted a seven year lease of the furnaces at Sowley and Funtley for £103 a year. These lease arrangements continued in one form or another into the 18th century.

In the year before his death the earl was attracted to another venture, that of manufacturing tin plate. From a letter dated 1623 we learn that John Tite had gone into partnership with the earl to manufacture tin plate. In the letter he wrote: "The mill which batters the iron is the Earl's of Southampton, he hath been at a £1,000 charge to build it and to fit it for this work."[127] There was agreement that a sum of £500 would launch the project and the earl contributed £200 for half the profit; the other half being shared by Tite and his active partner Thomas Jupp. It can be inferred that the mill was built at Wickham from a document of 1647.[128]

How much these industrial ventures contributed to the earl's income is largely a matter of guesswork. The iron mills by 1624 only brought in £100 a year and the proceeds from the tin plate mill at Wickham are unknown. Lawrence Stone conjectures that the total income from these ventures could be no more than £400 for £500 a year.[129]

It has long been believed that the short canal from the village to the sea was dug at the instigation of the 3rd earl of Southampton. This would certainly be in character and it is the kind of project he would have undertaken with enthusism. An estate map of 1610 does not illustrate a canal and yet in the following year there is this curious remark in the Titchfield Parish Register:

> the same day (24 June 1611) Titchfield Haven was shutt out by one Richard Talbotts industrie under gods permission at the costs by the right honorable the Earle of Southampton.[130]

This entry has been interpreted as closing off the estuary mouth and that the canal would henceforth carry all water transport. Dissenters from this view claim that "shut out" does not mean closed off but rather protected by a shingle bank, the spit that has probably grown over the years as more shingle is washed up against it. Such a bank would protect the haven and act as a kind of harbour wall.[131] This has given rise to a traditional view that the 3rd Earl of Southampton was the instigator of the Titchfield canal. At a date of 1611 this would make it one of the earliest such projects in the country.

The canal is manifestly there and is still evident today. Its construction, and indeed its purpose, remains a mystery. The Canal is a two-mile long stretch of water from the sea to Titchfield Mill. It is controlled by a sea lock. After its construction, the river estuary may have been neglected and eventually became difficult for navigation. It is now closed off from the sea by a sluice gate and has become a wildlife preserve. The canal was apparently not a success and the port of Titchfield, prominent in the middle ages, declined.

The location of the church and village of Titchfield on the west bank of the river Meon made very good sense. It was the first point on the river with a bank that would not flood in winter and easy access to water transport was available at all times. In medieval times roads and tracks were typically in poor condition and cartage, whether dependent on oxen or horses, was expensive and slow. Water transport was no faster, but a flat bottomed boat could carry a large cargo at low cost. Titchfield therefore became a port for the lower part of the Meon to carry grain and flour, hides and building stone. All traffic to Porchester, Southampton, the Isle of Wight, possibly Winchester and more distant coastal destinations would use this port.

The river was most likely navigable to Wickham at least, and possibly further north. It is quite wrong to assert, as some writers have done, that the river was not navigable above Titchfield because the bridges would prevent boats from passing. This assumes that bridges were level crossings, as they are today, but in an age when water transport had primacy, bridges over narrow rivers were 'hump backed' with a high arch to allow boats to pass underneath. The river served as an arterial highway with local tracks to cross country destinations. These tracks could cope with short-haul cartage; carts were drawn by oxen and later in the Middle Ages, once the flexible harness had been invented, by horses, but any road haulage was slow and never reached speeds above three miles an hour. Water transport, where available, was preferred. It was not much faster than by road but it was considerably cheaper. A single horse could tow a heavily laden barge along a river, whereas the equivalent cargo by road would require an expensive team of oxen or horses. Given Titchfield's natural advantages, merchants would look to the river first.

Titchfield did not get its first turnpike road until very late in the 18th century and a glance at earlier maps will show that the most

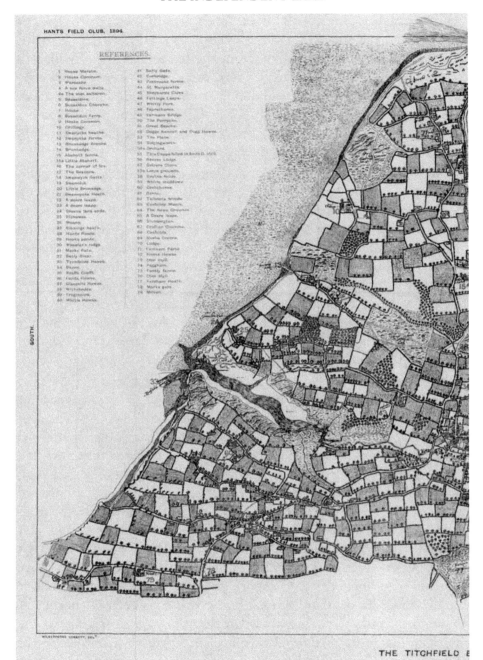

This estate map dates to 1610. It was copied by the Rev G W Minns and reproduced in 1906 by the Hampshire Field Club in their publication. The river in this map flows directly into the sea.

southerly cross country road passed through Wickham. There were practical reasons for this - river crossings over the Meon, the Hamble and the Itchen were much easier as the rivers narrowed. Nobody at Titchfield minded very much as the river had always been an easier method of carrying goods since medieval times.

As discussed earlier in this chapter, the 3rd Earl of Southampton became enthusiastic about iron production in 1605. Water transport must have been a key factor in founding these iron works at Sowley and Funtley. The transport of pig iron and finished iron goods was only practical if water transport was used. It is unlikely that the enterprising Henry Cort would have considered leasing the iron mill in the late 18th century without access to a navigable river.

There is a certain amount of regular sedimentary deposit in the Meon estuary but evidence shows that it is relatively light and regular dredging probably kept it under control. Thus it is reasonable to assume that the estuary had an open channel until at least the end of the 18th century.

All 17th century and early 18th century maps depict an open estuary at the mouth of the Meon. In 1759 a map drawn by Isaac Taylor shows what appears to be a canal, running in a straight line for about two miles to the village of Titchfield. The map also shows a spit protecting the estuary mouth and a road along the bank. The map is very close to the modern appearance, and it also accords with an undated chart[132] which is believed to have been drawn in the mid-18th century. However, we must treat this cartographic evidence with care as we do not know whether these maps were copies of earlier maps or whether the map maker made a survey.

No earlier map illustrates this. Maps drawn by Norden in 1607 and Speed in 1611 depict an open estuary and make a point of indicating Titchfield Bay. Bleau's map of 1645 shows no change and this is also true of Jannsen's map published a year later. Morden's map of 1695 and Kinchin's map of 1751 show no change in the traditional drawing of an open estuary.

It is difficult to draw any firm conclusions from this evidence. Cartographers did not always take a new survey and may have been tempted to copy information from previously published sources. Jannsen's map of 1646 is inaccurate in a number of details and cannot be relied upon. One general point may perhaps be ventured: that the

Above: The Jansson map of 1646
Below: The Taylor map of 1759, the first map to illustrate the canal.

cartographers understood the river to be navigable and not closed off to river traffic.

The canal is between 16ft. and 20ft. wide. A minimum width of 5 metres is therefore sufficiently wide for a conventional vessel and could conceivably allow two narrow barges to pass. Wider vessels might experience some difficulty. The depth the channel would have been a minimum of between 6ft. and 7ft., a sufficient draught for any laden vessel. There was certainly a wharf beside the tannery and when the new A27 road cut through Mill Lane some timbers were discovered by the river, suggesting that there may have been a wharf beside the corn mill. Unfortunately these were not recorded by an archaeologist so the evidence amounts to hearsay, but it is consistent with what we might expect.

There is a lock at the sea entrance which has been unused for many years. It has been theorised that the lock was open at high tides to allow passage of the boats along the canal. In the abstract, the canal makes good sense. Water traffic would theoretically move at a more efficient rate and there would no longer be a need to dredge the traffic lane in the estuary. The reality may not have been so successful. Passage of the boats would have to be well organised, with boats queuing up at high tide. It is a puzzle that the canal was not widened after the lock so that there could be a waiting bay for incoming boats. One writer[133] has argued that such operation was impossible as there would only be a few minutes when the water levels were equal and once open they would be difficult to close because of the high water pressure. There was also a risk of salt water flooding the fields and causing contamination. It is quite possible that cargo was transferred at the canal mouth from masted sea going vessels to horse-drawn barges. If so there would be no need to open the sea lock.

Some have suggested that the canal was intended as an irrigation ditch. Certainly that became its purpose in the 19th century. White's Directory in 1859 states that the canal was "chiefly for the purpose of drainage and irrigation, and not now used for the navigation of barges". George Watts commented that 'within living memory there were a regular series of small sluice gates along the canal, most of them now destroyed, which permitted the water in the canal to be used in this way.'[134] It would appear that the canal was later exploited for this use rather than intended as such. An irrigation channel, if that was its planned intention, need not have been dug so wide and there would likely have been a series of dykes branching at right angles to the main channel.

In the 17th century we discover references to a 'new river.' These would tend to support the idea that the canal was intended for transport rather than for irrigation purposes. These documents do, however, raise questions about the earlier date of 1611. In a letter of 1752, the land agent Clement Walcot refers to a change in the area of land leased to the Stares family, supposing that the land was originally surveyed "before the New River was made".[135] The original lease in this case goes back to 1640 and would have been held by copyhold by succeeding family members. It must be inferred from this that the 'new river' was not cut before 1640. The 1611 reference to Richard Talbot 'shutting out Titchfield Haven may also be put into another context as there is a lease to Richard Tamye dated 6th June 1614 includes amongst other things 20 acres of land "lately recovered from the overflowing of the sea".[136] Thus the construction of a sea wall, authorised and paid for by the 3rd earl may not necessarily be tied to the construction of a two-mile canal from the village to the sea. The Tamye lease supports the idea that the purpose of the sea wall was land reclamation.

There is some further evidence. On 4th October 1676 a volume of presentments at the Manorial Court of Titchfield[137] included the following recently discovered entries: "Wee p'sent that ye Lord of this mannor by Cutting ye new River hath taken away & doth detaine one acre of Land from John Cooper which belongeth to his Coppiehold. Also wee p'sent that ye said Lord doth detaine Two acres of Land from John Landy which belongeth to his Coppiehold, Taken away by Cutting ye said New River."

These references make a strong case for excluding the idea that the canal was built in 1611 and that the construction was more recent to the 1670s. A further court record from 1742 relating to William Churcher. The claim was that lands held in trusteeship by the Churcher family had failed to make payments to the Overseers of the Poor. William Churcher, in evidence, submitted that at some time after the death of his great-grandfather the River was diverted by the Earl's heirs or assigns "for their benefit" and the consequent loss of the River brought about the rapid and total loss of the woollen trade and a collapse in the revenues derived from it. Robert Churcher was buried on 4 June 1643 and this offers us another piece of evidence to suggest that the canal could not have been built before that date.[138] Given that no one was in a position to embark on such projects during the civil war period and the Commonwealth, when taxation was high and often arbitrary, it is unlikely that anything would happen before the Restoration, and during that period the 4th earl (1607-1667) was actively developing Bloomsbury and was much occupied with his duties as Lord Treasurer. The 4th earl, incidentally, when he came into his estates in the 1630s showed himself to be quite unlike his father. He was a practical businessman who recovered and built up the family fortune and showed little interest in the more creative projects that captured his father's imagination.

At his death in 1670 the estate was divided equally between his three daughters. The "Titchfield third" passed to his daughter Elizabeth and her husband Edward Noel, who later became the 1st earl of Gainsborough. He began to take an interest in Hampshire in these years. He was appointed Colonel of the Hampshire Militia in 1678. On 3 February 1681, he was created Baron Noel of Titchfield and entered the House of Lords. In 1682, he was given several local offices in Hampshire: Governor of Portsmouth, Constable of Portchester Castle, and Lieutenant of South Bere Forest. He succeeded his father in October as Viscount Campden and as Lord Lieutenant and Custos Rotulorum of Rutland, and was further honoured at the end of the year when he was created Earl of Gainsborough on 1 December 1682. If we accept the documents that indicate that the 'new river' was cut in the 1670s, perhaps we should look to the Earl of Gainsborough as the instigator. As a new landlord he might well have been tempted by ideas that would bring the estate "up-to-date." We can perhaps imagine that like many new managers he may have been seduced by the notion that he was the 'new man' who could drag Titchfield out of its medieval past. He may have taken advice from a local man who sold the benefits of such a scheme to a man who was completely unfamiliar with the Titchfield estate. He would not be the first or last man to endorse a scheme that accomplished the opposite of what he intended.

It may be also worth noting that the earliest use of the word "canal" in the sense of a waterway, according to the Oxford English Dictionary, is 1673, so although we today describe it as a canal, the Titchfield locals clearly understood it as a *new river*, the word canal not having come into general use in its modern sense.

Dating the canal to 1611 rests entirely on the interpretation of the words 'shut out' in an entry in the Parish Register. It has been inferred from this that the estuary was blocked off and of necessity the canal must have been cut at the same time. A date of somewhere in the 1670s rests upon four pieces of documentary evidence, and if we consider four documents as weightier evidence than two lines of hand-written text, then the later date has more plausibility. The cartographic evidence for both dates cannot be taken as definitive because we do not know whether they were based upon contemporary surveys or were simply iterations of earlier maps.

The new river may have been impractical, for the reasons outlined above. Sea locks can be designed to work effectively but this one was not. The canal may have been abandoned as a waterway and later adapted as an irrigation ditch. If the estuary had silted up the ironworks at Funtley may have been forced to transport their goods to Wickham, where they had a reasonably good road to Portsmouth. Even with this partial clarification, the canal remains a mystery.

In the village there is some folk memory that the canal had disrupted the lives of good people of Titchfield and this was blamed on the 3rd Earl of Southampton. In fact, this earl was a very benign landlord. From his majority until his death in 1624 he tended to allow copyhold leases to be renewed at their traditional rent and he never attempted any enclosures, which were then growing in popularity among the landed classes. The common, or the 'great waste' as it was sometimes called locally, would have to wait until the 19th century for any serious development. The breakdown of the three field system had largely been accomplished during the time of abbey control and the earls seemed content to go along with those arrangements. In contrast to his active interest in North American settlement, the iron and tin plate mills and his duties at court, he showed very little zeal for change in the traditional management of his estates and was broadly content to leave his stewards to manage these affairs. Although one can argue that it was in character for the 3rd earl to indulge in the experiment of the canal, it should also be noted that 1611 was the beginning of his sponsorship of the Virginia colony and that alone was probably sufficient to occupy his interest. There can also be little doubt that some well-to-do and established farming families would have raised lawsuits had their land been carved up in 1611, as indeed proved to be the case in the 1670s.

I would also have to agree with John Mitchell that 'shutting out" Titchfield Haven did not mean closing it off.[139] The words should rather be interpreted as protecting the mouth of the estuary, which is what the spit bank does. There was also an instance later in the century when the sea wall was breached and had to be repaired. The Taylor map of 1759 illustrates bridges at both the canal and estuary entrances. These would have been hump back bridges which would allow a barge, but not a masted craft to pass under. This does raise a question or two about how un-masted vessels were propelled along the coast. Was the cargo moved from sea-going vessels and vice versa? There is little evidence of a dock at the estuary entrance which would support such a theory. So once more this leaves us with unanswered questions unless there were lift bridges at the harbour and canal entrances.

Keith Hayward's revelation of the 17th and 18th century leases and letters makes a strong case that the new river was not constructed during the time of the earls but rather by his heirs and although he rightfully urges caution, the evidence supporting a theory of later construction stands up much better than the parish register entry which appears to pinpoint 1611.

On balance, construction during the 1670s appears to be a safer theory. The later date is also closer to the great age of canal building which began after the middle of the 18th century. The Titchfield 'new river' or canal did not present an engineering challenge; there were no steep slopes to negotiate by means of locks, tunnels and cuttings. Since it was entirely within the jurisdiction of a single landowner no Act of Parliament was required, and the landlord could authorise the project, which could then proceed quickly. £1,000 might have covered the cost of the project, a sum which was not beyond the revenues of the Titchfield estate, so it may have been paid for out of estate income with no special borrowing. This may explain the somewhat frustrating absence of any accounting for the canal construction.

We do know that the iron mill continued to operate into the 19th century and we have made an assumption that river transport was necessary to its commercial functioning. We also know that Titchfield's trade certainly fell into decline in the 18th century. These two facts may not be contradictory. The creation of turnpike roads in the 18th century may have given Wickham and Botley and Bishop's Waltham mills a strategic advantage in distributing their goods. Titchfield's mill remained dependent on tides and the inconvenient operation of the sea lock. Changing times may have been against Titchfield. Water transport, which was the preferred option in the middle ages lost precedence to an improved road network in the 18th century. In the same period nearby Hamble deteriorated to a poor fishing village and Bursledon became a dumping ground for hulks.

If there is any further information to be discovered about the Titchfield Canal a likely source may be documents from the time of the earl of Gainsborough. These eventually descended to the Dukes of Portland and their papers are mostly to be found in the Nottinghamshire archives.

9

MATTERS OF STATE

This day the Earl of Southampton was by his Majesty's special commandment sworn one of his Highness' Privy Council, sat at the Board, and signed letters as a Councillor. - Privy Council Register, 30 April 1619.

Although James had released him from his imprisonment in the Tower in 1603 and made him a Privy Councillor, and he appeared to be in favour, he was never quite at the centre of government. He was perhaps too independent-minded to suit James' style of kingship but there seems little doubt, once we examine Southampton's mature years, that he turned himself into a very skilful politician and contrived to become an effective voice even though the tide of English politics was heading towards doom. Rowse characterises him as a "leader of the Opposition" and there is some validity in this observation, but we must be careful in going too far with this comparison. English politics had yet to crystallise into government and opposition parties. Loyalties could be very fluid and personal.

A contemporary writer, Arthur Wilson, made this observation:

> Southampton, though he were one of the king's Privy Council, yet was he no great courtier. Salisbury kept him at bay and pinched him so by reason of his relation to old Essex, that he never flourished much in his time; nor was his spirit, after him, so smooth-shod as to go always the court pace, but that now and thence would make a carrier that was not very acceptable to them; for he carried his business closely and slyly, and was rather an advisor than an actor.[140]

Robert Cecil, 1ˢᵗ Earl of Salisbury, was a very clever politician who stayed at the forefront of two regimes until the last year of his life. He routed the Essex plot of 1599, in which Southampton was implicated, and saw off various plots against James, including the celebrated Gunpowder Plot of 1605. As Lord Treasurer he managed the finances of the state effectively despite James' tendency to extravagance. After he died in 1612, the kingdom slid towards ruin.

Salisbury kept Southampton at arms length because of his closeness to Essex, and as Wilson observed, the earl never had much opportunity to flourish politically during this period. After Cecil's death he had more scope than he had during the reign of the disapproving Elizabeth but his years in the tower had taught him the wisdom of being circumspect in his political dealings. But he was no longer the attractive young man of the last Elizabethan decade; in 1612 he was close to 40 and he was competing for attention with a new generation of bright young men, such as George Villiers, who was gaining the attention of the king in the second decade of the 17ᵗʰ century. This probably moved him towards a stance of becoming a wise and independent counsel.

Cecil was replaced as Lord Treasurer by Charles Howard, the Earl of Nottingham, and he held that position until he resigned in 1619. Southampton could have been a sensible replacement but George Villiers had became the king's favourite. Once he captured the king's attention in 1614 he was promoted rapidly though the nobility, becoming, baron, viscount, earl and marquess in rapid succession. By the time he was appointed Lord Treasurer in 1619 he was Marquess of Buckingham.

As part-recognition of his quality and usefulness, but also as a kind of consolation prize, Southampton was made a Privy Councillor in April 1619, and at the end of the same year Parliament was called. Southampton's eldest son, James, was elected the member for Callington, in Cornwall on 27 December 1620. Parliament began its sitting on 30 January 1621.

The reason for calling this Parliament was that the king needed money to pursue a foreign policy that was not necessarily to the liking of his people. Frederick, Elector of the Palatinate, and son-in-law of James, was under threat from the catholic Habsburg powers in Germany. The Palatinate comprised a collection of city states in south west Germany, later absorbed in the 18th century into the kingdom of Bavaria. The

Elector held some status as one of seven princes who could elect the Holy Roman Emperor, traditionally a member of the Habsburg family. James felt that he should support his son in law but also, ambiguously, sought friendly diplomatic relations with Spain. In this latter policy he had the active encouragement of Buckingham, who was promoting an alliance with Spain through marriage of Prince Charles to the Spanish Infanta. This was unacceptable to Protestant England, which saw Frederick as a natural protestant ally. James did not help his case by taking the Stuart position, continued by his son, that the motives of kings should never be questioned. No explanation was offered for the large sum of money required nor were satisfactory answers given for the disposition of that money. Accordingly, Parliament approved a much smaller subsidy which would have yielded a quite inadequate amount for a foreign adventure. They were rightly suspicious of the king's motives.

The Commons then turned to domestic matters. The matter of monopolies had grown worse since the ascendancy of Buckingham, in particular the licensing of inns and the manufacture of gold and silver thread. In each of these instances Buckingham's relatives were favoured and therefore prospered.

One of the most egregious cases of the period, which exemplified the corruption that festered during this period of James' reign, concerned a man called Sir Giles Mompesson.

Giles Mompesson had a family connection to George Villiers and used this to persuade Villiers in 1616 to allow him to become a commissioner of inns in 1617. Under this scheme Mompesson could levy fines against innkeepers for any violations of the law. Of all the money collected, 80% was to go to the treasury. Fulke Greville, then Chancellor of the Exchequer, spotted the flaw in the plan, but it was endorsed by Francis Bacon and Villiers and thus the king. Mompesson knew clearly at the outset that the more money he raised the greater his personal gain; there was every incentive to find ways of prosecuting innkeepers.

It became an extortion racket. Mompesson sent agents to inns posing as travelling customers, who would lure the innkeeper into some minor breach of the law and announce the following morning that they had caught the innkeeper red-handed. The favourite trick was to turn up at a tavern (which were not licensed as inns) and beg for a place to stay. The taverner would usually acquiesce and then be surprised to discover that his act of kindness had led him to break the law. The fines were not small and within a few years some 3,320 inns and taverns had fallen foul of Mompesson's practices.

Another of his schemes was to raise money for the Treasury by selling decayed timber from Royal forests. In his proposal to Villiers the scheme would raise £10,000 for the government and he would be allowed £2,000. At his trial it was revealed that he had pocketed £10,000 for himself.

The Commons started proceedings and would have continued but for the fact that someone raised the question of whether or not the Commons had the right to punish men for these offences. A search for precedences revealed none, so they referred the matter to the Lords.

At this stage Southampton emerged as a leader of the commission to investigate. They discovered that Mompesson had drawn some £200 a year as income from concealed lands - an illegal practice. Further, as described above, he had enriched himself through prosecuting innkeepers for the breach of obsolete statutes. Mompesson was caught dead to rights and the king and Buckingham, sensing the prevailing wind, made no effort to defend him. Before sentencing Mompesson was able to escape to France on 3 March 1621. In the following week the Lords voted to fine him £10,000, strip him of his knighthood and insist that he ride backwards on his horse along the Strand and then be imprisoned for life.

There is not much evidence that he was in any way punished. His estate was tied up in various ways and it was probably difficult to extract the fine. As he was in France he could not be publicly humiliated or imprisoned. He was back in the country in 1624 and seems to have spent the rest of his life in retirement in Wiltshire. He died in 1663 at the age of 80.

Soon after their success with Mompesson, parliament turned to the higher prize of the Lord Chancellor.

Sir Francis Bacon, or Lord Verulam as he became under James, was one of the great intellectuals of the period. He was born in 1561 and had served in various roles under Elizabeth. He was recognised as an accomplished poet and philosopher and when the craze for seeking aristocratic alternatives for the author of Shakespeare's work began in the 19th century, he was put forward as one of the candidates. Like many brilliant intellectuals he tended to be a little unworldly, and this was to bring about his downfall. There was a demonstrable gap between his public writing and his administrative practice. He wrote, 'the more you remove yourself from particulars, the greater peril of error do you incur.'[141] Wise and practical words indeed, but it appears that Bacon was happy to delegate to others without attending to the 'particulars' of their activity.

Many aspects of James's government were corrupt at this time and everyone knew it. The world had moved on since the time of Southampton's grandfather, when gifts to court officials and ministers were accepted as a means of getting things done. Such gifts had now become bribes because the intent behind them was to loot the public purse and with the nation's finances in a parlous state and a foreign policy that was teetering on the edge of war, many were becoming alarmed.

Under Southampton's leadership a schedule of 28 charges were sent by Parliament to Bacon to answer. It was probably then that the grand Bacon realised the extent of the doubtful transactions and bribes that were almost routine in his office. It was not necessarily the man himself, but the men under him, who were the perpetrators. One of them was John Churchill, the founder of the family fortunes that led to the great Marlborough dukedom, who, as registrar, had many instances of suspect dealings against his name. However, Churchill was canny enough to turn state's evidence in order to save himself, and was quite prepared to expose his master. Buckingham, who understood well enough his own vulnerability, kept his distance and no doubt welcomed the distraction from his own dodgy dealings. A short trial, which considered demotion from the peerage, exile and incarceration in the Tower, ended by allowing Bacon to retreat to his sick bed. He lived a further five years and played no further part in pubic affairs.

With these side shows out of the way the king wished Parliament to return to the business of granting him sufficient funds to prosecute war in the Palatinate. Questions from the Commons were countered with vagueness and assertions of the king's right. Buckingham wanted to lead the army and while both he and the king knew that this would be unpopular, they pressed for approval. Had they allowed Southampton to take charge, it is likely that the proposal would have been approved. The Venetian Ambassador observed"

The point consists inducing the King to agree to allow the Earl of Southampton, a leading nobleman, rich, experienced, with considerable influence, to go to the defence of the Palatinate.[142]

The ambassador went on to comment that the appointment would be popular. Nevertheless, the king was inflexible. It is possible that the earlier exchange of words between Southampton and Buckingham during the Bacon trial, which had escalated to a scuffle where the two men were on the point of drawing their swords, may have permanently prejudiced James again the earl. Even in middle age, Southampton's tendency to hot temper was never completely dormant.

Eventually James lost patience and adjourned the Parliament on 24 May. Some opponents were arrested. Walter Yonge wrote in his diary:

> Presently after Parliament was adjourned, the Earl of Southampton, Sir Edward Coke, Sir Edwin Sands and Wright, the Clerk of the Parliament, and Dr Bayley were imprisoned, Oxford for saying we should all turn Papists, Southampton for encouraging the Palsgrave in his wars.[143]

The Venetian ambassador further observed that the earl was "considered to be almost the only person capable of commanding an army."[144] It was not a view shared by Buckingham who was undoubtedly influencing James. James announced that it was not appropriate for a member of the Privy Council to involved himself in a matter in which he did not wish to declare himself, and appointed Sir Horace Vere to take responsibility for the levy. Southampton was sidelined and placed under house arrest.

He was to be held under the custody of the Dean of Westminster. His detention was not as restrictive as the Tower, but he was to be allowed no dealings with anyone else. When he protested that he should be allowed to correspond with his wife, this was allowed, provided that he was under supervision. The intention of James and Buckingham was to isolate their critics so that they could not nourish any alliances. Southampton was questioned of course but he was too careful and too experienced to fall into any traps. The record of the inquisition follows:

> 1. Whether his own conscience did not accuse him of unfaithfulness to the King in the latter part of Parliament, which his Majesty had cause to doubt both in. his own carriage in the Upper House and by the carriage of those near to him

in the Lower House?

Reply. He protested his conscience was free, and he thought his Majesty too just to charge him with the carriage of any one in the Lower House howsoever near to him.

2. Whether he was not a party to a practice about Easter to hinder the King's ends at that meeting, and were there not meetings and consultations held to that intent?

Reply. He neither was party to any such practice, nor knew of any such thing, nor of any meetings, nor consultations to any such end, yet he had inquired of it, because he had heard before the end of the Parliament that some such thing was conceived to have been done in that time.

3. Whether in the time of Parliament, some of the Lower House did not usually come up into the Committee Chamber of the Upper House, or design and plot to receive directions from him what to doe in their own House the same day?

Reply. Some of the Lower House came thither every day, some time to him sometime to others, when he went out to speak with them ordinarily and familiarly, as every one else did, and divers times of what was then doing in their house, and of other Parliament business, but yet he utterly denied that he had any design or plot in their coming thither.

4. Whether after the King had declared his purpose to adjourn Parliament, he had no practise with some of the Lower House to crosse the King either when he would have bills pass, or afterwards when he would have had Bills passed?

Reply. He knew of no such practice at either of these times.

5. Whether he had no practice with some of the other House to work that some of the Subsidies now granted might have been sent over to the King & Queen of Bohemia by order of the House, without coming at all into the Exchequer?

Reply. That question was the first word that ever he heard of any such thing.[145]

Thus inconclusive he was subjected to a second round of questioning with similar results. What was to be done?

Dean Williams, who was soon to become Bishop of Lincoln, was a friend of Southampton; they had both attended St John's college in Cambridge. He opened discussions with Buckingham and the king and eventually the king agreed to meet with Southampton, which they did on 21 July with Buckingham and Williams present. It appeared to be a satisfactory meeting and Southampton thought he was at liberty. Not so. He was allowed to go to Titchfield but only in the company of his keeper, Sir William Parkhurst. The confinement of Southampton was unpopular in both the city and the country and both the king and Buckingham were losing ground. He was released on 1 September.

Nothing ever came of these vague charges but he was now out of favour and deprived of some of the offices which had sustained him on his release from the Tower in 1603. Buckingham then resorted to another pressure point. Southampton was a pensioner of the Crown and that pension could be withdrawn and Buckingham set about doing so. Southampton's opposition cost him £2,000 a year.

It could be regarded as an act of political bravado or folly, and perhaps it was both. The earl was never completely free from the demon of rising anger. He certainly never lacked courage and was clearly prepared to stake everything on a principle.

He was mature enough to exercise caution. When Parliament eventually resumed on 21 November Southampton was absent, having been excused on the grounds of sickness. Other lords under scrutiny took similar steps to avoid any risk not offending the monarch. This did not go down well in Parliament, particularly in the Commons where noisy discontent was recorded about the absence of the lords 'from fear that they could not express their opinions safely.'[146] The Parliament met with the difficult issues of support for the Palatine and the unresolved matter of the Spanish marriage. The broadly Protestant Parliament would have voted for support of the Palatinate but would not begin to countenance a catholic marriage. James continued to be opaque about his intentions although almost all of Parliament understood the direction, but without a clear mandate they could not proceed one way or the other. Both houses drew up a Protestation to the king of their liberties. James ran out of patience and at a meeting of his Council tore up the Protestation document. He then dissolved Parliament

Buckingham was a clever and unscrupulous politician quite ready to throw overboard any of his supporters when he himself was under threat. Under James, for example, he quickly distanced himself from support for Sir Giles Mompesson and Sir Francis Bacon when they ran into political difficulties. Both cases involved Southampton.

Buckingham had been given free rein in Ireland where he controlled the farm of Irish customs, the patronage of titles and honours and along the way gathered many Irish estates for himself and his family.

The Parliament of 1621 continued acrimoniously. They insisted in a voice on foreign policy and James resolutely refused to budge, even issuing threats that he could proceed against individual members if he so wished. On 18 December 1621 Parliament issued a 'protestation' to insist that Parliament had an ancient right to have a voice on foreign affairs, the defence of the realm and matters of religion. James reacted with fury. He called for the record of the commons and ripped up the pages containing the protestation. He committed the leaders Sir Edward Coke and Sir Robert Phelps to prison and confined John Pym to house arrest.

A whole year had passed since the Habsburgs had exiled Frederick from Prague and the English had failed to come to the rescue. James may not have been too heartbroken about that outcome.

Heedless of public opinion, the desire to ally with Spain grew stronger in James, Buckingham and his heir Charles. Negotiations between Spain and England for the desired marriage were stalling, not least because the Spaniards knew well enough that the English public were hostile. They wanted assurances that catholics in England would be protected and they were minded to ensure that Charles himself returned to the Catholic faith.

Early in 1623 Charles and Buckingham approached James with a plan for the two of them should travel secretly to Spain to woo the Infanta and win her consent to the marriage. Hitherto, these complex negotiations were typically conducted by special envoys while the principals could stay above the nit-picking negotiations. The delusional Charles, offering an early illustration of his unfitness to govern, nevertheless believed, obviously encouraged by Buckingham, that he could manage this triumphantly. James could see the pitfalls and consulted with other courtiers who counselled against such a risky enterprise. Buckingham and Charles were adamant and James, weakened by poor health, conceded. Accordingly they left on 18 February 1623. Astonishingly, after just over two weeks of travel they arrived at the house of the English ambassador in Madrid. Their secret did not last long.

The Spanish now assumed that Charles' personal presence could only mean one thing, that he intended to convert to Catholicism. The infanta herself declared that she would never marry a heretic. Even Charles recognised the impossibility of this demand and his expedition had proved pointless and embarrassing. By May it was very clear that the journey to Madrid had been a complete waste.

In June 1623 the king was the guest of Southampton at Beaulieu and was expecting, looking forward to, the return of his son and Buckingham with the Spanish Infanta as his bride. There were many down sides to the match but one attractive feature was that it would bring Spanish gold to the depleted English treasury, The Venetian ambassador reported:

> The Ships are all at Sea in the Downs. In the matter of equipment and every excellence they are incomparably finer than any vessels which plough the seas. The King has told the Earl of Southampton that he shall have the honour of first seeing and receiving the Prince and the Infanta, because of their landing in the County of Southampton. These courteous words have been the more remarked, because the Earl was not always in favour with his Majesty.[147]

Ironically, the failure to cement a Spanish match was greeted enthusiastically in the country and Charles, for possibly the only time in his life, enjoyed some popularity.

The failure to bring Spanish gold to the Treasury meant that the king had to call Parliament once again, and on 29 January 1624, James, Lord Wriothesley was elected for Winchester. Parliament met on 16 February 1624 and after the King's Speech set down to business on 23 February. The Spanish issue was now dead and Southampton was therefore back in favour.

The Queen of Bohemia wrote to Sir Thomas Roe, from
The Hague, 1st March the day of good St David 1623-4.

> Since my dear brother's return into England, all is changed from being Spanish, in which I assure you that Buckingham doth most nobly and faithfully for me; worthy Southampton is much in favour, and all those that are not Spanish....

Your very affectionate friend,

ELIZABETH[148]

The Palatinate issue had also gone away. By default of any action by the English, the Spanish had overrun the Rhineland in south west Germany and Frederick was in exile. Parliament could now attend to domestic business. James had come to recognise that his appeasement policy with Spain would not restore the Palatinate to Frederick

Southampton's leadership qualities came very much to the fore. He had a good sense of the public mood and he enjoyed support in both the Lords and the Commons. James was willing to deal with him and on the surface Southampton bore him no ill will for his more recent harsh treatment. Nevertheless Parliament's course was clear; they wanted no conciliation with Spain. If anything the Spanish appeasement policy had led to a hardening of English hearts towards Catholics. Far from relaxing penal laws against Catholic the Commons now pressed to increase penalties for recusancy. On 5 March Southampton and the Archbishop of Canterbury advised the king to break with Spain. James was in no position to fight against this yet he hesitated, mainly because Buckingham and Charles sought to insulate him from good advice.

Parliament then concentrated their energy on the unpopular Middlesex, and as has been discussed earlier, Sir Edwin Sandys and others sought their revenge for what they saw as the unfair dissolution of the Virginia company. Buckingham and Charles, who were in effect operating a regency for the ailing King, did not bother to defend Middlesex who was crippled with a punitive fine of £50,000. James was perceptive enough to understand their mistake.

> By God, Steenie, you are a fool, and will shortly repent of this folly: you are making a rod with which you will be scourged yourself.[149]

And so it proved.

10

AN UNTIMELY DEATH

I am sure you have already heard the infinte loss we have all had of the brave worthy Earl of Southampton and his son the Lord Wriothesley; you know how true a friend I have lost in them both, and may imagine easily how much my grief is for them. – Elizabeth, Queen of Bohemia.

During the Christmas period 1623, the earl wrote to a friend. It was a commonplace letter containing nothing of great importance, but it is most interesting because shows the earl as a man at ease with himself, possibly for the first time in his life. He takes pleasure in his humdrum domestic life in Titchfield and had no special hankering for life at court. He was out of favour with James but unconcerned.

To my very assured friend Sir Thomas Roe.

You must not impute it to neglect that I have not written unto you since I saw you. I have been wholly a country man, and seldom seen either the Court or London, and you know that between Titchfield and Constantinople there is no ordinary correspondence. In this life I have found so much quiet and content, that I think I should hardly ever brook any other; sure I am I envy none, and shall unwillingly leave this if any occasion shall draw me from it. This last term going to London about some business I met with a letter from you which I was glad of, because it brought me the news of your well-being. I stayed there till the week before Christmas, when I came home to keep that time with my wife and children. I will write no news, because of things past you cannot want notice, and of any future, which we can know only by conjecture, there is no certainty; yet this I will say, I think the time is near wherein we shall see the crisis of our affaires. When I came from London, the opinion was we should have a Parliament very shortly. I have not yet heard that the day is appointed, but I believe it will sone be. God send the Lower House may be composed of discreet and honest men, else all may bee naught, but I hope the best and persuade myself I have reason to doe so. I have no more to say, but that you may be out of doubt that I wish you as well as any of your servants, and am and will be your very assured friend.[150]

H. SOUTHAMPTON

Titchfield the 24th December (1623).

The earl had every reason to feel sanguine. He had reached the age of 50 and exceeded the life spans of his father and grandfather. His eldest son James was coming of age and he had a 16 year old second son. His financial situation was reasonably stable. James was now able to take his proper role in the affairs of state and on 29 January 1624 he was elected as MP for Winchester. A few weeks later, on 16 February he joined his fellow MPs at Westminster. Parliament was almost immediately prorogued until 19 February when the King's speech was due.

Since he came to the throne in 1603, James had managed to steer clear of war, but in the last year of his life he was a sick man and had effectively abdicated his role to his son and his favourite "Steenie", the Duke of Buckingham. Foreign policy was therefore in the hands of this unwise duo. An attempt to secure an alliance with Spain through marriage in 1623 was something of a debacle and foreign policy swivelled to a French alliance soon after. In the course of negotiating the marriage of Charles and Henrietta Maria, Buckingham agreed to support the Dutch in their struggle for independence against the Spanish. A treaty with the Dutch was concluded in June 1624 and 6,000 volunteers were agreed to fight for the States General in Holland.

This had been the first opportunity for the Earl of Southampton to undertake military service since 1599 when he was part of Essex's Irish expedition, and where he had demonstrated some ability as a military commander. He must have looked forward to the new adventure. He raised his levy and departed for Holland on 7 August 1624. He took with him his eldest son James, who was also keen for the experience and they were able to meet Elizabeth, the exiled Queen of Bohemia.

Thereafter not much is known. There were no military engagements, and the soldiers spent boring and idle hours in military camps. The curse of confined army life, dysentery, spread throughout the encampments and many soldiers lost their lives without ever seeing armed struggle. James Wriothesley was one of that number and he gave up his life on 5 November at Rosendaal. His father contracted the same illness but, apparently having overcome the fever, left Rosendaal with the intention of returning to England with his son's body. However at Bergen-op-Zoom on 10 November he collapsed and died. Both bodies were carried by sea to Southampton.

It was an unlucky end.

The bodies of the two men were interred at Saint Peter's Church, Titchfield on 28 December 1624 in the vault commissioned by the 2nd earl. No monumental figures were added.

The Church Register has the entry:

> December 1624. The Right Honourable Henry Earle of Southampton, Knight of the most noble Order of the Garter, and one of his Majesties most Honourable Privy Council, was buried the 28th day of this month.[151]

The earl came into a substantial income in 1594 and then proceeded to dissipate it in wild living. By the end of the decade he had to sell off one third of his land holdings to repay debts. Were it not for the accession of King James in 1603 he would have been almost completely impoverished, but James was able to grant him substantial income opportunities from the Crown, which largely restored him to the income he inherited in 1594. The earl was very far from being a hard-headed businessman. He was content to manage his estates without land or rent reform and his creative mind was drawn to interesting ventures which probably cost rather than made him money. The sponsorship of overseas colonies usually resulted in a loss as one colony after another failed. There may have been some income from tobacco crops but it is hard to imagine that it contributed much to the earl's fortune. In a similar way his industrial ventures required large capital investment but may have yielded small returns.

In summary, we can say that from 1581, upon the death of the second earl, to 1624, when the third earl died of dysentery in Holland, the earldom was in decline. There was one seed which held the promise of recovery - the manor of Bloomsbury.

The first earl acquired the manor in the early 1540s. It was very much outside London and was completely undeveloped. The first earl also added to this property in 1547 through the acquisition of a large house and grounds bordered by Holborn and Chancery Lane. These properties were largely undeveloped until the end of the 16th century when the earl granted leases for building purposes. In 1616 the earl paid £600 for part of the manor of St Giles in the fields. Together these formed the core of what would become prime London property. This was the third earl's legacy to his son. But for this it would have been a hollow inheritance.

The third earl has enjoyed a favourable press in posterity due to his association with William Shakespeare. An almost casual agreement made at the age of 21, to act as patron for Shakespeare's narrative poem, *Venus and Adonis*, moved his name into the pantheon, and he has been of interest to Shakespearean scholars ever since. The formidable early feminist, Charlotte Carmichael Stopes, published a detailed 600 page biography of the third earl in 1921. The assiduous Elizabethan scholar, A L Rowse, turned his attention to the earl in a book, *Shakespeare's Southampton, Patron of Virginia*, in 1965. Three years later, a University of British Columbia professor, G. P. V. Akrigg, brought out his book, *Shakespeare and Southampton*. Various writers since have turned their attention to one or other aspect of the relationship between the young earl and the poet and playwright.

In general these biographies focus their attention on the earl's political difficulties and his later achievements and gloss over the near financial ruin that came to the house of Southampton.

The one aspect of the earl's life that should not be overlooked, and which may be his enduring legacy, was his unwavering commitment to the Virginia project. He may have sunk a great deal of money into the various attempts to settle the eastern coast of North America and if there were some returns from tobacco crops they were minimal. It is presently unfashionable to attribute any benefits to colonial enterprises from earlier centuries but we should acknowledge, for good or ill, that these early attempts at colonising distant lands led eventually to the world wide spread of the English language and English institutions.

It did take commitment, and more. The optimistic expeditions sponsored by Raleigh, Southampton, Sandys, de la Warr and others were mostly expensive failures, but each time lessons were learned and the promise of success never deterred the enterprising. Eventually, after the Virginia Company had failed, an expedition left Southampton and Plymouth in 1620 and landed at the tip of Cape Cod. Those settlers had strong leadership and a common cause, ingredients that were perhaps missing in the pioneering attempts in Virginia.

Five centuries have now passed since the Spanish government first sponsored an attempt to discover a western route to India. The ready access to gold transformed the Spanish economy and made them the richest country in Europe for a while. The English came late into the game and farming and fishing settlements in North America were the only ones open for development. The French entered the game too but lost interest in the 18th century. Thus the Spanish and Portuguese developed South America while the English were largely free to develop North America. That continent eventually achieved cultural and economic dominance entirely due to the pioneering expeditions sponsored by the likes of Henry Wriothesley, 3rd earl of Southampton.

This does seem to me to be a legacy of note, more so perhaps, than the casual patronage of an emerging poet in 1593.

THE
LAST EARL

PART 4

1

AN UNEXPECTED INHERITANCE

All Peace and Happiness, my very Honourable good Lord. It hath pleased God to make your Lordship heir unto your most noble Father, and therefore I think you have most right to these Tears which were shed for him, and your renowned elder brother. – W. Jones: The Tears of the Isle of Wight.

A week or so after the death of her eldest son on November 5th a message must have reached the countess, probably from her husband, to inform her of this tragic loss. Even in her grief she could not have imagined the double blow that would follow: her husband was dying at the very moment she was reading his last letter. Towards the end of November young Thomas Wriothesley knew that his unexpected destiny was to become the 4th Earl of Southampton

He may not have known in the middle of 1624 what his future might be. He had options of course, but succeeding his father as earl was not the one that was marked out for him. His older brother James had already served in Parliament, and by accompanying his father to Holland was being groomed for military experience and leadership. Like his future king, Thomas had grown up in the shadow of an older brother who was expected to succeed his father.

Thomas, born in 1607, was the fourth child in the family. Penelope was born in 1598, Anne in 1600, James in 1603, and Elizabeth in 1609. The family was later completed with the birth of Mary, whose burial was recorded in the Titchfield Parish Register 10 January 1616.

The baptism of Thomas Wriothesley was recorded in a most unusual place. Little Shelford in the county of Cambridge has this record:

1607 Thos Wryosley S. Henry and eliz. Wryosley. Erle and Countess of Southampton, baptised 2nd April.[152]

The village is far away from any Wriothesley landed interests, which were concentrated in Hampshire and London, and as far as we know, no land in Cambridgeshire was ever of interest to the first earl of Southampton. That the earl and countess were living there is not quire as quixotic as it first appears.

During James' slow journey from Edinburgh to London in 1603 he stopped over at Royston in Cambridgeshire. While there he was entertained by Robert Chester at his Priory House. The area struck the king's fancy and in the following year he rented Priory House and used it for his passionate pastime of hunting. Later he purchased two inns at Royston and converted them into a Royal hunting lodge, which he returned to every year. He was even there in January and February 1625, shortly before his death. In 1603 Southampton was now in favour after a decade in the political wilderness and he could scarcely run the risk of losing this important gain. It was therefore essential to be near the king at all times.

Fortunately, a suitable house was available for lease. Sir Horatio Palavicino (c. 1540-1600), an Italian born Anglophile who had many business dealings in England had built a splendid house in the Italian style. It was modern and palatial but Sir Horatio's son had little use for the property and was prepared to consider a lease. The mansion was an ideal property for use during the hunting season. They must have used it with some regularity, year after year. The industrious Mrs Stopes also uncovered evidence that two of Southampton's servants, John Cooke in 1608 and Valentine Metcalfe in 1615, had recorded burials in the Little Shelford register. This indicates that the house was in regular use and on a long lease, which may have concluded with the death of Henry Palvacino (Sir Horatio's son) who died in 1615.

We know practically nothing about Thomas's childhood. As a second son he would not be subject to the same expectations as his elder brother nevertheless, we can only assume that the two boys, close enough in age, grew up together, probably with the same tutor.

The unfortunate death of both his father and elder brother within a week of each other in November 1624 must have been a serious shock to the young man who, at the very best, might have expected to become Baron Titchfield and perhaps serve as a member of Parliament.

However, he was to prove to be more than equal to expectations and grew to be a better statesman than his father and grandfather and certainly developed into a man of whom his great grandfather would be proud.

He came into his earldom on the cusp of the accession of Charles I. The old king, who left no comment on the death of the 3rd earl, outlived him by only a few months and died on 27 March 1625, although the ailing monarch had effectively ceded power to his surviving son and his omnipresent aide, the Duke of Buckingham. Thus the adult career of Earl Thomas covered three reigns: the whole reign of Charles I, the interregnum of the Commonwealth and the first seven years of the reign of Charles II. Charles I made use of his talent somewhat begrudgingly and sparingly; Cromwell sought his help but was rebuffed on principle, and it was only after Charles II came to the throne in 1660 that he was able to hold one of the highest offices of state.

The new earl was almost 17 years old in 1624 and the wardship would not be a long one. Long enough perhaps, but compared to the 17 year wardship of his grandfather and the 13 year wardship of his father, four years was a light imposition. There was one complication. The third earl had not made a will. Unlike his father who had some premonition of his own death, he may have felt at the age of 52 that he still had some years ahead of him. The illness which abruptly shortened the life of his son James and subsequently himself could not have been anticipated. The tragedy could be considered an accident which came upon him suddenly while he was in a foreign land with no time to assemble lawyers. The economic impact on the Southampton estates was immediate. The two life annuities of £3,200 each that had been awarded to the third earl were suspended immediately upon his death, as well as a life interest in the Lyndhurst manor. The new earl could no longer count on the profits of office that his father had enjoyed as these would now go to another's benefit. For the next four years the young earl was under wardship, the profits of which were granted, predictably, to the Duke of Buckingham. In addition the king's third of £400 a year had to be paid out of the estate plus £2,000 to the Crown for the wardship and marriage of the young earl. In 1629 the dowager Countess had to pay a further £234 for the earl's livery.

On the brighter side, Elizabeth, Queen of Bohemia and daughter of the king, was a friend of the late earl and his family, and appears to have been instrumental in securing the guardianship of Thomas for the widowed Countess, a much more satisfactory arrangement for the Southamptons, as it kept control of the estate within the family. His memory was fresh in her mind as he had visited the exiled queen in Holland shortly before his demise and this recent renewal of contact between the third earl and the queen may have made her favourably disposed towards the widowed countess, and she put some effort into helping her. The Admor book in the PRO records this:

> Henry Wriothesley, late Earl of Southampton, deceased 1624. Power to administer his property and goods granted to Elizabeth, Countess of Southampton, Arthur Bromfield of Titchfield, Thomas Wriothesley of Cheltwood, co. Bucks, Armiger, 2nd June 1625.[153]

The new king in 1625, Charles I, was also a second son, and was a man by temperament and by training unsuited to the role, as he amply demonstrated over the next quarter of a century. He was in thrall to the charming and adventurous Duke of Buckingham, who was no friend to the 3rd Earl of Southampton.

After the failure to secure a marriage alliance with Spain, Charles returned to England, and for the only time in his life, to popular applause, such was the relief in England that the marriage would not go ahead. He would never again enjoy such popularity, as he set on a course of intransigent adherence to his own will. He never fully understood popular opinion in any case, nor was he sensitive to many of the courtiers closer to him. He was an extremely introverted man who constructed a carapace of self-belief around himself. Strong monarchs of the past knew the time to be resolute and understood that there were moments to compromise or make concessions. Charles never had that instinct; he was a weak man who believed that his adamantine refusal to deviate showed strength. As described in the previous chapter, the collapse of his Spanish marriage proposal turned him, without much thought, to France for a replacement bride. A French princess, Henrietta Maria, was offered on condition that she was able to maintain her catholic faith in a protestant country. This was agreed, although at some cost to the English, as Charles and Buckingham agreed to commit 6,000 troops to the Dutch war of independence. Buckingham believed that he had Richelieu's support to reclaim the Palatinate for Charles' brother-in-law, but when he returned to France to stand in for Charles at his wedding to Henrietta Maria he discovered that Richelieu had no such intention of wasting French resources on a war that had no interest for the French. The commitment of troops to to the Dutch war in 1624 proved to be a wasteful exercise, not least because it cost the lives of the third earl and his eldest son.

The new queen, after her proxy marriage, travelled to Titchfield in an echo of that other fateful queen, Margaret of Anjou, who came to Titchfield Abbey in 1445 to marry Henry VI. So the new earl found the new king and queen on his doorstep at Titchfield in August 1625. The Parish Register has left this record.

> King Charles and Queen Mary came to Titchfield place the xxth day this month and the Queen stayed there five weeks and three days.[154]

Royal visits were expensive and a mixed blessing. They conferred prestige on the host and might lead to future favour, but they were often ruinously expensive. Five weeks was a very long stay, but, after eating the earl and his countess mother out of house and home, the new king and his wife eventually left for London. Why the king chose to stay at Titchfield is not known; there were other great houses near to Southampton which could have accommodated the king's entourage. The old earl had died the previous year and the new earl was a minor with no influence. There were no obvious political advantages for the king, but none may have been considered. The land route up the Meon Valley to London was easier than some of the alternatives and this may have been the deciding factor.

One might expect some favour to fall on the Southamptons after their pleasant hospitality, but such warm feelings appear not have been in the make up of the introverted Charles. He was a thoughtless man. His assumption of what was his by right took no account of any sacrifices made by others and his general insensitivity to this was to characterise his kingship. He was not driven by malice in this instance: he was an inward-looking man, largely oblivious to the feelings of others. He could by no means, for example, be compared to the malevolent Mabel de Bellême, an 11th century French countess who deliberately descended on an abbey with her retinue and made sure that they used up all the abbey's provisions before leaving, as punishment to an abbot who had upset her. However, the actions of the king, and their consequences must be noted rather than the motivation behind them.

Once free of the burden of hospitality to the royal couple the new earl was able to get on with his life. Still three years shy of his majority, he had little authority in the administration of his estates; in any case, they could be competently managed by the stewards and the countess. He was free to plot his own course. He seems to have determined in the first instance to enter St John's College, Cambridge to complete his studies. Edmund Lodge, writing in 1838,[155] says that he went to Eton and Oxford. The Eton College Register records his attendance from 1617-1619. Oxford may be discounted as there was never any connection between that university's colleges and the Wriothesleys. He is on record as having attended St John's College at Cambridge and as this was the Alma Mater of his father this makes sense. He was certainly at St John's in the Michelmas term of 1625 when he was 18, an age which would have made him older than other undergraduates. This was a year after the death of his father and brother and leads one to wonder if this might be a voluntary act on his part, possibly sensing some deficiency in his education. Perhaps he had studied there a few years earlier.

He finished with St John's in 1626 and there is no record of the award of a degree. He then decided to travel to France, a sensible enough way of filling the time before he could take control of his inheritance. His sojourn would broaden his education and enable him to make contacts that might be of future value. He came to like it and although he retuned to England from time to time to take care of business he did not return permanently until 1634. He effectively 'dropped out' of English society for eight years and was content to leave the day-to-day management of the estates to his mother and their stewards, dropping in every now and then to give direction where it was needed. In retrospect this seems to have been a remarkably cool-headed decision. He had not been schooled to take over as earl; that had been the destiny of his older brother James. He must have known within himself that he was not ready. In any case he was a young man with a few wild oats to sow, and there is evidence that he shared his father's taste for gambling; far better to do that away from the prying and disapproving eyes of the English court and his family retainers.

This decision caused him to be absent from the political fray, which was beginning to become increasingly polarised in England. In retrospect, although he may have thought nothing of it at the time, he was able to bring some balance and detachment to his political counsel when he did enter the lists in 1640 as a mature man.

For most of his reign Charles favoured other interests over those of the 4th earl. Principal among them was George Villiers, Duke of Buckingham, who had captivated King James and continued to work his charm on his son. He was no friend to the Southamptons and enriched himself at the expense of the two earls on more than one occasion. It was quite conventional for close advisers to the king to become rich as well as powerful. The previous century had yielded high returns for Thomas Wolsey, Thomas Cromwell, Thomas Wriothesley and William and Robert Cecil as examples. Personal enrichment was acceptable but poor advice which impacted on the people of the country was not. Buckingham was a reckless adventurer who led his compliant monarch into several foreign policy fiascos. In 1627 Buckingham led an army to the port of La Rochelle on the west coast of France in order to assist the Huguenots who were in rebellion against Louis XIII. The ill-prepared and poorly disciplined invading force was no match for the French and many lives were lost. The Huguenots and the remnants of the English forces were pressed into the walled town, where they lay under long-term siege. Buckingham was entirely blamed for the failure and he became the most hated man in England. So much so that when he was assassinated in Portsmouth of 23 August 1628, his murderer became a popular hero. This rejoicing was evident in the village of Titchfield when the man responsible for the Parish Register wasted little time before recording this unnecessary this entry:[156]

> The Lord Duke of Buckinghame was slayne at Portsmouth the 23 day of Auguste being sattersday Generall of all the fleete by sea and land whose name was George Villiers Right Honerable.

The assassin was John Felton, a former officer who had some personal grievances against Buckingham. Buckingham was staying at the house of Captain Mason in Old Portsmouth High Street. The house is still there. Felton had travelled down from London fully intent on his deed and after breakfast on 23 August he stepped forward to the unguarded duke and plunged a knife into his chest. Felton's last words to the duke were, "May God have mercy on thy soul!" Felton made no attempt to escape and was eventually tried, sentenced and hanged, but not before receiving applause as a popular hero.

In one sense the duke's untimely death would have removed one obstacle from the progress of the House of Southampton. However, the king had a low emotional intelligence and instead of seeing the assassination as a signal that he should modify his policies, simply doubled down on his old entrenched position. One optimistic view, expressed on the day after the assassination, "the stone of the offence being removed by the hand of God, it is to be hoped that the king and his people will now come to a perfect unity."[157]

The hope was entirely fanciful. When Parliament opened in January 1629 Charles embarked on a collision course with the assembly on the role and power of the church. A century after the break from Rome England was now a Protestant country and nothing, short of invasion and conquest, would turn the country back. Charles' attempts to Romanise the English church met with stiff resistance. After a showdown and the imprisonment of leading members, Charles dissolved Parliament. It was not to be called again for eleven years.

Earl Thomas was at this time largely removed from such quarrels. He came into his majority in this year and. apart from occasional visits to England, was enjoying life in France.

The earldom was still at a financial low point. The great estate built up by the first earl had been put at risk, first by the extravagance of his son, and then by the youthful indiscretions of his grandson. It is to the credit of the young fourth earl and perhaps a testament to the resilience of the original portfolio, that matters could be corrected. His father had left heavy debts and the wardship of the 4th earl had enriched the Duke of Buckingham without addressing the debt issue. In addition, the widowed countess was entitled by law to one-third of the estate.

Already, in 1629, his first act when he came of age was to sell property to meet the debts incurred by his father. Walsworth was sold for £1,900. Dogmerfsfield, the great passion of his grandfather, was sold for £3,600. Itchell and Ewshott were traded for something in excess of £3,000 and the manor of Nettleton in Lincolnshire and West Meon were also sold. He also sold the two manors in East Horseley in Surrey, which he only three years earlier inherited from his great aunt Katherine Cornwallis.[158] Thus, on the only occasion when the Southampton earldom was enlarged through inheritance, it was immediately pegged back to manage debt. Laurence Stone estimates that the total amount raised through these sales came to £19,000.[159] With this money he was able to redeem property secured for £20,000, which had been conveyed by his father to Arthur Bromfield in 1611.

The sums raised were enormous but only went part way in dealing with the debt burden. He was still under pressure and in 1633 the wealth of the earldom was in a perilous position, as it had been for some years, so when the earl returned to England in 1634 he was immediately faced with some extreme choices. Top of that list was the potential sale of Beaulieu, which, if it had gone ahead, would have seriously diminished the earldom. Fortunately, there was an alternative. The Navy had an immediate need for timber for shipbuilding and he negotiated the sale of about 2.000 trees from. Titchfield Park. This was not without its setbacks. King Charles got wind of this and demanded that they be sold to the Crown for shipbuilding at a knock-down price, in this instance £2,294 10s, probably about half the value. He had also taken out mortgages in 1630 to the sum of £3,000. These were later paid off in 1641 through the sale of Soberton and Flexland to the bishop of Winchester.

This was much to the credit of the earl; however, he also inherited some of the headstrong traits of his father. His gambling habit drew him to the uncertain chance of wagering on horse racing. Almost inevitably he suffered losses and in 1634 he made a quick visit to Hampshire to sell his stud in order to settle these debts before immediately returning to France to marry.

Arthur Bromfield, who became steward for the 3rd earl has an interesting side story. He was the second son of William Bromfield of Monkton Farleigh in Wiltshire, and as such did not have much in the way of an inheritance. In fact he received an annual allowance of £6 13s. 4d., and while that was certainly enough for a young single man, it was well short of what a gentleman might need to marry and support a family.

Fortunately he was taken into the service of the Earl of Southampton and, as discussed earlier, almost immediately proved himself useful by arranging for the safe escape of the earl's friends, the Danvers brothers, who were wanted for murder in 1594.

He was a loyal servant and this alone cost him his liberty in 1599 when his master was arrested for his part in the Essex plot. Bromfield languished in prison until 1602 when he was granted his liberty on payment of a £40 fine - a heavy penalty at the time.

Bromfield had an entrepreneurial spirit and got involved in a number of business ventures. He even partnered the earl by investing in the Fontley iron works and had money to put into the Virginia company. As noted above, he was in a position to help the earl through a loan of £20,000 advanced in 1611. He also acquired properties in Southampton and London. In 1614 the earl made Bromfield steward of all his estates. He served as MP for Yarmouth IOW on three occasions, in 1604, 1614 and 1621, no doubt acting in his master's interest.

By his first marriage to Lucy Quinby he had a son, Henry and a daughter Elizabeth. She married William Beeston, about whom little is known, and they settled at Great Posbrooke. Her eldest son Henry became master of Winchester College and her second son William, showed some of his grandfather's entrepreneurial drive and went off to Jamaica to make his fortune. He eventually became governor of the colony and returned to England a wealthy man.

Arthur Bromfield lived with his family at St Margaret's until 1623, when the third earl appeared to have lost confidence in him. The cause of the falling out is not known, but Bromfield was evicted from St Margaret's and the earl refused to nominate him for his parliamentary seat.

Bromfield was resilient. He acquire the manor of Heywood through marriage to his second wife Mary Oglander. Like many, although there is no evidence that he supported either side in the Civil War, he suffered financial hardship and the 1640s were difficult and sometimes litigious. He was probably born at about the same time as the third earl, so he lived a very long life. He mirrored to some degree the enterprise of the first earl of Southampton, but in contrast to his master he started out with little more than some prospects and could only use his intelligence and energy to become wealthy man. He died on 26 May 1650 and is buried at Boldre in the New Forest.

In 1634 the earl was ready to put aside his youthful freedom and take full charge of his affairs. He returned with his new bride, Rachel de Massue. She was the daughter of a French Protestant, Daniel de Massue, Seigneur de Ruvigny and reported to be a very beautiful woman. Daniel de Massue was a prominent Huguenot, well placed at the court of Louis XIV, and his son Henri, Rachel's brother, became a leading statesman in the court of Louis XIV and was created Marquis de Ruvigny. However, life became increasingly difficult for the followers of the Reformed Church, which had enjoyed some kind of protection since the Edict of Nantes in 1598. The marquis' son, along with many of his fellow Huguenots, was compelled to seek a life in England after the Edict of Nantes was revoked in 1685. He did very well at the English court and was created the 1st Earl of Galway.

Rachel and Thomas were married at Charenton in France on 18 August 1634. It was a love match; she brought no dowry with her and from the earl's standpoint there were no financial benefits to the marriage. (This may not be uncommon, but it is at least curious that not one of the descendants of the 1st earl managed to add to the estates through marriage.) His choice of marriage partner was surely motivated by love. He was not without other marriage opportunities in the 1630s. Sir Thomas Thynne of Longleat had proposed his daughter with a very handsome dowry of £40,000, more than enough to settle all his debts, but marrying for love and placing his political career at risk was, in his mind, worth the sacrifice.

When the earl fully returned in 1634 he was a mature man ready to take on the responsibility of his estates. Without leadership, the Southampton estates had been in a holding pattern for a decade. Earl Thomas now approached his inheritance with energy and maturity. He immediately ran into trouble.

Charles I had by this time built up his own coterie of favourites and the earl was not one of them. His lack of favour at court left him vulnerable to Charles's predatory taxation policies. Without Parliament, which over centuries had become an essential mechanism in raising taxes the king was forced to raise money through various dubious measures. The granting of monopolies became a favoured method. For a fee, a company could be granted a monopoly on a product or service and the inevitable outcome of this was goods of higher cost and lower quality. Even an ordinary commodity like soap was subject to a monopoly. Established soap manufacturers were forced out of business; those who continued their trade were fined and in some cases imprisoned and their tools of manufacture destroyed. The monopoly product was more expensive and of poorer quality - at least from the general public's perception. A black market opened up for the old soap, which now had a higher price. Unsurprisingly there was enormous public resentment at Charles' policies.

Nobody was immune to inventive ways to get money into the

treasury once the avenue of general taxation was closed. In many cases old laws were resurrected or reinterpreted so that money could be claimed from people who had no idea that they were breaking the law. In 1635 Charles set up a commission to review the boundaries of ancient royal forests and the earl was one of many who became an easy target. The Crown decided the 2,236 acres of land at Beaulieu was royal forest. This ancient law gave the king forest rights and the earl's complaints and appeals against the decision fell on deaf ears. A forest court was instituted at Winchester in October 1635 which found for the king. Accordingly, rent paid by the Crown for the use of Beaulieu lands were reduced from £2500 to £500 per annum. After some protracted efforts the king agreed to relieve him of this imposition in July 1636.

If the king had ever held warm feelings towards his young host in 1625, they had long since disappeared. The marriage to Rachel de Massue may have been a factor as this did not sit well with the devoutly Catholic wife of Charles I, Henrietta Maria, who could not in conscience tolerate the Protestant Huguenots. Southampton may never have been in favour, but at this time he was certainly on the outside.

The earl could be excused for joining the lengthening list of men who became opposed to the rule of Charles I, yet he remained steadfast through the turbulent 1640s. He believed devoutly in the institution of kingship, despite his doubts about the present holder of the title.

He therefore spent the first decade of his majority restoring his estates to good order. He was remarkably successful. Since he was out of favour at court, where he held no offices, he could focus entirely on bringing his own estates into solvency. One is tempted to observe that the earldom had lacked this quality of leadership for over 80 years.

In this endeavour he demonstrated intelligence and creativity. The traditional approach to leasing land was for the lessee to pay a fine on entry and thereafter a low rent. Southampton transformed this policy by setting a low entry fine, or sometimes none at all, and charging a higher rent. One illustration of the benefits of this practice was a Beaulieu farm which had been leased at £10 per annum with a £50 entry fine in 1616, was granted a new lease at £20 per annum in 1639 with no entry fine at all. Thus the total income from this property from 1616 to 1639 was £280. The yield for the following 21 years would be £420. The consequence of this policy was that he considerably increased his revenue. So, although he had to sell off about a quarter of his estate after 1629 to pay his father's debts, his rental income in 1642 on the remainder of his Hampshire property was £2700 - £300 a year more than it had been in 1624!

His most inspired act, and the one which made a great fortune for one of his daughter's heirs, was to begin to develop the Bloomsbury and Holborn estates. When the first earl acquired the Bloomsbury manor in 1546 it was completely rural and undeveloped. The 4th earl found himself living at a time when London was expanding beyond its walls and the development of this property offered huge investment potential. One of his neighbours, Francis Russell, the 4th earl of Bedford, showed the way.

He was responsible for developing Covent Garden into a desirable residential area between the city and Westminster. The Russell family had been granted these lands, formerly belonging to Westminster Abbey, in 1552. Bedford House was built on part of this land with an entrance on the Strand. Behind it lay the convent garden. In 1630 Francis Russell obtained a licence from King Charles to build as many houses as he thought 'fit and convenient.' He paid £2,000 and work began in 1631. In some respects he set the standard for future development projects. At the insistence of Queen Henrietta Maria he imported Italian concepts of town planning with the idea of building around a piazza, or square, as it became known in England. He employed the fashionable architect and designer Inigo Jones, and work began on the project in 1641.

The English were learning a thing or two about town planning. The narrow and frankly filthy medieval streets of the city were deeply unpleasant to anyone with a sensitive nose, but even wealthy merchants on Cheapside lived in close proximity to the poor. The situation has worsened in the 16th century with the import of sea coal from Newcastle and soot and grime hung everywhere just as it did in 19th and 20th century London.

What the new builders discovered from the development of Covent Garden, Leicester Fields and Bloomsbury was that the air was much cleaner than in the city and that wider streets and squares did make a difference to day-to-day living. Although wealthy London merchants were still tied to their businesses and mansions in Cheapside, professionals, such as lawyers and physicians were more mobile. In any case, their clients would be drawn from the nobility who were building great new mansions in the district.

The Russells were already wealthy and their union with the Wriothesleys, as we will come to, made them extraordinarily so. William Russell, the 5th earl of Bedford was no stranger to extravagance. He would for example, make annual jaunts to Trinity College Cambridge. Detailed accounts which survive for one such visit show the cost of meals alone for himself and his entourage totalled £18 11s. over a period two days. One of his highest paid servants would have to work for years to afford this level of expenditure.

The development of the land between the city and Westminster was therefore too successful for Earl Thomas to ignore. In 1636 he approached the king for permission to demolish the old Southampton House on Holborn and build new tenements to augment his income. This was granted in 1638 and a row of buildings, including an inn, filled the frontage along Holborn. In 1640 the king gave him permission to build a new Southampton House and although it is believed that work started immediately the Civil War disrupted the development. In 1642-3 a fort for the defence of London had been built on Bloomsbury land, destroying a number of houses which represented a capital loss of £1,600, and an annual rental loss of £100. The earl estimated that £1,000 worth of damage was done to the new Bloomsbury House.

Despite this setback, the fortunes of the Bloomsbury estate continued to improve. By 1642 the London properties were already yielding about a quarter of his annual income. In 1603, when the 3rd earl was released from the Tower, rentals in Holborn amounted to only £113, about 6% of the total landed income. In 1624, when the 4th earl succeeded to the title, Holborn rentals had increased to £126 a year, while Bloomsbury rentals barely recorded £22 a year. By 1668 Bloomsbury's revenue was £1,980 and the Holborn properties brought in £997 a year. By that date the London properties accounted for 35% of all estate rentals.

London had grown with two centres since William Rufus decided to build his great hall at Westminster. Thereafter a commercial centre had developed in the old city, while a political centre grew around Westminster. Communication between the two was via the river and the space between remained agricultural. It is difficult today to imagine the busy streets of Holborn and Bloomsbury as an area that was deep in the countryside but Bloomsbury was little more than a country manor when Sir Thomas Wriothesley acquired it in the 1540s. It had been one of the properties of Charterhouse Priory. This proved a very shrewd investment; even in the 16th century there was a rising demand for suitable residences for country lords and businessmen who needed to be close to government, and the district between London and Westminster became attractive. However, the concept of smaller houses and shops for lease had to wait until the 17th century.

The earl's marriage produced issue. Almost a year after marriage, on 6 June 1635, Rachel gave birth to a son, who was named Charles, presumably to honour the king. He was not a strong child and he died a few months later on 20 November. A second child, this time a daughter, Elizabeth, was born at Holborn a year later. She later married Edward Noel, who later became the 1st Earl of Gainsborough, and became one of the inheritors of the Southampton estate. Another daughter, Rachel, was born in 1637. She first married Francis Vaughn who died in 1667. There was no surviving issue from this marriage; one miscarriage was reported and two children died in infancy. She remarried William Russell, son of the Earl and 1st Duke of Bedford in 1669, at the age of 32. The Dukes of Bedford descend from her. Another son, Henry, was born in 1638, but he died 4 years later. A third daughter was born in February 1640, but the birth was difficult and Rachel died after childbirth. The girl, baptised as Magdalene, lived to 7 December 1643.

It was a sad end to a marriage which, in the absence of any negative reports, must have been a happy one. Two of these daughters feature later in this story.

Two years later, in 1642, the earl remarried, this time to Elizabeth Leigh. She was a daughter of Francis Leigh, 1st earl of Chichester and. although her date of birth is not on record, she was probably born c. 1620. She gave birth to four daughters and only one of them, born in 1646 and named Elizabeth after her mother, survived infancy. The earlier daughters had been named Audrey, after her own mother, and Penelope, after the earl's eldest sister. It must have been somewhat odd to have two daughters with the same name in the same household. Southampton now had three daughters who lived to become adults: Elizabeth (1636-1680), Rachel (1637-1723) and Elizabeth (1646-1690). The elder daughters' marriages have been already mentioned. The younger Elizabeth married Josceline Percy, 11th Earl of Northumberland, in 1662.

His second wife died in 1658 and in May of the following year he married for the third time, Frances Molyneaux, widow of Viscount

Molyneaux of Maryborough. She was born Frances Seymour, the daughter of the 2nd Duke of Somerset. Her date of birth or baptism is unrecorded but it was probably after 1618. She did not give birth to any children by her first husband and by 1659, when she married Southampton, she must have been around 40 years of age.

2

LOYALTY

The earl of Southampton, a person of great prudence, and of a reputation at least equal to any man's, - Earl of Clarendon.

At the beginning of 1639 the earl's detached position from national politics came to an end. Charles was faced with another potential invasion from Scotland and like an early medieval king sought to raise his army by feudal means. All of the peers of the realm were commanded to meet the king in York with their retinues. Mercenaries were also raised in the midland to complement this force. They were not fighting men and were leaving their work as ploughmen and bakers without any military experience. It must be assumed that the men assembled by the peers had some training but many were reluctant and it is quite likely that they recruited men who equally lacked enthusiasm. Men raised from Hertfordshire in particular refused to be conscripted and fought against their officers before returning home. Conscripts from other parts of the country pillaged villages and tore down enclosures which had appeared in recent years. Some opened up the gaols to free prisoners. Those with a religious axe to grind attacked and looted churches. After a decade of direct rule by the king his oppressed people were in no mood to risk their lives for a royal cause.

It must be assumed that the earl of Southampton dutifully raised his force of men. As a relatively benign manager of his estates he would have no difficulty in calling on his supporters. In addition, he would not have been among those lords who were by this time in direct opposition to Charles. The king now demanded an oath of allegiance from all the lords. Lord Brooke and Viscount Saye refused to take the oath unless it was approved by Parliament, which of course was not possible since Charles has disbanded that institution ten years earlier. Charles responded by arresting the two men and sought to charge them with treason. He was then advised that Brooke and Saye had broken no law; they had merely asked that Parliament approve the oath, so Charles was obliged to back down.

The military activity went no better. One force sent out against the Scots retreated at first sight of a superior army. The Scots in the meantime were careful not to attack while they knew that the English forces was not supportive of their king. They waited while Charles depleted his treasury and came to a truce of sorts in July.

The earl of Southampton's involvement in all this is unrecorded. We can assume that he responded to Charles' summons in January and that he brought men from Hampshire with him. It seems unlikely that they experienced any military engagement and that they returned to Hampshire having achieved nothing. As far as we can tell, this was the only time that the 4th earl was connected to any military action. When serious military conflict broke out during the Civil War he reserved his talents for the diplomatic table.

The king eventually had to concede that he could not cope alone with the Scottish problem and grudgingly conceded to advice to recall Parliament. Elections were held and the new Parliament assembled on 13 April 1640. Southampton would have been amongst the Lords. If Charles imagined that appeals to fight for king and country would be sufficient to gain the endorsement of Parliament he was in for a surprise. All of the grievances of the previous eleven years, the ship money tax, the monopolies, the extension of royal forest laws now tumbled out in speech after speech and Parliament wished that these issues could be addressed before tamely agreeing to raise a tax to subsidise the king. The king put forward his request five times in slightly different forms but each time the Commons either demurred or rejected the proposal. On 5 May, having achieved nothing, Charles dissolved Parliament. It is known to history as the 'Short Parliament'; it achieved nothing but to set the country on a path to civil war.

There is no indication at this stage that Southampton was beginning to emerge as a figure in the political life of the day. He was 33 years old and had held no office, not even a minor one. One man, who was to play a large role over the next 30 years was noticed. His name was Oliver Cromwell.

England was clearly a divided nation and the Scots seized their opportunity. The Scottish army crossed the River Tweed in July and occupied Northumberland with no resistance. Charles set out from London with his army on 20 August 1640 and from York sent out an army to repel the Scots. The two forces met at Newburn and the English retreated ignominiously after the first shots were fired. Hardly any Englishmen, it appeared, was willing to put his life on the line for this unpopular king. The news of the defeat was greeted with celebrations in London; presumably other parts of the country, after a decade of royal monopolies and unjust taxes felt the same. It must have been obvious to wiser heads that the king had lost his own country.

Charles then summoned the peers of the realm to York and for the second year in a row the earl of Southampton made the journey to York. Their advice to the king was that he should recall Parliament in order to agree a peace treaty. Charles resisted at first but with the Scots demanding sums of money that only Parliament could approve, Charles bowed to the inevitable. His experiment in ruling like an Angevin king was over.

The news was greeted with joy in the country as people were generally optimistic that the restoration of Parliament would bring back the country to normalcy and send the Scots back across the border. But the scars left by the summary dissolution of the 'Short Parliament' remained and. if anything, those elected to the Commons were more belligerent and steadfast in opposing the king than before. Grievances had piled up and the House of Commons, under the leadership of John Pym, still wanted the king to address them. The new Parliament, known to history as the 'Long Parliament,' took up the cause which had been so rudely interrupted in the Spring and Charles was now in a much weaker position and forced to make concessions. One rumour that made things worse was the belief that Charles would bring troops from Ireland to England to restore order. This was known as the 'army plot' and the king's chief advisor, the unpopular Thomas Wentworth, Earl Strafford, was implicated. Strafford was the leader of those who encouraged the king in his hard line policy. He was a doomed man, but of interest here is that only two peers refused to agree to the Commons protest about the army plot or to the attainder of Strafford. One of them was Southampton, who was firm in his principles. According to Clarendon he had 'a particular prejudice' against Strafford, whom he saw as badly advising the king; nevertheless, he did not allow personal dislike to overcome his principles.[160] Strafford was accused of treason and many of the charges were trumped up. Obviously Southampton saw through that and was prepared to stand up for what he believed to be right. In reality it was the king's policies and his inflexible attitude that enraged the Commons and Stratfford was in many ways a surrogate target. Charles could have saved him from execution, but that would have meant making concessions. So Strafford went to the scaffold and nothing was resolved.

Parliament did agree to a payment of £300,000 to the Scots, but only after a number of concessions from Charles. The puritanical faction in Parliament, having tasted power, began to press for more, and this had the effect of pushing more moderate voices, such as the earl of Southampton, in to the royalist camp. Moderate voices, naturally enough, were critical of the king's policies, but at the same time had no interest in a revolution which would mean handing the government of the country to Parliament. The effect of Parliament's more extreme proposals during this year was to push people, who had hitherto not supported Charles, into the royalist party.

One outcome from this latest debacle was that Charles belatedly recognised the worth of Southampton as a supporter, and after years of neglect, appointed him gentleman of the bedchamber on 30 December 1641 and made him a Privy Councillor a few days later on 3 January 1642. This may have been one of his wiser appointments. The earl was intelligent and diplomatic but he was no mere yes man.

And indeed he was (according to Clarendon) a reluctant convert to the king's cause. Charles had granted no favours to Southampton during his 15 year reign and might have been considered hostile to the earl's interests, as we have described.

Southampton emerges during this period as a man with a gift for statesmanship. This in itself is remarkable. After spending his twenties living in France and the period after 1634 restoring good management to his estates, he was a very late entrant to the political world. But his voice was listened to from the first. He must have had impressive gifts. Once he cast his lot with the monarchy he stuck to it out of firmly held principle. He afterwards accompanied the King to York and to Nottingham, and was present at Edgehill. His counsel was always to seek peace and compromise and after the king raised his standard in June 1642, Southampton advised him to talk to the Parliamentary side.

Eventually, and after running out of other options, Charles agreed and he sent Southampton together with Edward Sackville, Earl of Dorset, Sir John Culpepper and Sir William Uvedale to carry the message of "his constant and earnest care to preserve the public peace."[161]

Charles was not believed, but he did at least understand that Southampton was respected by the other side and kept Southampton for any peace-making role over the next few years. Southampton was one of the commissioners who tried to negotiate the Treaty of Oxford (Feb-Apr 1643). In January 1643 Parliament asked for talks. The king agreed and the Parliamentarians came forward with the same proposals they had put to him in York in June 1642. The king's commissioners received them and there was a delay until March when the Parliamentary commissioners were allowed to return. The negotiations did not go well and were frustrated by Charles' prevarications and changes of mind. Even though there were extremes on both sides, there was potential for a compromise. Such a proposal, supported by Clarendon and Southampton, was to shelve the issue of the abolition of bishops and to skirt round Parliament's objection to the king's control of armed forces by appointing the earl of Northumberland as Lord High Admiral. The queen scuppered this as she detested Northumberland, so these negotiations ended in April with no agreement. In any case, Queen Henrietta Maria had just landed from the Netherlands with money and reinforcements and with the prospect of winning a battle the king had no incentive to compromise.

The next round of negotiations were conducted at Uxbridge between 29 January and 22 February 1645. They were tripartite, with representatives of Parliament, representatives for the king and representatives of the Scottish government. Southampton was one of 19 commissioners for the king. Once again the talks proved to be fruitless as both side felt that their military forces had been strengthened.

In this assessment the Parliamentarians were proved right. The two armies met at Naseby in Northamptonshire on 14 June 1645 and the New Model Army won a decisive victory. The king was still not ready to recognise this reality and it was not until 20 June 1646 that he was eventually willing to surrender. For much of the Civil War Oxford became the temporary capital for the king. London was hostile and although the citizens of Oxford were not supportive, most of the colleges were. The city was placed under siege three times during the Civil War and it was only after the third in 1646 that Charles capitulated. Southampton was one of the privy councillors who signed the articles of capitulation.

Clarendon made this comment about his friend Southampton's dedication: "although a person naturally loving his ease, and allowing himself never less than ten hours' repose, he was then never more than four hours in bed; bending his whole soul towards effecting an union which he never ceased to consider as the greatest blessing which could befall his afflicted country." [162]

After that, Southampton played no active part in the war, choosing to abide by the articles he signed. The same could not be said for Charles who, as ever, was looking for ways out of the predicament he had largely created for himself. The earl held to a principled position; he had agreed to and signed the document of June 1646 and the matter was therefore closed. His decision also turned out to be a prudent one; after the war many royalist supporters were heavily fined, but Southampton seems to have escaped such punitive measures. It would appear that Southampton was respected by the Parliamentarians even though he ended up on the losing side.

The last years of Charles reign were conducted while he was held in captivity. For a time he was kept under house arrest at Hampton Court Palace, but wary that some of the more extreme Parliamentarians might put his life at risk, he resolved to escape to a safer environment. One November night in 1647 he slipped away from Hampton Court with a small party. They rode through Windsor Forest and reached Farnham in the early hours of the morning, 12 November. From there it was the intention to proceed to Bishops Sutton. near Alresford, and from there make their way to the Isle of Wight, where Charles believed that he had sympathisers. He may also have intended to escape to France. However, they learned that Bishops Sutton was occupied by Parliamentarians and there was a change of plan.

The main party was to continue to the Isle of Wight, while Charles and a single companion diverted to Titchfield, where the fourth Earl of Southampton could be counted on to accommodate him. Thus it was that Charles returned to the house where he had honeymooned with his young bride 22 years earlier.

Robert Hammond was Governor of Carisbrooke Castle and the Isle of Wight at this moment. He had served in Cromwell's New

Model Army and was ranked as Lieutenant Colonel. Charles believed that Hammond was sympathetic to the royalist cause and had charged his men with negotiations. Hammond realised that this put him in a very difficult position but agreed to travel with Jack Ashburnham, one of the king's close attendants, to meet the king at Titchfield. There he explained that he was in no position to assist the king with his escape plans but he was prepared to offer him safe custody at Carisbrooke Castle. The king felt that Hammond could be trusted to act with honour and agreed to accompany him back to the island. Thus began a long period of incarceration for Charles, from 13 November 1647 to 29 November 1648. The king was at least safe from the extremists, the levellers, who would have no compunction about taking the king's life. Cromwell was probably content to have the king tucked away from active interference in government, but Charles, incorrigibly, continued with his secret manoeuvres with both factions of the army and the Scots. He contrived to sign an agreement with the Scots which guaranteed the establishment of of Presbyterianism as the state religion. In return a Scottish army would march to London to enforce 'a full and fair parliament.'

Towards the end of March 1648, Viscount Saye and Sele and several Commons allies — including Sir John Evelyn, William Pierrepont, and possibly Oliver Cromwell — attempted a personal approach to Charles I. Their difficulty was that Parliament had passed a vote in January, known as the 'vote of no addresses' which asserted that there should be no further communications with the king They tried to enlist Southampton's help as an intermediary, believing that this would excuse them from breaking the Parliamentary vote, but the earl refused to become implicated in such a contravention of Parliament. In the end he informed them bluntly:

> my lords, I must tell you that I shall as a sworn privy councillor to his Majesty give him such advise as is best and safest for him, but my lords you shall not hear nor be privy to what I say.[163]

The king's continued machinations led to uprisings in South Wales, Kent and Essex in the Summer. These were easily suppressed by Cromwell's New Model Army and he then had to deal with an invading force from Scotland, which he soundly defeated at a bloody battle at Preston on 17 August 1648.

In the next months Charles finally began to realise that he should make concessions and did so to Parliamentary representatives in a document known as the Newport Treaty, but it was far too late. On 1 December he was removed to the less comfortable confines of Hurst Castle on the mainland. A few days later, on 5 December, the army effectively engineered a military coup. Any Parliamentarian likely to be sympathetic to Charles was removed or prevented from entering the chamber. The ones who were left, about 200 or so, became known as the Rump Parliament. It took almost two months of argument to bring everything to a conclusion, possibly an outcome that few wanted, but made inevitable by events, the beheading of the king on 30 January 1649.

Southampton was among the few peers permitted to attend the trial of the king. Following the king's execution, he obtained leave to stay in the palace of Whitehall, where it is said that he witnessed Cromwell approach Charles's corpse, consider 'it attentively for some time', and then mutter the words 'cruel necessity'.[164] Finally, Southampton attended the king's funeral at Windsor on 8 February.

One has to admire Southampton's steadfastness to the idea of kingship. He was not alone; the overwhelming majority in the country understood monarchy to be the only effective way of running a government, and in the 17th century they were probably right. Government by Parliament was the solution of dreamers and could not work, as Oliver Cromwell soon discovered when he had to assume the role of a king without the title. There was nothing in Charles's behaviour towards the earl over a period of 24 years that could cause the earl to love him, in fact, as we have seen, Charles sometimes behaved very badly towards him. Nevertheless, loyalty to the anointed monarch was a principle he would never discard.

Parliament's treatment of Southampton's estates was relatively lenient. In November 1645 the committee for the advance of money had assessed him at £6,000, although there is no evidence that this sum was ever paid. In the autumn of 1646 he begged to compound under the Oxford articles and was assessed at the rate of one-tenth, or the value of two years' income from his estates, and on 26 November his fine was set at £6,466. In the autumn of 1648 the Commons confirmed his composition fine and ordered him to be pardoned for his delinquency and the sequestration to be taken off his estates. There is, however, no evidence that this fine was ever paid, and thereafter the committee for compounding apparently ceased to pursue him.

Even so, the Civil War and its aftermath did some harm to the Southampton estates. £980 worth of iron was seized from the Beaulieu furnace and wood to the value of £235 was cut down, and, as earlier mentioned, there was damage to the new buildings at Bloomsbury.

After the king's execution Southampton lived in retirement in Hampshire. Although the council of state kept an eye on him, his political activities were extremely limited throughout the 1650s.

His only political intervention during these years was to offer assistance to the young Charles II, to whom he remained deeply loyal. He played no part in the forlorn attempt to overthrow the Parliamentary regime but after the battle of Worcester in October 1651, he sent word from Titchfield that he had a ship ready for Charles. The king had already secured a boat to take him to France but he 'ever acknowledged the obligation with great kindness, he being the only person of that condition who had the courage to solicit such a danger'. After the king's escape Southampton 'had still a confidence of His Majesty's restoration'.

Yet Clarendon thought the earl 'of a nature very much inclined to melancholic.' [165] We should treat this remark with care. Melancholy was regarded by many in the 17th century as a serious mental disease, and Robert Burton had published *The Anatomy of Melancholy* in 1621 as a serious treatise to examine causes, symptoms and possible cures. In some instances people believed that melancholy could lead to madness, but there is no other indication that the earl seriously suffered mental turmoil. He would certainly be depressed by the eventual outcome of Charles' kingship, and there would be moments when he mourned the tragic loss of his first love and the loss of his son. Earl Thomas was a man who was seriously committed to the natural order of society, with the king acting through God for the betterment of mankind. The outcome of the 1640s must have left him disillusioned and in 1649 it would have been hard for him to imagine a good outcome. He apparently believed that there was little chance of overthrowing the republic in the immediate future. His advice to young Charles was always 'to sit still, and expect a reasonable revolution, without making any unadvised attempt', and he

'industriously declined any conversation or commerce with any who were known to correspond with the King.'[166]

Southampton declined to recognise the republican regime, and was not among those royalists known to have engaged with the new government.

Earl Thomas had signed an agreement with Parliament in June 1646 and he intended to honour it and until the Restoration in 1660 he remained politically inactive. He did not for a moment deviate from his belief that the Parliamentary regime was illegitimate, but he determined to remain neutral - he would neither support nor work against the new regime. Various overtures were made to bring him on side but he rebuffed each of them. There was even an occasion when Cromwell was in the New Forest and thought to visit him. The earl got wind of this and arranged to be unavailable.

> He could never be persuaded so much as to see him; and when Cromwell was in the New Forest, and resolved one day to visit him, he being informed of it or suspecting it, removed to another house he had at such a distance as exempted him from that visitation.[167]

Southampton was never a career politician. As already noted, he steered clear of political activity until 1642 and then exempted himself after 1646. He responded twice to calls from his king to bring his talents to government, the first to bring his counsel to Charles I at his moment of desperate need, and the second, to be discussed in the next chapter, to take high office for Charles II at the Restoration. In both cases he was a reluctant recruit whose only motivation appears to be a willingness to act out of a sense of duty. He was a rare man.

The only time he got into trouble was when he took a stand on a matter of principle. Parliament had assessed a decimation tax in November 1655. Southampton claimed that this violated the Oxford articles under which he had surrendered in 1645 and refused to give particulars if his estate. He was briefly imprisoned in the Tower, but released shortly when Parliament realised that they did not have legal case in this instance.

On his release he continued his policy of staying out of any royalist conspiracies.

3

THE RESTORATION

Great joy all yesterday at London, and at night more bonfires than ever, and ringing of bells, and drinking of the King's health upon their knees in the streets, which methinks is a little too much. But every body seems to be very joyfull in the business, insomuch that our sea- commanders now begin to say so too, which a week ago they would not do. And our seamen, as many as had money or credit for drink, did do nothing else this evening. -Samuel Pepys, Diary May 2nd 1660.

On the Restoration of the monarchy in 1660 Southampton was one of the first to be called into the new government. Time had made him something of a rarity. In 1660 he was one of only two who had ever served the king on the Privy Council on a list of 70 presented to Charles II when he reached Canterbury. Charles had no difficulty in accepting him. His loyalty to the crown was unquestioned and he was also a man of great ability. He was immediately appointed to the Privy Council and made a knight of the Garter. On 8 September he was appointed Lord Treasurer, an office he was to hold with distinction until his death. He was not in the least tempted by the opportunities for peculation and corruption, a fact that was noted in his day. 'He was an incorrupt man, and during seven years management of the Treasury he made but an ordinary fortune out of it'[168]

He came to an agreement with the king that he would take a fixed salary of £8,000. This was a large amount of money, but in comparison with conventional practice this represented a model of restraint, a practice not emulated by the king and many of his courtiers who continued to waste money for their own pleasure. He did try to warn the king that 'the revenue is the centre of all your business', but his caution went largely unheeded.[169]

In government, as with his father Charles I, he tried to become a voice of moderation. He argued for magnanimity towards the king's opponents and against replacing one extreme with another. The military government of Cromwell had led to excesses by the authorities and he felt the new regime would be better advised not to follow the same path.

> They had (he said) felt the effects of a military government, though sober and religious, in Cromwell's army: he believed vicious and dissolute troops would be much worse: the King would grow fond of them, and they would quickly become insolent and ungovernable: and then such men as he was must be only instruments to serve their ends.[170]

Charles II continued in the manner of Stuart kings by being profligate with public money. In some respects he was worse than his straight-laced father. He had great need of a man like the earl who could raise sufficient money for domestic extravagances and foreign adventures, such as wars with the Dutch. Earl Thomas had a hard job. Parliament was generally reluctant to raise taxes and the Stuart expedient of loans, used by both Charles I and Cromwell, became a great headache for the Treasurer. He complained to Pepys:

> 'What will you have me do? I have given all I can for my life. Why will people not lend me their money? Why can they not trust the king as well as Oliver.'[171]

Pepys was struggling to find money on the occasion of recording this exasperated remark to pay sailors in the navy and he was having to deal with riots. He concluded that the solution was either 'money or the rope', realising that the second option was the only long-term solution. Earl Thomas could only sympathise and was clearly frustrated at his relative impotence. The unspoken answer to Southampton's questions was that Oliver Cromwell held one card that Charles II could not play - the threat of execution!

He was not in an easy position. While the wealthy were willing to loan money to Cromwell out of fear or respect, the decadent lifestyle of Charles II and his court may have given many of them pause. The court was soon mired in scandal. The king ran through a succession of mistresses and his followers in the court sought to do likewise. Their behaviour was often unrestrained. Pepys tells a story about Sir Charles Sedley, one of Charles II's close confidants, how he presented himself naked on the balcony of the Cock Inn in Bow Street where he enacted 'all the postures of lust and buggery that could be imagined.' He took a glass of wine and 'washed his prick in it' drank the draft and then squatted to 'excremetize.'[172] To a degree the population went along with such shocking behaviour because they were in sympathy with cutting loose after the restrictions of the Commonwealth. In the 20th century the austerity of World War I was succeeded by the 'Roaring Twenties' and there was a similar explosion of hedonism in the 1950s and 1960s after World War II. After the closing of the theatre and bans against dancing, the English were happy to grant Charles the soubriquet of the 'merry monarch.'

Earl Thomas was now in his fifties and had little inclination for such frivolities; he was ready for the serious work of government. His continued friendship with Clarendon was a factor in ensuring that his advice was heeded. Clarendon, as Lord Chancellor, was the most powerful man in government.

Edward Hyde was almost an exact contemporary of Thomas Wriothesley, being born at Dinton in Wiltshire in February 1609. He was also a younger son so like his friend he grew up with no expectations of inheritance and would have to make his own way in the world. He also shared with Thomas the fate of succeeding to his father's estate through the early deaths of brothers - in Hyde's instance two elder brothers. His original destiny was to take orders in the Church of England; instead, he redirected his study to law at the Middle Temple. He had considerable intellectual abilities and he was an excellent public speaker, and after being called to the bar in 1633, quickly established a thriving practice.

Hyde was first elected to the Short and then the Long Parliaments in 1640. He was initially critical of Charles, but as a moderate could not countenance the extreme reforms of many parliamentarians and therefore placed his support behind the king.

After the royalist cause was lost in 1646, he went into exile in Jersey. Like Southampton, he did not approve of Charles' underhand dealings with the Scots that led to the second civil war of 1648. During the next decade he wrote his *History of the Civil War*.

Charles II appointed him Lord Chancellor and he held that office until 1667 and in that respect his time in high office mirrored that of his friend Southampton. Soon after the Restoration he was made Baron Hyde and in the following year Viscount Combury and the Earl of Clarendon.

It has been observed that all political careers end in failure and a series of events, not all of his own making, brought about his downfall. The year of the Great Plague, 1665, was followed by the Great Fire of London in 1666 and then the English fleet in the Medway was attacked by the Dutch in 1667. He also lost the confidence of Charles II, who became tired of his lectures about his profligate lifestyle. He was exiled and spent his last years in Rouen, where he died in 1674. One interesting footnote about Edward Hyde is that one of his daughter's, Anne, married James, duke of York, and thus Edward Hyde became the grandfather of two future monarchs.

Edward Hyde became the dominant figure in the new government but two other men, Sir Edward Nicholas and James Butler, who became the 1st Duke of Ormond, became principal secretaries to the king. Together with Southampton, this quadumvirate, formed a core council to the king. New men, who came over from 'the other side' and had been instrumental in the Restoration joined the council.

As Lord Treasurer, Southampton had the key role financing government and given the unfortunate relations between the earlier Stuart kings and Parliament, this was by no means an easy challenge.

Despite the civil war and the contest between Parliament and the King, England was developing into a modern mercantile state a long way removed from the government of the Tudor period and certainly the medieval system out of which it had grown. Whatever one's opinion might be of the wastefulness of the Stuart kings, government had become more complex, and therefore more expensive. Worse still, from Southampton's viewpoint, he only had responsibility for raising money; he had no say (except as a member of the Privy Council) in the spending of that money. For many years now this country has had an exchequer which controls both income and expenditure. In 1660 that system did not exist. In addition, there was no reliable mechanism to calculate the amount of money a particular tax measure might raise, and indeed the results were always short of expectation. The old medieval approach of farming tax gathering only worked with a relatively small number of tax gatherers. Usually the crown could define an amount and it was then up to the farmer to make what he could. However, the number of new taxes introduced by the early Stuart kings, particularly by Charles I who sought to circumvent Parliament, meant that tax gathering was thinly spread amongst many people throughout the country; not all were reliable.

In 1660 there were pressing and large demands on the Treasury and the most important of these was the imperative was to disband and pay off the army. If soldiers were not integrated into normal society they would become a menace and most likely a destabilising force. This matter was resolved by an immediate tax on personal property.

The new regime was able to excuse itself from any responsibility for loans authorised by the Protectorate. Any outstanding loans undertaken by Cromwell's government were simply ignored as illegal and therefore those who backed the regime had to swallow their losses. The converse of this argument was that Charles II headed a government in exile from 1649 to 1660 and therefore any debts he accrued during this period should be repaid. The same argument held true for any outstanding debts incurred by Charles I.

Finally, but not unimportantly, money was needed for the ordinary running of the machinery of government.

The Earl of Southampton's financial experience in 1660 amounted to the management of his own estates. He had never been privy to any of the revenue-raising schemes of the government of Charles I, so it could be argued that he was a novice when he undertook the responsibility for the state treasury in 1660. In addition, as touched upon above, many of the financial instruments that we now take for granted in state management had yet to be invented. Nevertheless, this 'novice' demonstrated a great capacity for creativity. His great grandfather, by far the most financially astute of the Wriothesleys, would have cheered from his grave.

600 years after the Norman Conquest, the concept of the king owning all the land and those below holding land in tenancy still prevailed, although in practice this concept had become much eroded. The system of knight service and wardship for minors was still in place and remained a source of revenue for the Crown. Now there was to be a new arrangement, agreed to by Charles II, that the king would surrender all of these hereditary feudal dues in return for an annual

income of £1,200,000.

Sadly, although this sum was huge in 1660, it was never to be sufficient and Southampton was always under pressure to find further sources of revenue. Some windfalls helped. The king initially paid his dowry of £180,000 into the exchequer. Clarendon arranged to sell Dunkirk to the French for £400,000. This too went into the Exchequer's maw. The sale was not popular in the country but the maintenance of the garrison cost at least £100,000 a year, so that also provided some relief. Hundreds of thousands pounds were raised through the sale of crown lands. At every stage government finances were in deficit.

Opposition to any form of authoritarian government was a deeply held principle with Southampton. He had argued unsuccessfully against the uncompromising policy of Charles I and had witnessed that tragic outcome. Equally, the Protectorate had become a military dictatorship. Neither were to Southampton's taste and the more liberal regime of Charles II, for all its flaws, was a path he was content to follow.

A similar magnanimity characterised Southampton's attitudes towards the church. Burnet praised his commitment to 'moderating matters both with relation to the government of the Church and the worship and ceremonies.'[173] Southampton sought to make the Church as comprehensive and inclusive as possible, and hoped that at least the more moderate presbyterians could be encompassed within it. He was one of the peers who tried to soften the terms of the Act of Uniformity, although their efforts were only partially successful. There is some evidence that his stance did not endear him to some members of the Restoration episcopate. Equally, he wanted such comprehensiveness to be established by statutory means and, like Clarendon, he strongly resisted the king's attempts in 1662–3 to introduce a bill that would have enabled him to issue dispensations from the Act of Uniformity. Both Southampton and Clarendon 'were very warm against it, and used many arguments to dissuade the King from prosecuting it.'[174] Both actively opposed the bill when it came before the Lords and helped to ensure that it was dropped. According to Clarendon, Southampton even expressed the view that the Indulgence Bill was 'unfit to be received … being a design against the Protestant religion, and in favour of the papists.'[175] Southampton regarded such use of royal prerogative powers as unacceptable, and clearly remained profoundly attached to a vision of royal powers tempered by the rule of law. Indeed, Burnet later claimed that Southampton blamed 'all the errors' of Charles II's reign on his 'coming in without conditions,'[176] and even criticised his friend Clarendon for giving so favourable an impression of the king in 1660 that such conditions were not deemed necessary.

As we have described, the third earl, in the first two decades of the 17th century, started to pay attention to this development. Southampton House grounds were first taken up for shops and houses. In 1613 the earl began to lease lots for building on the Bloomsbury manor and in 1616 he purchased part of the manor of St Giles in the Fields for £600, which enabled him to further extend his frontage along Holborn. The rentals from Holborn and Bloomsbury were starting to inch upwards in 1624 but even so only accounted for 6% of all estate rentals.

The fourth earl continued the development of Bloomsbury which he had started in the 1640s. First he had built Southampton House for his own occupation, a large mansion on a site called the Long Field. After the restoration and with new income at his disposal he could afford to build on a grand scale. In the open space on the south side of his house on Great Russell Street he created a piazza in the Italian style. It was known as Southampton Square, although today it is called Bloomsbury Square. In the crowded cityscape of London this square must have been a delight. An 18th century drawing by John Stow, shows the grand Southampton house and the square to the south, with elegant terraces on either side. The square is crossed by diagonal paths as well as paths through the middle. Samuel Pepys described this small suburban town as 'a very great and noble work' after he visited in 1684.

This whole area between the city and Westminster was completely transformed by the developers in this century. That intrepid horseback traveller and diarist Celia Fiennes (1662-1741), left her observation of this development at the end of the 17th century;

> 'There was formerly in the City the houses of several noblemens with large gardens and out houses . . . but of late are pulled down and built into streets and squares and called by the names of the noblemen.'[177]

The table below[178] illustrate the dramatic rise in income from the Bloomsbury manor in the 17th and 18th centuries. Bloomsbury was not a rental property in 1601 and in 1624, when the fourth earl succeeded his father, the annual income from rental was £22, little more than a small country manor. By 1668 this income had risen almost 100 fold to £1,980. A century later, in 1765, this had increased to an astonishing £7,800. The Dukes of Bedford, through the marriage of William Russell to Rachel Wriothesley, became the beneficiaries of this, and their income today from their London properties must be astronomical by comparison to the 17th century. The seed of this great wealth was planted by the first Earl of Southampton.

The figures also show that the income from the Bloomsbury manor and the adjoining properties at the time of the earl's death was approximately one-third of the income from all estates, and this was the division agreed to by the earl's three surviving daughters. Its potential very soon outstripped the Hampshire manors and the inheritor of this estate, as noted above, became the greatest beneficiary.

Year	Holborn	Bloomsbury	Total London rental	Total Land rental
1601	£113		£113	£1,873
1624	£126	£22	£148	£2,524
1642	£550	£414	£984	£3,733
1668	£997	£1,980	£2,977	c. £8,500
1701	?	£2097		
1732	?	£3,700		
1765	?	£7,800		

In some respects the earl's long period out of public office was a great advantage to the development of the estates. When he inherited in 1624 the estates were still encumbered by debt and his father had largely survived on generous pensions and sinecures from the crown. These sources of revenue dried up in 1624 and the new earl was forced to live within his means. He proved to be creative and astute, and, largely due to the Bloomsbury and Holborn development, had recovered the family fortune at his death. He only held public office for about 4 years in the 1640s and for the last years of his life from 1660.

William Wriothesley, Sir Thomas Wriothesley (1st earl) and Henry Wriothesley (2nd earl) lived short intense lives. The longest lived of those three was Thomas, who died at the age of 45. The third earl was set to live longer but died of dysentery in 1624 at the age of 51. Thomas, the 4th earl, stands out as the only male to live to almost 60 years.

Towards the end of 1666 he became gravely ill and after a lingering illness he died at Southampton House on 16 May 1667. After his death they cut open his body to reveal an enlarged kidney and a large stone in his bladder. He endured his final months with considerable stoicism. Samuel Pepys reported that he prepared himself for the end by 'closing his own eyes and setting his mouth, and bidding Adieu with the greatest content and freedom in the world.' Pepys could identify with the pain the earl. must have felt as he himself had suffered from an enlarged bladder stone. The pain became so excruciating that at the age of 25 he submitted to an operation without anaesthetic whereby iron forceps removed a stone 'the size of a tennis ball.'

As Pepys left Southampton House he discovered the porter in tears. No doubt the emotion was genuine, but Pepys was a practical man and reasoned that his opportunity for tips was much diminished by the death of his master: 'he hath lost a considerable hope by the death of his Lord, whose house will no more be frequented as before.' So Pepys gave the man a large tip and it was probably the last time he had occasion to visit Southampton House.[179]

The body was prepared and taken to Titchfield where he was buried on 18 June 1667. The parish register made this record:

> June the 18th 1667 Then Buried Thomas Ryothizley Eirle of Southampton High Treasurer of England to Charls the 2

Earl Clarendon had this to say about his friend and colleague. 'He was a person of extraordinary parts, of faculties very discerning and a judgement very profound.'[180]

He was the most statesmanlike Wriothesley since his great grandfather and namesake. The third earl, his father, had many gifts but was prone to being erratic and quarrelsome. His grandfather effectively exempted himself from any consideration at court by his uncompromising position on religion. All of these Wriothesleys were highly intelligent men but it was the fourth earl who understood the virtues of accommodation and compromise.

This engraving, drawn in 1754, shows Southampton House facing Bloomsbury Square. At that date it was still on the very northern edge of London with open fields behind it. Highgate and Hampstead are shown in the distance.

4

THE INHERITORS

Lord Southampton died in 1667. His thoughtless and unfeeling master had, for some time, been desirous to snatch from his dying hand the treasurer's staff which he still held, that he might place it with those, to whom he could with less shame and less fear of remonstrance confide the opprobrious secret of his political dishonour. The disgrace of Clarendon, which happened within a few months after the death of his friend, seems to have formed a melancholy era in the avowed venality and profligacy of the court of Charles. His daughters thus became considerable heiresses. – Some Account Of The Life Of Rachael Wriothesley Lady Russell.

As previously mentioned the fourth earl was survived by three daughters, Elizabeth (1636-1680), Rachel 1637-1721) and Elizabeth from the second marriage (1646-1690). The Southampton estates were divided three ways: the Titchfield estate, which included manors on both sides of the Meon Valley, the Beaulieu estate in the New Forest and the Bloomsbury manor on the edge of London which attached the Stratton manors in north Hampshire. They were more-or-less equal in value at the time, and although, the Bloomsbury manor was under development and rising in value, it would have taken a very far-sighted person to predict the future worth of suburban property between London and Westminster. The three sisters agreed to draw lots to determine who got which third. The eldest daughter drew the Titchfield estate; Rachel got Bloomsbury and the second Elizabeth, the Countess of Northumberland, received Beaulieu. There is no indication that either of the three women were unhappy with the outcome of the draw.

TITCHFIELD ESTATE

Had there been a fifth Earl of Southampton it is likely that the old Elizabethan house would have given way to some suitably splendid 18th century pile, possibly a Palladian mansion built on higher ground at the end of a long driveway. As it turned out it became a secondary estate to Edward Noel, who became the first earl of Gainsborough, and when his male line died out, it was subsumed into the extensive properties of the Bentinck Dukes of Portland. This secondary status had its long term impact.

Edward Noel was heir to Viscount Campden, who held estates in Rutland. He married Elizabeth in May 1661 and had five children together, four daughters and a son. The son, who was born c. 1665, was named after his two grandfathers Baptist Wriothesley Noel and succeeded to his father's titles in 1689. Viscount Campden had been a strong royalist supporter during the civil war and after the restoration the family returned to royal favour. Edward Noel was appointed to a number of Hampshire offices by virtue of his marriage, and after his father's death in 1681 he assumed several Rutlandshire offices. At the end of 1682 he was created the first earl of Gainsborough. James II dismissed him from all his Hampshire and Rutlandshire offices in December 1687 in a purge of all those in opposition, but he was largely restored in the following year when that unfortunate king was expelled from the country. Edward Noel died in January 1689 and his only son Baptist died in the following year leaving two very young daughters. It appears that the Titchfield association with the Wriothesley family came to an end in 1690, and thereafter Place House at Titchfield assumed secondary importance.

The two daughters of Baptist Noel and Elizabeth Wriothesley were named Elizabeth (1688-1737) and Rachel (1690-1709). Elizabeth married Henry Bentinck, who became the first Duke of Portland. Rachel married into the Somerset family who were Dukes of Beaufort and died the day after giving birth to her third son. That boy became the fourth Duke of Beaufort and the male descent continued uninterrupted until the 10th Duke of Beaufort died in 1984 without a male heir.

In 1741 the manor and Place House was purchased by Peter Delmé, son of a highly successful and therefore wealthy London merchant. The Delmés were a Wallonian family. At some time after 1780 the family acquired Cams Hall and the Tudor house was abandoned. After more than 200 years the house must have been in desperate need of modernisation, and, as with many other properties of the period, it was cheaper to give it up rather than restore it. Cams Hall itself was not a new property, possibly being built in the 1620s. In 1665 the Hearth Tax roll recorded 15 fireplaces. However, Peter Delmé resolved to update the building and it was lavishly expanded into a large Palladian mansion. Cams Hall lay at the heart of a 500 acre tract of land and was attractive for its relative privacy. Some of the stone from Titchfield was transported to Cams Hall to be used in its construction, but it is possible that the ruins became a quarry for local builders and that stones from the old house can be found today in some Titchfield properties.

The gatehouse which had been built by Sir Thomas Wriothesley in 1539 has stood as an impressive shell for several hundred years. Cams Hall was unlucky. It was requisitioned by the Admiralty during World War II and they occupied it until 1948. Two years later the unoccupied building was seriously damaged by an explosion of munitions nearby and the ruined shell was left to deteriorate for forty years. A £4 million restoration was completed in 1996.

THE BLOOMSBURY INHERITANCE

Rachel Wriothesley lived into her 80s and had the time to have a more varied life. Her first marriage to Lord Vaughan ended on 2 March 1667 when he died during an outbreak of plague. Her father's death two months later transformed her into a wealthy widow. Consequently she was pursued by several men, including William Russell, a younger son of the fifth earl and later first duke of Bedford. Young William was certainly good looking but was an impetuous character with a reputation as a womaniser. Nevertheless, Rachel fell in love with this man, who was two years younger, and they were married on 20 August 1669.

The marriage worked out surprisingly well. William became a reformed character and was thought to be a model husband and father. Rachel developed an interest in public affairs. At first they lived at Stratton House in Hampshire and after the death of the dowager Countess of Southampton moved to Southampton House in Bloomsbury. Rachel bore four children: Anne (1671), Rachel (1674) Catherine (1676) and Wriothesley (1680). Anne died in infancy.

Rachel was admired for her good looks and her quick wit. It was said that she spoke very quickly and it was if her thoughts were ahead of her words as they tumbled out of her mouth. One admirer said that 'he never knew man or woman speak better.'[181]

In 1678 William's older brother died and William became heir to the Bedford dukedom. Since his father was still alive he was given the courtesy title of Lord Russell.

However, William's tendency to impetuosity got him into trouble three years later when he became involved in a failed plot to raise a rebellion against James II. He was arrested on 26 June 1683 and tried and condemned to death on 13 July. Eight days later, on 21 July, he climbed the scaffold for execution. Rachel was certainly implicated in her husband's activities and she openly tried to defend her husband and get him a reprieve. Her plea was ignored but no proceedings were taken against her, even though there was evidence that could have been used against her. The service to the state by her father and the fact that she was a woman, counted in her favour.

She was very unhappy after the loss of her husband and many letters that have been preserved testify to her genuine grief and her determination to restore his good name. She set herself the task of managing his estate and business affairs with great competence and preparing her son for his future role as the 2nd Duke of Bedford. She took a keen interest in the development of Bloomsbury Square.

When Lady Rachel married Lord William, her father's 'little town' was already growing. Rachel remained in Bloomsbury and continued its development and management. She proved to be politically astute. She backed William of Orange and his wife Mary during the so called "Glorious Revolution" of 1688-9 and became an important voice within the inner circle of the new regime. The attainder of her husband was immediately reversed in 1689 and further, in 1694 she was rewarded by a successful campaign to get her father-in-law's status raised from earl to Duke. Thus her son was destined to become the second Duke. She pulled off the same trick in 1703 when she successfully petitioned for her son-in-law to be made Duke of Rutland. She was also instrumental in promoting her candidate as Archbishop of Canterbury. She was a formidable political operator.

Rachel's one third of the Southampton estate included the Stratton manor in North Hampshire and there they had a country house. Lady Russell divided her time between Stratton and Southampton House, mostly spending the winters in London, where she could stay at the centre of social and political life. She worked hard to ensure good settlements for her children. She achieved a marriage settlement for her daughter Rachel with William Cavendish in 1687, who became the second Duke of Devonshire. Catherine was married to John Manners, who became the second Duke of Rutland. Her son, Wriothesley, was contracted to Elizabeth Howland who came from a wealthy merchant family. The agreed dowry was £50,000. The 1st Duke died in 1700 and was succeeded by his grandson, Wriothesley, son of Lady Rachel and Lord William. The Russells had their own London mansion on the north side of the Strand, but it was close to the noisy Covent Garden market and Wriothesley did not like the location. This house was abandoned and demolished and by 1706 Southampton Street had been developed on this site, all the way to Southampton House in Bloomsbury. This became the principal London residence of the Dukes of Bedford. Wriothesley died in 1711 but Lady Rachel continued to manage the Estate until her death in 1723.

She had reached a very great age, when she died on 29 September 1723 at the age of 87 at Southampton House. She had outlived her son who died in 1711 of smallpox and her younger daughter Catherine who died in childbirth in the same year. She was a wealthy woman at her death and it is estimated that the Bloomsbury rental brought in £3,000 a year and the Stratton estates about a similar amount - equivalent to the annual income of the entire Southampton earldom at the time of her father's inheritance. The fortune of the dukes of Bedford were greatly enriched by this one third of the Southampton estates. Bloomsbury continued to develop and become a richer asset. In 1668 the London rental income was approximately one-third of the Southampton estate, so the division at the death of the 4th earl was not at all unfair.

She could feel some pride in the fact that her three children were either dukes of duchesses.

BEAULIEU

The final third of the Southampton legacy was the Beaulieu estate. Beaulieu was the site of a monastery founded by King John and at the dissolution in 1538 it was granted to Sir Thomas Wriothesley. It was a prosperous estate of 10,000 acres with abundant woodland resources and a navigable river to the sea. A house was created from building materials salvaged from parts of the abbey but it is thought that its principal function for many years was a hunting lodge. The earls of Southampton had primary country residences at Titchfield and Dogmersfield as well as London residences and Beaulieu may have been too far distant from London to be attractive for regular use. At the fourth earl's death in 1667 his daughter by his second marriage, Elizabeth, inherited the Beaulieu third. She had first married the earl of Northumberland but after being widowed in 1670 married his cousin Ralph Montagu three years later. He later became the first Duke of Montagu. Elizabeth, bore four children, a daughter and three sons, of which, the youngest, John, succeeded his father as the second Duke of Montagu in 1709. She died some months after the birth of John in September 1690 at the Montagu country seat of Boughton in Northamptonshire. This line continues, in a rather complicated fashion to the present Lord Montagu of Beaulieu.

Ralph Montagu was a very rich man. A Huguenot historian wrote that he 'lived with a greater Splendour and Magnificence in his Family, than any man of Quality perhaps in Great Britain.'[182] He was appointed by Charles II as his ambassador to the French court and apparently lived in Paris in great opulence. His time there was curtailed by scandal after his affairs with the Duchess of Cleveland (also one of Charles's mistresses) and her daughter Lady Sussex. He left Paris after this scandal in 1678.

The one-third of the Southampton estate that he inherited through his marriage in 1673 did no harm to his fortune and he acquired some land from his sister-in-law in the newly fashionable suburb of Bloomsbury, where he built a splendid mansion designed by Robert Hooke. After James II succeeded his brother, Montagu found himself out of favour and spent some years in political exile in Montpellier. While abroad he rented Montagu House to the Earl of Devonshire and during his tenancy the house was destroyed by fire in 1686. Undeterred, Montagu set about rebuilding the house on his return in 1689 and he hired French architects to restore the mansion in new splendour.

The Montagu's seat was at Boughton in Northamptonshire, where they had most of their financial and political interests. Although his marriage to Elizabeth Wriothesley in 1673 added considerably to his overall wealth there was no compelling reason to develop Beaulieu. Ralph Montagu succeeded his father as Baron Montagu in 1684. He was politically prominent in the reigns of both Charles II and James II and he was politically adaptable, surviving well enough in the reign of William of Orange, who create him Duke of Montagu in 1705. Their son John, born in 1690 was married at the age of 15 to Mary Churchill, daughter of the Duke of Marlborough. Four years later, at his father's death, he inherited the estates.

John Montagu died in 1749 without a male heir and the Beaulieu estate, amongst others, was shared by his two surviving daughters. The manor later came into single ownership. Its descent became complex and in 1885 it was granted to the second son of the Duke of Montagu, who in 1885 was created Lord Montagu of Beaulieu.

The present Palace House, originally a modest house adapted from the abbey gatehouse, finally received serious attention in the 19th century and the buildings were enlarged and transformed into an impressive Victorian mansion. Beaulieu is famous today for its house, abbey ruins, and the celebrated motor museum, the latter due to the entrepreneurship of Edward, Lord Montagu, who inherited the estate in 1951, and who, in common with his distant relative, the Duke of Bedford, transformed the stately home into a tourist attraction.

THE EARLS OF SOUTHAMPTON

Thomas Wriothesley
1505-1550
1st Earl of Southampton
1547-1550

Henry Wriothesley
1545-1581
2nd Earl of Southampton
1550-1581

Henry Wriothesley
1573-1624
3rd Earl of Southampton
1581-1624

Thomas Wriothesley
1607-1667
4th Earl of Southampton
1624-1667

CODA

There were only four Wriothesley earls of Southampton and the earldom lasted only 120 years, from 1547 to 1667. The first earl had only one surviving son and his son left only one son when he died in 1581. The third earl did father two sons who reached adulthood but unluckily, the eldest died a week before his father while on a military expedition to Holland. Thus the younger son, Thomas, inherited the earldom. His marriages produced no sons who survived infancy and there were no co-lateral male descendants to claim the earldom, which then became extinct.

It is a statement of the obvious to say that if the fourth earl had been survived by a male heir, there would be a continuation to this story, but only according to the 'rules' of male primogeniture. The fourth earl did have daughters who themselves bore children into some of the premier families of the kingdom. It was the earldom rather than the Wriothesley bloodlines which came to an end in 1667. The earldom would have become a very wealthy one in the 18th century. The escalating revenue of the Holborn and Bloomsbury developments would have placed the family in the first rank of the nobility and they almost certainly would have been created Dukes at some point. The 16th century house at Titchfield would have become inadequate to meet the needs of a wealthy 18th century family and would most likely have been torn down to make way for a larger Palladian mansion.

The Wriths/Wriothesleys illustrated a new path to power in the 16th century. Throughout history there have always been openings for clever people from modest backgrounds to rise to power, but until the Tudor reigns there were mostly only two channels, the military or the church. There were already signs in the 14th century that clever men from merchant families could make their way at court. Geoffrey Chaucer was one such. His father was a London merchant and Geoffrey, although he is now famed for his poetry, became a career diplomat.

Once he established this platform his son became a prominent London politician and his granddaughter became a duchess. The Hull merchant family, the de la Poles, followed an even higher trajectory. They followed traditional conventions by acquiring lands and proving themselves in military conflict, and rose to become earls and then dukes of Suffolk. Other families such as the Nevills, the Woodvilles and the Howards had risen in the 15th century by conventional routes such as land acquisition, opportunistic marriages and military expertise.

The church had also lost its place as a nursery for men of talent, and Thomas Wolsey may have been the last of his type, an extremely bright man of modest origins who could rise to the pinnacle of power. By the time Henry VIII came to the throne promising men such as Thomas More and Thomas Cromwell could achieve office by establishing themselves as secular lawyers.

The civil war of the 15th century exhausted and depleted the old warrior class and a new crop of men emerged from what might be called the English gentry and London merchant families. In this second group could be found the Wriths who had established themselves as drapers in London in the 15th century. Some members of this family, as we have seen, found openings for themselves as Heralds. In many respects this was a safe inroad; such positions were important but not politically controversial and almost all the heralds kept their heads on their shoulders.

So it was that Thomas Wriothesley found himself working with other new men who had neither had to raise a sword in battle nor bother to take holy orders.

When Thomas Wriothesley entered government he undertook the humdrum work of preparing documents. Before long he was marked for his intelligence and diligence and was entrusted with tasks which required managerial ability, such as preparing contracts for Cardinal Wolsey's great Oxford college. By 1530, at the age of 25, he was operating at a senior level in Thomas Cromwell's office and he was carefully filling up his strong, locked chests with coin. A few years later the dissolution of the monasteries offered him (as well as others) a great opportunity and he was astute enough to seize the moment. At his death in 1550 he was a wealthy man and was able to pass on the title of Earl of Southampton to his only surviving son.

In other circumstances we might have expected better from Henry

Wriothesley, the 2nd earl, but he was brought up by a single dominant parent, who, with the best intentions, limited his education. As a young man the earl ran counter to the prevailing wind of protestantism and was unable to take his expected place in government circles. Accordingly he is known only for his building projects and the tomb at Titchfield.

The third earl was only eight years old when his father died but he benefited from being a ward of Lord Burghley, which exposed him to a more rounded education. He did inherit his father's stubborn and independent streak, which got him into trouble on more than one occasion during the reign of Elizabeth and he spent the last years of her reign in the Tower with his cat Trixie. He was lucky to have been spared execution and if he had been executed in 1600 with Essex and others we would only know him now for the dedications in Shakespeare's two narrative poems. Ironically it is this association (which cannot have seemed important at the time) which has brought a lot of posthumous attention to the third earl.

Yet his real achievements were to begin in 1603 when James released him from prison and began to reward him with income opportunities. The earl had a restless mind and was readily attracted by risky projects. He built iron mills at Sowley and Funtley on his estates and a tin plate mill at Wickham He even projected another iron mill at Botley, although this did not come to pass. He was drawn to the sponsorship of voyages to North America and to investment in the East India Company and as an inveterate gambling man was unafraid to stake his money on high-risk ventures.

His most notable achievement must be his sustained willingness to invest in North American settlement, that part of the eastern seaboard known at the time as Virginia. He put a great deal of money into successive expeditions which either failed or were never entirely successful. Nevertheless these experimental ventures laid the foundation for a permanent settlement and the eventual creation of the United States of America. He has a village on Long Island named after him and a county in the state of Virginia; some recognition perhaps but not quite at the level of one of his associates, Lord de la Warr, who had the state of Delaware named after him.

The last earl may not have had the attention from historians that he deserves, and I am not sure that my modest contribution advances his cause much further. This lack of interest may lie in his apparent

THE SOUTH EAST VIEW OF TYCHFIELD ABBY, IN HAMPSHIRE.

Tychfield. Abby was founded by Richard Ripetous Bishop of Winchester in y.e 16.th of K. H. 3. for Premonstratension Canons, the Marriage of K. H. 6. with Margaret of Anjou was here solemniz'd. It was y.e seat of Wriothesly Earl of Southampton, but he dying without Issue Male, it came by Marriage of his Daughter to Edward Lord of Gouerhough, and for want of y.e Issue Male again to two Daughters. The present Proprietors are his Grace y.e Duke of Beaufort y.e Grace y.e Duke of Rutland, &c &c { S.S.o to S.Foot. S.S.o to S.Foot.

S.W.th Buck delin. et sculp. 1733.

detachment from a political life. The old truism about political careers ending in failure did not apply to Earl Thomas; he died in office, arguably at the peak of his political career. Most men who have tasted political power are reluctant to leave it and are often ready to compromise themselves in order to retain office. Such considerations do not appear to have touched the fourth earl. Remarkably, he was able to take government office when it came and walk away without regret.

He was at the centre of politics for only two short periods in his life: during the Civil War from 1641 to 1645 and on the Restoration in 1660 he was invited to become Lord Treasurer. He held this office until his death seven year later.

He had of course grown up without expectations of prominence. His older brother James was groomed to succeed his father and before his early death in 1624 had already been twice selected as an MP. Thomas, after his unexpected accession to the earldom almost immediately took off for France and made no serious attempt to take his place as earl of Southampton until 1634. At the time one might have judged him to be a man without ambition. And perhaps he remained so all his life but on those occasions when duty called him he plainly had the intelligence and the character to take on the required roles.

The earl comes to us with scant information about his life, possibly because of his long detachment from affairs of state, but it is not unfair to conclude the he was a highly intelligent and resourceful man without any ambition to make his mark on the world. When he came into his earldom his first thought was to complete his studies at Cambridge and once this task was completed he opted to spend time in France, enjoying life out of the view of disapproving Englishmen. He must have returned to Titchfield from time to time to attend to estate matters but he made no attempt to fully return and take on his responsibilities until he was married.

He had much to take up his attention. The Southampton estates were still encumbered by debt and had not been creatively managed since his father's death in 1624. There is much evidence that he spent those years in the 1630s attempting to place the estates on a sound footing. This was not without being hampered by some of Charles more outrageous acquisitive policies to raise revenue in the absence of Parliament.

In 1641 the desperate Charles was persuaded to take on this man of evident character as one of his Privy Councillors and during those war years the earl became a respected negotiator by both sides. After the Treaty of Uxbridge in 1644 he withdrew from political life. As far as he was concerned he had signed up to an agreement with Parliament and he intended to stick to it. Charles of course continued to wriggle out of agreements but this was not the earl's way of doing business and he remained true to his principles.

He took the same attitude during the years of Cromwell's regime. Cromwell was not his anointed king and despite offers, would not join his government. He did nothing to oppose or undermine the Commonwealth but he would never betray his principles by becoming an active supporter.

In 1660, at the age of 53, he was one of the few men still alive who had supported Charles I and Charles II did not hesitate to employ him. He was a man whose loyalty to the crown was unquestioned and who was also extremely able. He was made Lord Treasurer, a difficult job as we have seen, but one which he was able to accomplish with distinction.

Although Rudyard Kipling may not have known about Earl Thomas he could have been a model for the advice he offered in his poem *If*:

If you can keep your head when all about you

Are losing theirs and blaming it on you,

If you can trust yourself when all men doubt you,

But make allowance for their doubting too;

If you can wait and not be tired by waiting,

Or being lied about, don't deal in lies,

Or being hated, don't give way to hating,

And yet don't look too good, nor talk too wise:

. . .

If you can meet with Triumph and Disaster

And treat those two impostors just the same

Nobody is as entirely sanguine as this in real life and Clarendon did record that he had his moments of melancholy, which would suggest that there were times when he despaired, but in his political dealings he does appear, on balance, to have conducted affairs with a level head on his shoulders.

The four earls were all highly intelligent men who came into the world with many gifts. The first earl Thomas must be rated as an extraordinary man. He was a very able court official who was prevailed during the uncertain politics of the reign of Henry VIII and who was astute enough to use his position to create a great fortune. His only surviving son may have had potential, but was spoiled by an over-protective mother and his short life was largely detached from reality. His son, perhaps the most famous because of his association with William Shakespeare was gifted and imaginative and willing to take a chance on uncertain enterprises. Although he somewhat spoiled his opportunities during the last years of Elizabeth's reign, he thrived well enough during the reign of King James.

His second son Thomas represents a contrast. While he seems to have inherited some of the playboy traits of his father he proved to be very practical in matters of business and politics

Two of the earls, the 1st and 4th, held some of the highest offices in the land, and the 3rd has to his credit, the pioneering of colonies on the west coast of North America.

There is a fine 16th century portrait of the 1st earl at Palace House at Beaulieu. The earl is not looking at the painter, but over his shoulder into the distance, as if looking beyond the present to a better future. Thomas Wriothesley must have been under 40 years of age when he sat for his portrait by Hans Holbein, who was then at the pinnacle of his profession. Since Holbein was known for drawing a good likeness we can take it that this is an accurate depeiction of the earl. Some art critics believe that Holbein was capable of imbuing his portraits with a sense of personality and perhaps from the sharp eyes and the jaw raised somewhat aggressively we can take from this some sense of this ambitious man. This is the visible record of the man who founded the dynasty.

The Hampshire Estates
The shaded areas show the extent of Wriothesley land holdings in Hampshire alone. The largest concentration was in the lower Meon Valley, with the lands of Hyde Abbey in central Hampshire. Quarr Abbey on the Isle of Wight was quickly sold and Dogmersfield was acquired in the 1540s.

APPENDICES

1 A MAN OF PROPERTY

By any measure the accumulation of wealth by Thomas Wriothesley in less than two decades was spectacular. The 1530s were not only a period of profound political significance but also a period which transformed Sir Thomas Wriothesley from a modestly placed court official into a man of property.

The Earl of Southampton's grandfather, Sir John Wrythe was a man who had achieved some prosperity at his death, leaving land and property in Wiltshire, Middlesex and Chichester as well as a library, which in itself may have been worth a great deal. His eldest son Thomas was able to build a large mansion in Cripplegate and it must be concluded that he improved upon his father's inheritance. We know less about the earl's father, William, but we might infer that he left his widow and children in comfortable circumstances after his early death, although he would not have had the inheritance that his elder brother had. It is reasonable to assume that the young Thomas started out in his career with not much more than a very good education and the contacts that came from his position. It was all to do.

As we have seen in his public career, Wriothesley was astute in financial matters and to some degree was never happier than when he was managing money. When he became Chancellor in 1544 he still retained an interest in financial matters and extended what was hitherto a legal function into a fiscal one. So we can assume with some justification that he was equally assiduous in managing his private financial affairs. As a government official he was in a position to receive gifts from suitors to government and as he rose in government ranks his services were worthy of more considerable donations, shall we say. He had acquired a house and property in London but there is little evidence of other purchases until he embarked on his energetic acquisition policy during the 1530s and 1540s. At his death he held a portfolio of extensive holdings in London, Berkshire, Hampshire and the West Country and established the great wealth of his descendants.

The great opportunity came at the dissolution of the monasteries and, as we have seen, Wriothesley was in a good position to do some insider trading and take first pick of many of the properties coming on to the market. Wriothesley set his sight upon Hampshire estates. There is no apparent reason for this. His own family had its origins in Wiltshire and Somerset and there is no sign that he held any Hampshire property until he focussed on the monastic spoils in 1536. He may have coolly assessed the situation and decided that there were few competing interests in that part of the world. Much of Hampshire at that time was either owned by the king or the Bishop of Winchester. The rest was owned by various monastic orders, all of which were about to come under the hammer.

At this time Wriothesley must have built up a substantial treasure chest, because, although these monastic properties represented a good buy, they were not necessarily assessed at an underpriced value. The situation may have been akin to the sale of public utilities in the 1980s when a market price was set for the shares. The purchasers saw an almost immediate return on their investment. We can imagine him literally filling secure treasure chests of silver coins in the 1530s ready to make his property investments. He may not have acquired all the money he needed to make his very extensive land purchases in the late 1530s but it was probably easy for him to borrow money and to defer payment to the crown in some instances while he paid money out of income. Thus he could meet the capital outlay in part through revenues. For example he paid £1,381 for Beaulieu - a vast sum of money - but the annual revenue of the former abbey was in the region of £400. A simple mathematical calculation would show that he paid off his investment in just over three years and could therefore enjoy considerable income from the property. Beaulieu was largely left unmolested and used only as a hunting lodge until the 19th century. Even today Beaulieu draws significant revenue from its land and river rights.

At his death in 1550 his property portfolio was very large and included Titchfield and its estates, Hyde Abbey and its many manors in central Hampshire, Beaulieu and its estates, Quarr Abbey on the Isle of Wight and its associated manors, the manor of Bloomsbury and parts of Holborn, some properties acquired from his son-in-law, Sir Richard Lister, properties in and around London, a manor in Essex, Dogmersfield in North Hampshire and some scattered manors in Wiltshire, Dorset and Devon.

As can be tallied from this extensive acreage across one county he was quite properly styled the Earl of Southamptonshire. He may not have been rivalled in Hampshire in the spread of his estates.

The practice of what we would now call "insider trading" gave him the advantage. He was working for Cromwell during the period of the monastic dissolution and his good friend and colleague, Sir Richard Rich, was the first chancellor of the Court of Augmentations, a post he held from April 1536 to 1544, a critical period in the disposal of former monastic holdings. Indeed the two men who benefited most from the disposal of these lands were none other than Rich and Wriothesley. Sixty per cent of all these lands went to either members of the royal household or government office holders.

Henry VIII was able to reward Wriothesley for good service and he did so with sone frequency. At first the grants were small. In 1530 he was given the proceeds of the office of Bailiff of Warwick and Snitterton.[183] The following year he was given a pension of £5 a year from the lands of St Mary's Abbey in York.[184] It was not a great deal for a man of Wriothesley's aspirations, but £5 could support a peasant family for a year, so it was not negligible.

Five years later, in 1536, the rewards were larger. On 4 January 1536 he was appointed coroner and attorney to the king's bench, and was made joint constable of Donnington Castle, a position shared with Lord Sandys. These offices brought significant opportunities for income. In May of that year he was appointed 'graver of the irons appertaining to the coinage', surely a sinecure of sorts, but one which paid him £20 a year. He obtained a 61 year lease of Hyde Abbey and lands around Micheldever. Quarr Abbey on the Isle of Wight fell into his hands in the same year and at the end of 1537 he took ownership of the Titchfield Abbey with several attendant manors. Titchfield had no fewer than 15 manors. Here he chose to build his own country house. In 1539 the manor of Dogmersfield was appropriated and passed to the Court of Augmentations. By 1547 it was in Wriothesley's hands.

In the 1540s he enjoyed a large income. He received an annuity of £100 as Secretary and £400 as Chancellor. In addition he had accumulated a number of offices. He had more than enough to support his family in some comfort and, although we do not know the exact nature of his finances, we might judge that he was prudent in his expenditure and lifestyle. It has been calculated that he spent £2,700 on property acquisition in the years 1548-9. This was a very large amount and could only have come from savings. The estimate of his wealth at the time of his death was £1,300. Some consider this to be a serious underestimate. Lawrence Stone believes that it was probably an expression of rental income in 1550 and since fines paid on renewing leases would substantially affect income, he guesses that the total income lay between £2,000 and £3,000.[185] Both his son and grandson had long minorities and income was drawn from the estates by wards for many years, but despite this, and the two young men's propensity to spend extravagantly once they came to the age of majority, the estate was still enormous in the 1590s when the third earl settled some of his debts.

Both Quarr Abbey and Hyde Abbey were plundered for their building materials. Wriothesley used a short lease on Hyde to pull the buildings down in 1539 and sell the materials. Only the gatehouse survived this demolition. In a similar manner most of Quarr Abbey's stone were sold to build blockhouses at Cowes on the Isle of Wight. Later, in 1545, the king granted most of the lands formerly belonging to Hyde Abbey to Wriothesley 'in consideration of the good counsel and service.' He seems to have been given these valuable lands for nothing 'to hold of the king's gift without any account to be rendered therefor.'[186]

After Cromwell's downfall in 1540 Wriothesley was granted the great mansion of Austin Friars in London. He acquired further interests in Hampshire in the 1540s - constable of Southampton Castle and the custody of the manor of Freefolk. He became constable of Porchester Castle in 1542. But for the bishop of Winchester, he became Hampshire's most important landowner, and all this happened in a very short space of time

The forced dissolution of the monasteries mean that a lot of property came on to the market at one time. However, it was not a disorderly process. Engineered and managed by Cromwell, the dissolution proceeded largely without the disruption to the economy that might be expected from the dismantling of what was, in effect, a large scale medieval industry. The first act of 1536 forced the dissolution of all monasteries with an annual income of under £200. Thus the smaller foundations were dealt with first. Usually the abbots and priors got benefices somewhere else and most of the monks received pensions. Presumably these were paid for from the proceeds of the sale of the monasteries' possessions. The property in the first instance went to the crown.

However, the government was in need of liquid assets and the former monasteries were put up for sale. There was no auction and the final decision rested with the king, so those with an inside track were able to put forward their offers. Sir Thomas Wriothesley was one of those close enough to the king to put his bid forward for consideration and in this he was very successful.

The payment for these properties can be estimated at approximately three times the assessed value of the property - a bargain perhaps. Wriothesley was assiduous in putting himself forward.

Wriothesley's elevation to the earldom of Southampton after Henry VIII's death brought with it lands to the annual value of £300. How this was contrived is unclear, but they were significant additions to his now considerable estates. He was, it appears, regularly buying and selling land, probably showing a profit on his sale. In 1546 he acquired the former priory of Southwick and the monastery of Abendon. A few days later he sold Abendon to his friend Edward Peckham, presumably at a nice profit. He negotiated the purchase of some more properties in Hampshire and land on Hampstead heath from the Marquis of Hertford in May 1546. In August of that year he transferred some property at Painshill in Hampshire to Richard Lister, who married his daughter Elizabeth. In 1547 he acquired a manor at Woodham Water in Essex and sold that in the following year to the Earl of Sussex. Even up to the moment of his death he was engaged in land purchases. Seven days before he died he demised the land on Hampstead heath to a man called Thomas Raynes for twenty years at an annual rent of £10. It appears that once he got going in the late 1530s he was constantly trading in land. His main objective, apart from acquiring his London properties, was to consolidate his land in Hampshire.

2 THE ACQUISITIONS OF 1538

TITCHFIELD ABBEY

It is not immediately obvious why Thomas Wriothesley settled upon Titchfield as his country seat. Titchfield was no more nor less favoured than any other location he may have chosen. In its favour it had a pleasant siting in the Meon Valley and was within reach of plenty of heath land for hunting. The river streamed into the Solent two miles

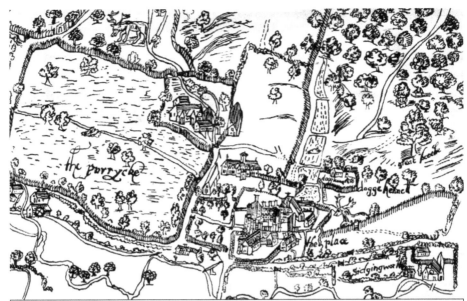

Place House at Titchfield
This map of 1610 offers some impression of the house and building complex which had developed since 1540.

Place House at Titchfield
The abbey buildings were adapted into a substantial Tudor house in 1540. Most of this house was later dismantled and the materials re-used in other buildings. The impressive gatehouse stands as a reminder of the former splendour of the house.

away, making both Southampton and Portsmouth accessible by boat. While Titchfield is midway between Southampton and Portsmouth today, the road linking the two, the A27, is relatively modern. In the 16th century the road between these towns went through Wickham and Botley before descending into Southampton. The more direct route required several ferry crossings.

Similar claims could have been made for Beaulieu Abbey, which he acquired at about the same time. Beaulieu had a good location and was accessible by sea. The abbey was certainly a good deal larger and richer and had more potential as a grand house. However, it was at the remoter end of Wriothesley's estates and interests and Titchfield was more central and a good few hours closer to London, where of course his attendance was required. Perhaps we should not ignore the fact that the route up the Meon Valley is a relatively easy road to London. henry VI chose Titchfield as a location for his marriage to Margaret of Anjou in 1445, presumably because the road to London was easier than those to the east and west.

The formal surrender of the monastery, after long negotiation and asset stripping by the monks, was not signed until December 22nd 1538. The grant to Wriothesley was immediate and preparation began in January 1538 to sell off materials that were left and to begin the conversion to a splendid 16th century country mansion. The speed of action would suggest that Wriothesley intended this outcome from the outset. Before long a surveyor was at the site to determine what could be salvaged and reused. The paving stones in the nave were taken up but many were badly worn and only a percentage were salvaged. Men from Overton came to inspect the south aisle with a view to using the stone to build a tower for their parish church. It was estimated that the bells would fetch £60. The tower at that time had a steeple and the surveyors felt that it should come down and after much deliberation it did. The altar and several marble stones were sold to nearby Titchfield residents. New building stone was imported from Caen in France - a favourite quarry since the Norman Conquest and a grade of stone that can be found in many south coast buildings.

The new building had two wings, based upon the abbey church nave, and was divided by a gatehouse - which still stands today. Curiously, the final result was asymmetrical, with the west side somewhat shorter than the east side. The new owner was able to build three levels of floors in the nave conversion, making a substantial roomy mansion. The cloisters housed kitchens, the buttery, store rooms, and wells. They continued to be used and this is one reason why the ruins survive today. The east side of the abbey was levelled. The choir and transept went as did the library and chapter house and the dorter, frater and the refectory.

The work was undertaken by Thomas Bartewe, a master mason who had completed a lot of fortification work for Henry VIII., and was later to build Southsea Castle in 1544. In the Tudor period we enter an age where the names of builders begin to be recorded, unlike the builders of our great cathedrals who have remained mostly anonymous. It should not be surprising however that these builders had a thorough knowledge of materials and building techniques that had been handed on through the centuries, nor should it surprise us that these men had the ability to design imaginative buildings.

Titchfield Abbey was one such. It was a conversion, but it appears to have made good use of the pre-existing structure to create a contemporary Tudor mansion, or palace as the contemporaries would have liked to call it. The scheme was to take the nave of the church and bisect it with a turreted gate house. The Gate House provided an entrance to the courtyard and access to the two wings of the house. The west wing accommodated the gate keeper on the ground floor and according to G P V Akrigg, the Canadian Scholar, had a playhouse above it. The east wing was converted into apartments for the family. The refectory was converted into a hall and the cloister buildings used for kitchens, storage and servants accommodation.

It was thought to be an impressive building in its day and John Leland, the travel writer, recorded in 1540:

> Mr. Wriothesley hath buildid a right stately house embatelid, and having a goodeley gate and a conducte castelid in the middle of the court of it.[187]

The abbey was founded in 1222 with the endowment of the manor of Titchfield and some neighbouring manors. Further grants of land enlarged the abbey's holdings so that by the time of the dissolution most of the land between Stokes Bay and the River Hamble, together with manors at Portchester and Cosham and along the New Forest side of Southampton Water, were under the sway of the abbey. Further up the Meon Valley, parts of Wickham, Soberton, Corhampton and West Meon were annexed to the abbey, with the later addition of a manor in Berkshire. It had become quite a wealthy abbey, and the canons could even afford to maintain a large library. In 1400 224 volumes were recorded, putting it on a par with the very wealthy abbey of Reading, which had 228. The commissioners of 1535 who undertook the complete survey of religious houses determined that the gross annual income of the abbey was £280 19s. 10½d. And they placed a value on the abbey and all its holdings at £249 16s 1d. Two years later it was practically worthless. What happened?

The abbott at the time of the 1535 assessment was John Maxey, Bishop of Elphin. He stepped down in 1536 and was succeeded, briefly, by John Simpson. He was offered a pension of £20 but offered to resign if he could get the living of Horsted in Sussex.[188] Presumably this was arranged for him because another abbot was in place almost immediately. This one, John Salisbury the last abbot, was consecrated Bishop of Thetford on 19 March 1536 and later in 1537 the abbey was voluntarily "surrendered" to the crown, thus avoiding any fines that Cromwell might seek to impose. One suspects that there had been some collusion and deal-making between the abbot and the crown in this matter. The abbey was intended for Wriothesley and indeed after the commissioners report the whole lot was granted to him. He seemed to have been unconcerned about protecting the moveable assets. It would stretch the imagination to believe that Wriothesley, who had taken a close interest in this abbey, was unaware that the abbey was being stripped of its assets, but he may have concluded that this relatively trivial loss was a worthy exchange for having the canons go quietly. Wriothesley in the end acquired a large amount of land and the ensuing income for a relatively small investment.

When the kings commissioners, John Crawford and Rowland Latham, came to survey the abbey and take possession in late 1537 they found that the abbey had been stripped bare. All that remained were some vestments that Wriothesley had donated and two old chalices. There were no livestock on the lands, the library books had disappeared, together with the plate and anything else that could be sold off. In effect the abbot and the canons were allowed time to sell everything off and look after their own future. Crawford and Latham assessed the value of what was left at 40 shillings. There were also unpaid debts of £200.

One suspects a willingness to turn a blind eye to this asset-stripping. It may have been a small price to pay for encouraging the monks to go quietly. The crown was content because the treasury had been enriched; Sir Thomas Wriothesley must have been happy to secure lands that would bring him considerable income in the years to come; and the abbot and monks acquired sums of money that would secure their future. This seems like a reasonable explanation and a recently discovered document detailing payments made to monks in the dissolution of the abbey of Furness supports this view.[189]

The dissolution of the monasteries was not a mindless land grab by Henry's ministers. There were plainly efforts, as the Titchfield situation may illustrate, to achieve a level of compensation for the dispossessed monks. Sometimes these were in the form of jobs, at other times in the form of pensions. 8 priests at Titchfield were awarded pensions of £6 13s. 4d. each for the rest of their lives - quite enough to live on in those days. The abbots came out of it well. Some monasteries were so debauched and corrupt that they were indeed given summary treatment by Cromwell and his ministers, but it would appear that most came through the situation in a proper legal fashion. For many it was probably not unlike property coming under a compulsory purchase order today. It would never be totally satisfactory to the person at the receiving end but they would get appropriate compensation.

None of the "arrangements" made between the abbot and Sir Thomas Wriothesley were written down. We would not expect them to be. But from what happened we can infer that verbal understandings had been reached prior to Wriothesley's takeover.

It does appear that the new management was welcomed. The surveyor called a meeting of all the tenants and informed them that the abbey had been freely surrendered to the king who had then granted it to Wriothesley and his heirs for ever under his great seal. He reported the response: "whereof every man is glad, and wishes it had been done seven years before, and all are sworn to you."[190] One imagines that the tenants were relieved after two or more years of neglect while the old enterprise was being run down. They must have welcomed the new management.

There is no record of what Wriothesley paid for this. Unlike Beaulieu, where a sum was paid to the Crown, there is no record for Titchfield. Thus we can only speculate. The best guess, given that much was arranged in advance, is that Wriothesley himself took responsibility for all of the costs of acquisition. He took on the pensions for the canons, paid off the debts and any other expenses associated with the takeover. £50 a year covered the pensions, which, allowing for an outside average of 20 years, amounted to £1,000. There was a debt of £200 (as mentioned above) and there may have been other costs, such as presents for the commissioners and others who helped with the takeover. The total may have approached £1400. By any measure this was the deal of the century. The outlay would be recovered in five to six years income from this huge estate - 15,000 acres.

Wriothesley lost little time in putting his plans into effect. Most of the old monastery buildings were dismantled. Stone and marble were sold off as were the abbey bells. The work of building the new palace or place could now begin.

A drawing of the building, dated 1733, survives to give us an impression of how the frontage once appeared., (see page 262.) The new house was not designed merely to house the new grandee and his household staff but also intended to impress and entertain the monarch on visits to the south coast. Today, all that is left of this Tudor mansion is the ruined gatehouse.

BEAULIEU

In 1217, the Cistercian monks of Beaulieu Abbey made an offer to inter the body of the deceased King John at Beaulieu. It was ignored and the king was buried at the abbey at Worcester, now Worcester Cathedral. This may have been the only recorded time the Beaulieu monks showed much interest in their founder and benefactor. They left no chronicles to record the munificence of the king who presided over 17 turbulent years of English history.

In 1203, King John granted the manor of Farringdon in Berkshire to the abbey of Cîteaux and a year later improved on his offer by establishing the monastery of Beaulieu in the New Forest. There was provision for 30 monks and the Farringdon house became a cell of the abbey at Beaulieu. He granted 100 marks towards the construction of the abbey and gave them 100 cows and two bulls. In addition he gave them a gold chalice. It was a generous bequest. In 1206 the king launched an appeal to all Cistercian houses to provide funds for the construction of the abbey. He also made a gift of a tun of wine and made further grants of oxen and corn.

John's political troubles with the Church brought about an end

Beaulieu
Above: Palace House at Beaulieu. The house is mostly 19th century development of a smaller and older building.
Below: Part of the ruins of the old monastery.

to the abbey's building activities while England was under a Papal Interdict, which lasted from 1208 to 1214. Thereafter, until the end of John's reign, the king's disputes and civil war with the barons took his attention away from the abbey.

Royal interest resumed with John's son, Henry III, who made many grants to the abbey and eventually, on 12 June 1246, the monks were able to occupy the new conventual buildings. It is assumed that they had used wooden buildings for the first forty years.

These buildings, the ruins of which are visible today, became a home for the Cistercians for almost 300 years. They enjoyed almost continuous prosperity and the *Valor Ecclesiasticus* of 1535 assigned a gross annual vale of £428 6s. 8¼d. In the first wave of dissolution in 1536 the monks of Netley Abbey were sent to Beaulieu. They were not there for long. On 2 April 1538 the compliant abbot Thomas Stevens signed the surrender document to the Crown. The site was immediately granted to Sir Thomas Wriothesley. Stevens was awarded an annual pension of 100 marks and given the living of Bentworth, a village near Alton. He did not part on good terms with his monks, who he felt had unjustly accused him of letting out the mill and the parsonage for his personal benefit. In a letter to Wriothesley he complained about his 'lewd monks, which now, I thank God, I am rid of.'[191]

The abbey held the manors of Colbury, Hilton, Ippley, Holbury, Frencourt in Fordingbridge, the rectory of Beaulieu and scattered lands and properties in Southampton, Lymington, Esthamlode, Goorley, Blayshford, Bremmer and Avon and Newchurch, on the Isle of Wight. The manors of Great and Little Farringdon, Inglesham, Shilkton and Wyke in Berkshire, Langford and St Kirian, Tregtonan and Helston in Cornwall and a messuage in Southwark.

For all of this Sir Thomas Wriothesley paid £1340. Lord Lisle was anxious to acquire the spoils and although he petitioned Cromwell on two occasions, Wriothesley got the nod.

According to the conditions attached to the purchase the religious building either had to be converted or demolished. St Swithun's at Winchester was converted to a cathedral and Twynham and Romsey re-purposed as parish churches. Titchfield, Netley and Mottisfont were transformed into country houses. There was no obvious use for Beaulieu, so it was largely demolished, with the exception of the Domus, the Refectory and the gatehouses which were adapted to secular purposes.

QUARR ABBEY

Quarr Abbey was not a big abbey but it was doing well enough. The annual income of the house was determined as £134 3s. 11d. in 1535. It appears to have been a well-ordered house with no blemish on its record. The abbot, who had headed the house since 1521, wrote to Cromwell to appeal against the prospective dissolution. Unfortunately the appeal fell upon hard hearts. The author of the VCH acerbically remarks that "Thomas Wriothesley, the great devourer of monastic property in the west, obtained most of the manorial rights of the abbey by grant from the Crown."[192]

Quarr Abbey was of little practical use on the island and Sir Thomas chose to dismantle the buildings and sell off the materials. The stonework from the abbey was used to make two blockhouses on either side of the river at Cowes for defensive purposes. Some perimeter walls survive from the medieval period but almost all has been destroyed by later building, including the construction of a road from Cowes to Ryde.

The abbey was founded by Baldwin de Redvers, Lord of the Isle of Wight, in 1131. It was a Benedictine foundation. The abbot held an important position on the island, and because of the strategic importance of the Isle of Wight was often called upon to help with England's defences. In 1366 Edward III granted the abbey a licence to crenellate and it is possible that the seaward side of the abbey resembled a castle after that date.

At the time of the dissolution the monastery held the manor of Quarr with the site of the abbey and the manor of Newenham there; the manors of Arreton, Staplehurst, Sheat in Brixston, Shaldcomb, Newport, Comley, Forewod cum Forewey; the granges of Compton, Haseley, Lovecombe, Hampstede, Roughbarowe, Bydeborough, Charke in Rowner; the rectory of Caresbrook; messuages, rents, etc., in Newport, Whippingham, Newchurch, Southwick, Portsmouth, Christchurch, Swey, Milford, and tithe of salt in Lymington.

Sir Thomas took little interest in the manors on the Isle of Wight, nor the actual site of the monastery, and the tithes from Arreton were granted to one John Mylle of Southampton.

Some walls from the original monastery remain but the abbey had an interesting after life. In the late 19th century the French government enacted one of its periodic purges against monasteries in that country

Quarr Abbey
The top photograph shows the present-day monastic buildings, which are entirely 20th century. Underneath, some walls which may be remnants of the medieval abbey.

and to continue their foundation the Benedictine Abbey of Solesmes relocated to Appledurcombe House on the Isle of Wight in 1901. Subsequently they acquired the site of the old Quarr Abbey which had for many centuries accommodated an old manor house. the monks moved in 1907 and through a benefactor they were able to build a very fine looking abbey church. This was completed in 1912.

HYDE ABBEY

Sir Thomas Wriothesley was presented with a similar problem at Winchester. Hyde Abbey had valuable estates in the hundred of Micheldever and this was the main asset for Sir Thomas. Most of the buildings were dismantled, with the exception of the gatehouse which remains today, and the re-usable materials were sold. Much of the former abbey land has been developed as north Winchester, but the abbey church in part survives as a rather imaginatively designed outline.

The abbey was a venerable institution founded in 901 at a location next door to the Old Minster, presently known as Winchester cathedral in its latest incarnation. The abbey of the Holy Trinity, the Blessed Virgin Mary and Saint Peter to give its full name was founded by King Edward the Elder according to the wishes of his father King Alfred. It was known as the New Minster. It was endowed with much land in central Hampshire. King Alfred was re-interred in the New Minster.

The two monasteries did not live harmoniously in such proximity and in 1109 the monks of the New Minster left their old location for a new site outside the north city walls in Hyde Meadow.

The abbot who was appointed in 1534 was John Salcot, who was a theological soul-mate of Thomas Cranmer and a supporter of Thomas Cromwell. There was no opposition to the dissolution and Salcot was immediately appointed Bishop of Salisbury. The senior monks received annual pensions of £10 and the remaining monks £6. They were well-satisfied.

The demolition of the abbey buildings began immediately in 1538 and when Leland visited in 1539 he could find little evidence of the abbey and William Camden could only report on the existence of some ruinous outhouses, a gateway and a great barn which may have been the abbot's hall. The gatehouse survives today.

The great prize was the land, which included practically the entire hundred of Micheldever and lands in the Worthys and the Candovers - all in all, some of the richest land in Hampshire.

Hyde Abbey
The abbey buildings were soon demolished after dissolutio, leaving only the gate house, shown here.

3 SOME LATER AQUISITIONS

BLOOMSBURY

One of the most famous areas of London is the former manor of Bloomsbury. On the outskirts of London in the 16th century it was mostly rural and was held by the Carthusian monks of Charterhouse. At the time of the monastic dissolution it was appropriated by the Crown. Later, in 1545, Henry VIII granted it to Sir Thomas Wriothesley. At the time it may not have appeared to be a significant acquisition. The Titchfield and Beaulieu estates were worth much more, as were many of the Hampshire lands that Wriothesley had been assiduously acquiring during these years, but as London began to expand, the fourth earl saw the potential a century later and began to develop it. One of his daughters, who married into the Russell family, inherited this part if the Southampton estates and under her successors the development continued. It became, and remains, a huge source of income for the Dukes of Bedford.

The name Bloomsbury derives from William de Blemond, who acquired the manor in 1201. It thus became Blemond's burgh, or Bloomsbury. Edward III came into possession of the manor and granted its use to the monks of Charterhouse.

The first earl died in 1550 before much could be done and his heir went through a long minority and in his short adult life was more preoccupied with the development of Dogmersfield, so it was not until the 17th century that the third earl began to pay attention to this property and it was really during the time of the fourth earl that the potential of Bloomsbury was exploited to salvage the family fortune.

DOGMERSFIELD

Dogmersfield in North Hampshire was one of the later acquisitions of the first earl. It is north east of Odiham, for many years a royal manor, and Dogmersfield at times passed into royal hands. It was here that Henry VII met with Catherine of Aragon prior to her marriage with Prince Arthur. At that time she spoke no English and Henry and his son were equally at a loss to speak Spanish. It was reported that 'there were the most goodly words uttered to each other, in the language of both parties, to as great joy and gladness as any persons conveniently might have.'[193] Some tears later the Bishop of Bath and Wells sold the manor to King Henry VIII. He leased it to members of the Wallop family until he granted it to the Earl of Southampton in his will. There are many aspects of Henry's will that have been disputed by historians but there is no doubt that Edward VI confirmed the grant in 1547.

The manor enjoyed some favour with the family, certainly with the second earl who grew up there as a boy and used it a lot in his adult life. Once out of confinement in 1573 he devoted a great deal of time, and much money, to developing the property. In the last seven years of his life Dogmersfield became his main preoccupation and he certainly had great visions for it. In his will he instructed his executors to continue with the building, which he estimated would take a further eight years. It is doubtful that the executors made any attempt to pursue the project.

The third earl showed little interest and was content to use Titchfield as his principal country residence. This history of this project is very murky. Eventually, the fourth earl sold the manor in 1629.

Whatever existed as a medieval bishop's palace has long since disappeared. That it was substantial can only be inferred from the fact that Henry VI stayed here often and the first meeting between Prince Arthur and Catherine of Aragon was arranged at this venue. No information survives about the second earl's house, finished or otherwise. There must have been something there as the manor passed through several hands in the 17th century, eventually reaching to the St John family in 1727. It was immediately resolved to create a new house on the site in 1728 and this great Palladian mansion survived until 1981, when it was destroyed by fire.

4 THE COST OF THE 2ND EARL'S FUNERAL IN 1581.

The 2nd Earl of Southampton planned a lavish funeral for himself, and it was organised by the College of Heralds. By chance a sheet of paper recording the costs of the funeral survives. Here is a transcription. Currency values have been added in brackets.

THE CHARGES FOR THE FUNERALL OF THE R. HONORABLE ERLE OF SOWTHAMPTON VNTO THE OFFICERS OF ARMS, AND THE PAYNTER.[194]

To Mr. Garter, Princypall King of Arms, for his fee   x li. (£10)
Item for his Lyverye of black clothe for himselfe for vj yeardes of clothe   vj li. (£6)
Item for his 4or. servantes   iiij li. (£3)
Item for his Journey and transportation, at xij d. the myle (120 miles)   vj li. (£6)
Item to three other herauldes of arms for ther fees and lyveryes of black clothe to eache of them vj li. xiij s. iiij d xx li. (£5 13s. 4d. ; £20)
Item for three servantes' lyveryes for the servantes of eache of them
                          xxx s. (30s), iiij li. x s. (£4 10s.)
Item" for the Journey and transportation to eache of the [three] said herauldes for viij d. the myle (120 miles)   xij   li.

(£12)

Item the hearse and Rayles with all the blackes thereon, the velvetes, silke pawle, etc., the honourable and accustomed fees to the same officers of arms or ...... erasure probably   xxxix li. xs. (£39 10s.)

Somm   cj li. (Sum £101)

Item iiij^{or}. Dozen eschucheons on bokeram

Item iiij^{or.} Dozen on Paper in mettall

Item v Dozen on Paper in coullors

Item one Dozen of small eschucheons on

Item one Brace of Iron for the helmett

Item vj Braces of Iron

Item vj Staves for the Banners

Item vj Staves for the Officers

TO THE PAYNTER.

Imprimis for A great Banner	xl s. (40s.)
Item for A Standard	xl s. (40s.)
Item iiijor. Bannerolles	v li. vj s. viij d. (£5 6s. 8d.)
Item one Cote of Arms of Damask	iij li. (£3)
Item one Cote of Arms of Sarcenett	xxvj s. viij d. (26s. 8d.)
Item A Targett of Arms	xiij s. iiij d. (13s. 4d.)
Item A Sword gylt and Skaberd of velvett	xiij s. iiij d. (13s. 4d.)
Item A helmett of Steele gylt	xv s. (15s.)
Item A Creast carved in wood	x s. (10s)
Item Mantelles of velvett (an ermine spot), with knops and tasselles	xx s. (20s.)
Item A Wrethe of silke of his coullors	iij s. iiij d. (3s. 4d.)
item A great eschucheon on bokeram	x s. (10s.)
Item vj eschucheons on pastboord	xl s. (40 s.)
Item vj eschucheons on sarcenett for the Corps	xxx s. (30s.)
Item viij Dozen Penselles	iiij li (4)
Item iiijor. Dozen eschucheons on bokeram	iiij li (£4)
Item iiijor. Dozen on Paper in mettall	iij li. iiij s. (£3 4s.)
Item v Dozen on Paper in coullors	iij li. (£3)
Item one Dozen of small eschucheons on bokeram	xij s. (12s.)
Item one Brace of Iron for the helmett	iij s. (3s.)

Item vj Braces of Iron	x s. (10s.)
Item vj Staves for the Banners	vj s. (6s.)
Item vj Staves for the Officers	iij s. (3s.)
Somm	xxxvij li. vj s. iiij d. (Sum 37 6s. 4d.)
[Funeral charges—forward ci li. (£101)	
Total	cxxxviii li. vj s. iiiid. (£138 6s. 4d.)]

5 THE MONUMENT

As the outcome of several years of preparation a team of experts were able to open up the Wriothesley momument at St Peter's Church, Titchfield in September 2021. The findings will obviously be of great interest and I hope to publish them in an appendix in a future edition of this book. In the meantime, here is a press release issued on 5 September 2021.

Press Release
Monday, September 6, 2021
From: The Shakespeare Southampton Legacy Trust
To: The Titchfield History Society

Content to be published or distributed as written with no alterations.
Copyright ©The Shakespeare Southampton Legacy Trust

On behalf of the Shakespeare Southampton Legacy Trust, Lord Montagu of Beaulieu and the St Peter's Parochial Church Council, I am pleased to report that a team of experts successfully completed a site survey and structural inspection of the Southampton Chapel, monument and vault to inform their future conservation and care.

The work, which was supported by extensive historical, architectural, legal and conservation research, was performed by The Skillington Workshop Ltd, a leading firm with extensive experience in conserving monuments in an ecclesiastical setting. Dr David Carrington will be supervising the sympathetic restoration of the Southampton and Lady Mary monuments sponsored by the Shakespeare Southampton Legacy Trust.

The subsurface investigations confirmed that the Southampton Monument is supported by a vaulted Tudor passage running its entire length to the north. Access to the Wriothesley vault was re-established through the original access point on the chapel floor near the organ. Access involved lifting one stone slab that was fully reinstated upon completion. The investigations also confirmed that the vault does not have an external entrance from the churchyard. The location of the suspected exterior access has been confirmed to be a grave.

The Inspecting Architect and a structural engineer thoroughly examined the mortuary complex finding it in excellent condition with no structural concerns. It comprises a broad vaulted Tudor passage which empties into a vaulted brick chamber. It is presumed that the original staircase leading to the subsurface was removed during modern interventions in the 1950s.

Access to the vault chamber by the archaeologists did not involve risk or disturbance to the vault fabric or its contents. The recording of the vault contents was carried out with great care and solemnity by Dr Julian Litten and Adrian Miles, two of the UK's foremost funerary vault experts, assisted by an advisor from Historic England. The inspection of the vault contents was purely visual and will result in a written and photographic inventory of the visible contents.

I am pleased to report that no project overruns were necessary and that the Church opened at its regular hours of operation Monday morning. At the September 5th Church Service, the Churchwarden thanked Lord Montagu and the three generations of his family, who have taken such an active role in ensuring the monument and vault remain such an essential part of St. Peter's heritage.

A special thank you to Reverend Susan Allman, who kindly returned to bless the proceedings. Lord Montagu has asked me to pass on his gratitude to everyone at Titchfield who has assisted with the realisation of the project, the findings from which will significantly inform the future care and conservation of the chapel, monument and vault.

The works were sponsored jointly by St Peter's Parochial Church Council and the Shakespeare Southampton Legacy Trust (SSLT), a charity founded by Lord Montagu of Beaulieu, a senior hereditary descendant of the Wriothesley Earls of Southampton. Visit thesslt.org for more information.

I look forward to sharing the results of this historic initiative with the Titchfield History Society in the fullness of time. Please direct any questions or comments to Laura Matthias, Managing Trustee of the

Shakespeare Southampton Legacy Trust. laura.matthias@beaulieu.co.uk.

Laura Matthias | Project Coordinator
Southampton Monument & Vault Initiative
Shakespeare Southampton Legacy Trust, Managing Director
Palace House, Beaulieu
Brockenhurst Hants SO42 7YL

The Wriothesley tomb is housed in a south side chapel of the Church of St Peter's. Titchfield. This view shows the dowager Countess Jane lying on the top altar. On the second table is her son Henry, 2nd Earl of Southampton. Below, kneeling in prayer, are his two children Mary and Henry, the 3rd earl.

THE INSCRIPTIONS ON THE TOMB

I. HEERE LIETH YE BODYE OE YE RIGHT HONORABLE Sr THOMAS WRYOTHESLYE SONNE OF WILLIAM WRYOTHESLYE ESQVIRE : WHO FOR HIS VIRTVE AND WORTHYNES WAS CREATED KNIGHT OF THE HONORABLE OHDER OF YE GARTER BARON OF TYTCHFYLDE EARLE OF SOVTHAMPTON : CHANNCELLOR OF ENGLAND ONE OF YE HONORABLE PRYVIE COVNSELL VNTO KLNGE HENRIE THE 8 AND KINGE EDWARD THE 6 AND ONE OF THE ESPECIALLIE CHOSEN AND TRVSTED EXECVTORS OF THE LAST WILL & TESTAMENT OF KLNGE HENRIE THE 8 . BY LADY JANE HIS WIFFE HE HAD ISSVE HENRIE EARLE OF SOVTHAMPTON ELISABETH MARYED VNTO THOMAS FITZWATERS AFTERWARDES EARLE OF SVSSEX MARYE MARIED VNTO RYCHARD LYSTER ESQVIER KATHERINE MARYED VNTO THOMAS CORNEWALI.YS ESQVIER & MABELL MARYED VNTO SYR WALTER SANDES KNYGHT BESYDES DIVERS OTHER CHILDREN WCH DYED VNMARIED . THIS THOMAS EARLE OF SOVTHAMPTON DYED THE 30 DAYE OF Ao Do 1551

II. HEERE LYETH YE BODYE OF YE RIGHT HONORABLE HENRY WRYOTHESLY BARON OF TITCHFYELDE & EARLE OF SOVTHAMPTON WHO TOOKE TO WYFE MARYE BROWNE DAVGHTER OF SYR ANTHONIE BROWNE VISCOVNTE MOVNTAGVE & OF YE LADYE JANE RATCLYFF HIS WYFE, ONE OF YE DAVGHTERS OF ROBERT EARLE OF SVSSEX . BY WCH MARYE HE HAD ISSVE YE RIGHT HONORABLE HENRIE EARLE OF SOVTHAMPTON NOW LIVINGE MARIE MARIED VNTO THOMAS ARVNDELL ESQVIER SONNE & HEYRE OF S" MATHEW ARVNDELL OF WARDER CASTELL IN YE COVNTIE OF WYLTE : KNIGHT . THIS HENRIE EARLE OF SOVTHAMPTON ENDED HIS LYFE AT HIS HOWSE AT YTCHELL YE FOVRTH DAY OF OCTOBER IN YE 36 YEARE OF HIS AGE &IN YE,YEARE OF YE RAIGN OF OVR SOVERAIGNE LADY QVEENE ELIZABETH & IN YE YEARE OF VOR LORD GOD.1

III. HEERE LYETH YE RIGHT HONORABLE LADYE JANE COVNTIS OF SOVTHAMPTON DAVGHTER OF WLLLIAM CHEYNIE OF CHESSAMBOYES IN YE .COVNTY OF' BVCKINGHAM ESQVIER WYFE VNTO YE RIGHT HONORABLE SR THOMAS WRYOTHESLYE KNIGHT OF THE MOST HONORABLE ORDER OF YE GARTER, BARON OF TYTCHFYELDE EARLE OF SOVTHAMPTON AND LORDE CHAVNCELLOR OF ENGLANDE : WHICH LADYE JANE DYED THE I5 DAY OF SEPT IN THE YEARE OF OVR LORD GOD 1574.

6 THE RENTAL BOOK OF 1546-1547

By 1546 the estates of Thomas Wriothesley had grown significantly and in that year he charged his stewards with the task of accounting for everything. The documents are in the Hampshire Record Office. The Titchfield records have been translated from the Latin and transcribed for a publication Titchfield Rentals 1546-7, ISBN: 978-0-993421-31-0. A single page, with a translation and transcription opposite is reproduced here.

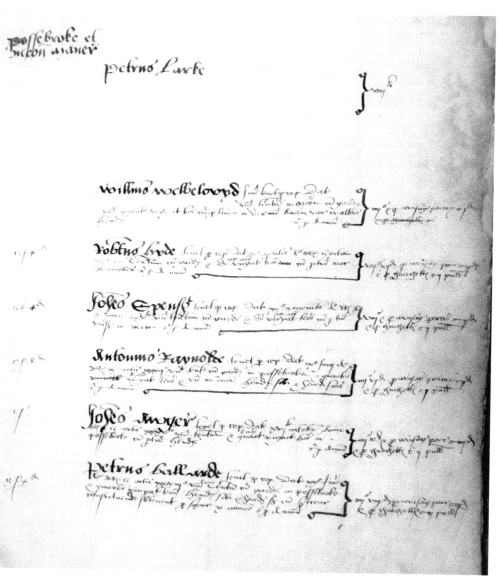

POSBROOK and **MEON** Manor

PETER LARKE   8s [entry ends]

WILLIAM WELBELOVYD junr holds by copy given   [blank] one tenement in **MEON** with garden

& one quarter virgate of land with appurtenances in the Baronial tithing called **WALKERS** to be held at the yearly rent of 4 shillings and for the right to pannage ^{2v}1d and for church scot [blank]

In margin [later hand] 13s 4d

ROBERT HYDE holds by copy dated the 10th of April in the 12th year of the reign of King Henry VIII

one tenement with garden and a half a virgate ^16 acres^ [later hand]with appurtenances called

MAUCELLES [or MANCELLES] at a yearly rent of 7s 11d for right to pannage 2d and for church scot of 2 pullets

In margin [later hand] 13s 4d

JOHN SPENSE holds by copy dated the 12th November in the 25th year of the reign of Henry VIII one tenement and garden and half a virgate of land ^16 acres^ [inserted above in a later hand] with all appurtenances in **MEON** at a yearly rent of 8s & for right to pannage 2d and for church scot 2 pullets

In margin, later hand 6s 8d

ANTONY RAYNOLDE holds by copy dated the 9th June in the 33rd year of the reign of Henry VIII one tenement and garden in **POSBROOK** and a quarter virgate of land ^8 acres^ [inserted in a later hand] and one marsh [or moor] to be held to himself and his heirs at the yearly rent of 4s 6d for right to pannage 2d and for church scot 1 pullet

In margin, later hand 6s 8d

JOHN AWGER holds by copy dated the 16th of October in the 35th year of the reign of Henry VIII one tenement and a quarter virgate of land ^8 acres^[inserted in a later hand] In **POSBROOK** with appurtenances to be held at a yearly rent of 4s 5d for right to pannage 2d and for church scot of 2 pullets.

In margin, later hand 13s 4d

PETER BALLARD holds by copy dated the 20th of June

in the 28th year of the reign of Henry VIII one tenement and garden in **POSBROOK**

and a quarter virgate of land to be held to himself and his heirs with licence

to let to a sub tenant for the space of 10 years at the yearly rent of 4s 8d for right to pannage 3d and for church scot 2 pullets

7 MONEY

For many centuries until currency was decimalised in 1971 money was accounted for by what became known as pounds, shillings and pence. This practice derived from an accounting system used by Italian banks. They accounted for money in three columns: lira (£), solidi (s) and denarii (d). The English unit of currency was the penny and for accounting purpose this was equated to the denarius and the *d* symbol was used for pennies and the £ symbol was used for the pound. The pound was essentially an expression of weight since 240 silver pennies actually weighed one pound. It says much for the innate conservatism of accountants and lawyers that these symbols survived until 1971. The Anglo-Saxon shilling, at one point a gold coin, was eventually standardised as the equivalent of 12 silver pennies.

For most of the middle ages the penny was sufficient for most transactions. Occasionally it could be cut in two to make a half penny or even further to a quarter penny - a *fourthing*, conventionally spoken and written as a farthing.

I have made no attempt to express 16th and 17th century sums of money as modern equivalents. Some historians in the 1970s started to provide these estimates in brackets, but at the end of that inflationary decade those estimates were already dated. In any case, it is difficult to draw comparisons between how people might spend their money in earlier centuries than today. Most people grew a substantial portion of their own food. Transportations costs were practically zero for most people as one could and did travel by foot. Fine clothing for the aristocracy was monstrously expensive compared to the simple clothing of the ordinary person. Taxes did not loom large in the budgets of ordinary people. In sum, the role of money in the economy was not equivalent to the way we use money today.

Property ownership was limited to very few people in the 16th and 17th centuries. Sir Thomas Wriothesley was remarkable in that he was able to enter this privileged circle. The vast majority lived out their lives without owning the property they lived in, even if they built the premises themselves. Prosperous men like William Beeston and Arthur Bromfield, as two examples, were content to lease from the Earl of Southampton for their whole lives. Housing costs may therefore have represented a small percentage of the household budget.

Therefore it my be more useful to relate the value of money to its own period. A poor family could get by on £5 a year in the 16th century and if you use that as a yardstick an income of £400 or £1,000 a year is huge by comparison.

Many of the land transactions were made for sums of £1,000 more or less. This is a relatively trivial amount today, but at the time, it was enormous.

The other wrinkle to take into account is the use of the term 'mark'. A mark was never an actual coin but was reckoned at ⅔rd of a pound. Thus 1 mark equalled 13s 4d.

However, there is a very useful website www.measuringworth.com which can express monetary values from the 16th and 17th centuries in terms that relate better to present day values.

BIBLIOGRAPHY

Acheson, A. *Shakespeare's Lost Years in London, 1586-1592, giving new light on the pre-sonnet period.* (New York: Brentano's, 1920)

Ackroyd, Peter. *Civil War.* (London: Macmillan, 2014)

Ackroyd, Peter. *Shakespeare: The Biography.* London: Vintage Books, 2006)

Ackroyd, Peter. *Tudors.* (London: Macmillan, 2012)

Ackroyd, Peter. *The Life of Thomas More.* (London: Vintage Books, 1999)

Acts of the Privy Council of England. ed. J. R. Dasent (London 1890-1907)

Akrigg, G. P. V. *Shakespeare and the Earl of Southampton.* (London: H. Hamilton 1968)

Asquith, C. *Shakespeare and the Resistance*: *The Earl of Southampton, the Essex Rebellion, and the Poems that Challenged Tudor Tyranny.* Public Affairs. (2018).

Aubrey, John. *Brief lives: A selection based upon existing contemporary portraits.* (London: The Folio Society, 1975).

Bate, Jonathan. The Genius of Shakespeare. (London: Picador, 2008)

Black, J. Bennett. *The Reign Of Elizabeth, 1558-1603.* Oxford History Of England. (Oxford: Oxford University Press, 1959)

Bray, W. 'An Account of the Confinement of Henry Wriothesley, Earl of Southampton, by Order of Queen Elizabeth, in 1570, first at the house of Alderman Becher, in London, and then at Loseley in Surrey, the seat of Wm. More, Esq. (afterwards Sir Wm.) taken from Original Papers there preserved, and now in the possession of James More Molyneux, Esq. the representative of that Family (1819.) Communicated by Wm. Bray, Esq. Treasurer.... '*Archaeologia Volume 19, 1821, pp. 263 - 269.* (Published online by Cambridge University Press, 2012)

Burgess, G., R. Wymer, & J. Lawrence. *The Accession of James I: Historical and Cultural Consequences.* (London: Macmillan, 2006)

Byrne, Muriel St. Clare, ed. *The Lisle Letters.* (London: Secker and Warburg, 1983)

Cadwallader, Laura H. *The Career of the Earl of Essex from the Islands Voyage in 1597 to His Execution in 1601.* (Philadelphia: University of

Pennsylvania, 1923)

Calendar of the Cecil Papers in Hatfield House: Volumes 1-24, (London: HMSO, 1888-1976)

Calendar of State Papers Foreign: Edward VI 1547-1553, ed. William B Turnbull (London, 1861), British History Online http://www.british-history.ac.uk/cal-state-papers/foreign/edw-vi

Calendar of State Papers Relating To English Affairs in the Archives of Venice, Volume 4, 1527-1533, ed. Rawdon Brown (London, 1871), British History Online http://www.british-history.ac.uk/cal-state-papers/venice/vol4 [accessed 25 November 2021].

Calendar of State Papers, Spain (Simancas), Volume 1, 1558-1567, ed. Martin A S Hume (London, 1892), British History Online http://www.british-history.ac.uk/cal-state-papers/simancas/vol1

Calendar of State Papers, Spain (Simancas), Volume 1, 1558-1567, ed. Martin A S Hume (London, 1892), British History Online http://www.british-history.ac.uk/cal-state-papers/simancas/vol1

Calendar of State Papers, Spain (Simancas), Volume 3, 1580-1586, ed. Martin A S Hume (London, 1896), British History Online http://www.british-history.ac.uk/cal-state-papers/simancas/vol3

Calendar of State Papers, Spain (Simancas), Volume 4, 1587-1603, ed. Martin A S Hume (London, 1899), British History Online http://www.british-history.ac.uk/cal-state-papers/simancas/vol4

Calendar of State Papers Relating To English Affairs in the Archives of Venice, Volume 4, 1527-1533, ed. Rawdon Brown (London, 1871), British History Online http://www.british-history.ac.uk/cal-state-papers/venice/vol4 [accessed 25 November 2021].

Calendar of State Papers Domestic: James I, 1623-25, ed. Mary Anne Everett Green (London, 1859), British History Online http://www.british-history.ac.uk/cal-state-papers/domestic/jas1/1623-5

Carisbrick, J.J. *Henry VIII.* (London:Eyre Methuen 1981)

Carroll, D. A. 'Reading Names in an Elizabethan Allusion: Henry Wriothesley, Earl of Southampton, and Thomas Nashe.' Names, 46(1), (1998) 29-36.

Chandler, John. *John Leland's Itinerary.* (Stroud: Sutton Publishing, 1993)

Child, L. M. *The biographies of Lady Russell, and Madame Guyon.*

(Boston: Carter, Hendee & co. 1832)

Chrimes, S.B. *Henry VII.* (London: Eyre Methuen, 1981)

Clark, Sir George. (1987). *The Later Stuarts 1660-1714.* Oxford History Of England. (Oxford: Oxford University Press, 1956)

D'Aubigne, J.H. Merle. *History of the Reformation of the Sixteenth Century.* (Ada, Michegan: Baker Publishing. 1986)

Daugherty, L. (2013). *The Assassination of Shakespeare's Patron*: Investigating the Death of the Fifth Earl of Derby. Cambria Press.

Essex, R. D., & Southampton, H. W. *The arraignment, tryal and condemnation of Robert, Earl of Essex, and Henry, Earl of Southampton: at Westminster the 19th of February, 1600 [i.e. 1601] and in the 43 year of the reign of Queen Elizabeth : for rebelliously conspiring and endeavouring the subversion of the government, by confederacy with Tyr-Owen, that popish traytor and his complices, of whom, these following, viz., Sir Christopher Blunt, Sir Charles Danvers, Sir Gillie Merrick and Henry Cuffe, were the 5th of March following, by a special commission of Oyer and Terminer, arraigned, condemned, and executed : the peers had to their assistance the learned judges, counsel for the queen, Sir Henry Yelverton. Sir Edward Cook. Mr. Bacon.* (London: Printed for Tho. Basset. Sam. Heyrick. and Matth. Gillyflower, 1679)

Davies, Godfrey. *The Early Stuarts 1603-1660.* Oxford History

Of England. (Oxford: Oxford University Press, 1959)

Duncan-Jones Katherine. *Shakespeare's Sonnets.* (London: Bloomsbury, 2010)

Edmondson, Paul. *The Shakespeare Circle.* (Cambridge: Cambridge University Press, 2020)

Erickson, Carolly. *Bloody Mary* (London: Robson, 1978)

Elton, Geoffrey. *The Tudor Revolution in Government.* (Cambridge: Cambridge University Press, 1962)

Florio, John. *A World of Wordes: Or Most Copious, and Exact Dictionarie in Italian and English.* (https://www.resolutejohnflorio.com/2019/09/19/a-world-of-words/)

Florio, John. *Firste Fruites.* (https://www.resolutejohnflorio.com/2019/09/19/first-fruits/)

Flower, R. 'The Wriothesley Manuscripts.' *The British Museum Quarterly*, 82-85. (1938).

Gajda, A. *The Earl of Essex and Late Elizabethan Political Culture.* (Oxford: Oxford University Press, 2012)

Gibbons, Geoffrey. *The Political Career of Thomas Wriothesley, First Earl of Southampton, 1505-1550.* (University of Warwick, 1999)

Gillespie, Stuart. *Shakespeare's Books.* (The Arden Shakespeare, 2016)

Green, M. 'The Pronunciation of Wriothesley.' *English Studies, 86*(2), 133-160. (2005)

Greenblatt, Stephen. *Tyrant.* (London: The Bodley Head, 2018)

Greenblatt, Stephen. *Will in the World: How Shakespeare became Shakespeare.* (London: The Bodley Head, 2016)

Greene, R. (1883). *The Life and Complete Works in Prose and Verse of Robert Greene. collected and edited by Alexander B. Grosart. The* Huth *Library.*

Gunn, S. J. 'The accession of Henry VIII.' *Historical Research, 64*(155), 278-288. (1991)

Gurr, Andrew. *The Shakespeare Company, 1594-1642.* (Cambridge: Cambridge University Press, 2010)

Gurr, Andrew. *The Shakespearean Stage, 1574-1642.* (Cambridge: Cambridge University Press, 2010)

Guy, John. *Tudor England.* (Oxford: Oxford University Press, 1990)

Hamill, J. 'Looney and Mythmaking.' *Shakespeare Oxford Newsletter, 56*(3), 11-14. (2020)

Hampshire record Office, 5M53 Wriothesley Deeds and Papers.

Harris, R. W. *Clarendon and the English Revolution.* (London: Chatto & Windus, 1983)

Hibbard, G. R. *Thomas Nashe: A Critical Introduction.* (Cambridge, Mass: Harvard University Press, 1962)

Hibbert, Christopher. *The English: A Social History, 1066-1945.* (London: Guild Publishing, (1987)

Historical Manuscripts Commission, *Bath and Longleat Manuscripts,* Seymour Papers, vol 2 (London, 1907)

A History of the County of Hampshire: Volume 2, ed. H Arthur Doubleday and William Page (London, 1903), British History Online http://www.british-history.ac.uk/vch/hants/vol2

A History of the County of Hampshire: Volume 3, ed. William Page

(London, 1908), British History Online http://www.british-history.ac.uk/vch/hants/vol3

Hoak, D.E. *The Kings Council in the Reign of Edward VI.* (Cambridge: Casmbridge University Press, 2009)

Honan, P. 'Wriothesley, Henry, third earl of Southampton (1573–1624).' *Oxford Dictionary of National Biography*, (2004)

Hutchinson, Robert. *Elizabeth's Spymaster: Francis Walsingham and the Secret War that Saved England.* (London: Phoenix, 2007)

Hutchinson, Robert. *The Last Days of Henry VIII: Conspiracies, Treason and Heresy at the Court of the Dying Tyrant.* (London: Weidenfeld & Nicholson, 2005)

Hutchinson, Robert. *Thomas Cromwell.* (London: Phoenix, 2008)

James, Southampton, H. W., Bonoeil, J., & Kingston, F. (1622). *His Maiesties gracious letter to the Earle of South-Hampton, treasurer, and to the councell and Company of Virginia heere : commanding the present setting vp of silke works, and planting of vines in Virginia : and the letter of the treasurer, councell, and company to the gouernour and councell of state there for the strict excecution of His Maiesties royall commands herein : also a Treatise of the art of making silke. together with instructions how to plant and dresse vines and to make wine. and in the end, a conclusion, with sundry profitable remonstrances to the colonies.* London: Printed by Felix Kyngston.

Jardine, D., Throckmorton, N., Norfolk, T. H., Parry, W., Essex, R. D., Southampton, H. W. et al. (1847). *Criminal trials, supplying copious illustrations of the important periods of English history during the reigns of Queen Elizabeth and James I; to which is added a narrative of the Gunpowder plot with historical prefaces and notes.* London: M.A. Nattali.

Klause, J *Shakespeare, the Earl, and the Jesuit.* (Madison, New Jersey: Fairleigh Dickinson University Press, 2008).

Koenigsberger, H.G. *Europe in the sixteenth century.* (London: Longman, 1989)

Lacey, Robert. *Robert, Earl of Essex: An Elizabethan Icarus.* (London: Weidenfeld & Nicholson, 2001)

Lacey, Robert. *The Life and Times of Henry VIII.* (London: Weidenfeld & Nicholson, 1972)

Lee, Christopher. *1603: A Turning Point in British History.* (London: Headline Book Publishing, Review, 2003)

Letters and Papers. Foreign and Domestic of the Reign of Henry VIII, J. Gairdner, ed. (1861-3)

Letters and Papers, Foreign and Domestic, Henry VIII, Volume 4, 1524-1530, ed. J S Brewer (London, 1875), British History Online http://www.british-history.ac.uk/letters-papers-hen8/vol4 [accessed 25 November 2021].

Lincoln, Margarette. *London and the Seventeenth Century: The Making of the World's Greatest City.* (New Haven and London: Yale University Press, 2021)

Mackie, J.D.*The Earlier Tudors 1485-1558.* Oxford History of England. (Oxford: Oxford University Press, 1952)

Marius, Richard. *Thomas More.* (London: J.M. Dent and Sons, 1984)

Massey, G. *The Secret Drama of Shakespeare's Sonnets Unfolded.* (London: R. Clay, sons, and Taylor, printers, 1872)

Matusiak, John. *James I.* (Stroud: The History Press, 2018)

McGinn, Donald J. *Thomas Nashe.* (Boston: Twayne Publishers, 1981)

Montaigne, Michel de. *Shakespeare's Montaigne: The Florio Translation of the Essays*, Greenblatt, Stephen. (ed) et al. (New York Review Books Classics, 2014)

Nash, Thomas. J.B Steane ed. *The Unfortunate Traveller and Other Works. (*London: Penguin, 1972).

Miller, Helen. *Henry VIII and the English Nobility. (*Oxford: Basil Blackwell, 1989)

Nicholl, Charles. *The Reckoning: The Murder of Christopher Marlowe. (*London: Vintage Books, 2002)

Nicholl, Charles. *The Lodger: Shakespeare On Silver Street.* (London: Allen Lane, 2007)

Penn, Thomas. *The Winter King: The Dawn of Tudor England.* (London: Allen Lane, 2011)

Ponet, John. *A short treatise of politicke power,* (Menston: Scolar Press, 1970)

Purkiss, Diane. *The English Civil War: A People's History.* (London: Harper, 2007)

Questier, M. C. *Catholicism and Community in Early Modern England.* (Cambridge: Cambridge University Press, 2006)

Ridley, Jasper. *The Statesman and the Fanatic: Thomas Wolsey and Thomas More.* (London: Constable, 1982)

Roe, Richard Paul, *The Shakespeare Guide to Italy.* (London: Harper Collins, 2011)

Rowse, A. L. *Shakespeare's Southampton, Patron of Virginia.* (London: Macmillan, 1965)

Rowse, A.L. *Eminent Elizabethans.* (London: Macmillan, 1983)

Rowse, A. L. *Shakespeare the Man.* (New York: Harper Row, 1976)

Rowse, A. L. *The Expansion of Elizabethan England.* (London: Palgrave Macmillan, 2003)

Rowse, A. L. *The England of Elizabeth.* (London: Palgrave Macmillan, 2003)

Russell, L. R., & Berry, M. *Some Account of the Life of Rachael Wriothesley, Lady Russell.* (London: Longman, Hurst, Rees, Orme, and Brown, 1820).

Schofield, John. *The Rise and Fall of Thomas Cromwell: Henry VIII's Most Faithful Servant.* (Stroud: The History Press, 2011)

Shapiro, James. *1599: A Year in the Life of William Shakespeare.* (London: Faber and Faber, 2006)

Shapiro, James. *1606: William Shakespeare and the Year of Lear.* (London: Faber and Faber, 2005)

Slavin, A. J. 'The fall of Lord Chancellor Wriothesley: a study in the politics of conspiracy.' *Albion: A Quarterly Journal Concerned with British Studies,* 7(4), 265-286. (1975)

Slavin, A. J. (1968). *Henry VIII and the English Reformation. Edited with an Introduction by Arthur J. Slavin.*

Snow, V. F. 'New Light on the Last Days and Death of Henry Wriothesley, Earl of Southampton.' *The Huntington Library Quarterly,* 59-69. (1973)

Starkey, David. *Henry: Virtuous Prince.* (London: Harper, 2009)

Starkey, David. *Elizabeth.* (London: Vintage Books, 2001)

Starnes, D. T. 'John Florio Reconsidered.' *Texas Studies in Literature and Language,* 407-422. (1965)

Stone, L. *Family and Fortune: Studies in Aristocrtic Finance in the Sixteenth and Seventeenth Centuries*. (Oxford: Oxford University Press, 1973)

Stopes, C. C. *The life of Henry, Third Earl of Southampton*. (Cambridge: The University Press, 1922)

Anglo, Sydney. *The Great Tournament Roll of Westminster: a collotype reproduction of the manuscript*. (Oxford: The Clarendon Press, 1968).

Tomalin, Claire. *Samuel Pepys*. (London: Penguin UK., 2003)

Trotter, Stewart. *Love's Labour's Found: Shakespeare's Criminal Passions*. (Ashford: Geerings, 2002)

Walker, E., C. R. L. Fletcher, H. B. Butler, & B. Rogers. *Historical Portraits*. (Oxford: Clarendon Press, 1909)

Wells, Stanley W. *Shakespeare: For All Time*. (London: Macmillan, 2002)

Wells, Stanley W. *Shakespeare and Co.: Christopher Marlowe, Thomas Dekker, Ben Jonson, Thomas Middleton, John Fletcher and the Other Players in His Story*. (London: Penguin Books, 2007)

Williams, Neville. *Henry VIII and his Court*. (London: Cardinal, 1973)

Wilson, D. Harris. *King James VI and I.*, (London: Jonathan Cape, 1956)

Wilson, Derek. *In the Lion's Court: Power, Ambition, and Sudden Death in the Court of Henry VIII*. (London: Hutchinson, 2001)

Wilson, Derek. *England in the Age of Thomas More*. (London: Hart Davis McGibbon 1978)

Wilson, John Dover. *The Essential Shakespeare*. (Cambridge: CUP, 1937)

Wriothesley, Charles. (1875). *A Chronicle of England During the Reigns of the Tudors, from AD 1485 to 1559* ((1)). Camden society.

Yates, Frances A. *John Florio: the life of an Italian in Shakespeare's England*. (Cambridge: CUP, 1934)

Yates, Frances A. *A Study of Loves Labour's Lost*. (Cambridge: CUP, 1936)

Yates, Frances A. (1969). *Theatre of the World*. (New Yor: Barnes & Noble, 2009)

ENDNOTES

Abbreviations

APC	Acts of the Privy Council
CSP	Calendar of State Papers
HMC	Historical Manuscripts Commission
HRO	Hampshire Record Office
LP	*Letters and Papers*
PRO	*Public Record Office*

1   *The Receyt of the Lady Kateryne*, ed. Gordon Kipling, (EETS, o.s. 296, Oxford, 1996) pp 15-18.

2   ibid. pp 28-9.

3   ibid. pp xxii-xxiii.

4   Houlbrooke, R. 'Prince Arthur's Funeral', in Steven Gunn and Linda Monckton, eds., *Arthur Tudor, Prince of Wales: Life, Death and Comemoration,* (Woodbridge, 2009) p. 72.

5   Kipling, pp 81-5

6   *Great Chronicle of London,* eds. A H Thomas and I D Thornley, (London, 1938) p. 321.

7   There is a will in the Provincial Court of Canterbury, dated 20 April 1529, lodged by a Thomas Wriothesley, Haberdasher. He appears to have been a merchant of some substance and he made bequests to his brother Henry, to be divided between his sons John and Thomas. Further bequests are made to his married daughters. I infer that these Wriothesleys were Writh cousins of the court family who must also have decided to change their name to the Tudor elaboration.

8   from Thomas Heywood. cited in G. P. V. Akrigg. *Shakespeare and the Earl of Southampton. (*London: Hamish Hamilton, 1968) p. 3.

9   G. P. V. Akrigg. *Shakespeare and the Earl of Southampton. (*London: Hamish Hamilton, 1968) p. 3.

10   Commonly pronounced 'Chumley' and 'Fanshaw.'

11   B.J. Greenfield. 'The Wriothesley Tomb in Titchfield Church', (Hampshire Field Club 1889) p. 65.

12   "He was not precisely a novus homo." A L Rowse. *Shakespeare's*

13   John Leland was first commissioned in 1533 to record the contents of all the monastic libraries in the country. After the dissolution he continued this work but made notes broader in scope as he travelled the country. His notes were not published until the 18th century. Unlike his school fellows at St Paul's Leland did not acquire great wealth. He was a church pluralist and so lived comfortably but he acquired no land to speak of.. His notebooks are his lasting legacy.

14   *Letters and Papers, Foreign and Domestic, Henry VIII, Volume 4, 1524-1530,* ed. J S Brewer (London, 1875) (2), 2735.

15   Geoffrey Gibbons *The Political Career of Thomas Wriothesley, First Earl of Southampton 1505-1550,* (Studies in British History). (Edwin Mellen Press Ltd., Oct 2001) p. 15.

16   John Schofield, *The Rise and Fall of Thomas Cromwell. (*The History Press, 2011)

17   Calendar of State Papers Spanish, 1529-30, no. 224, pp. 349-50; no. 232, pp. 366-7; LP 4 (3), no. 6307.

18   CSP Span., 1529-30, no. 445.

19   CSP Span., 1531-3, no. 598.

20   PRO, State Papers, 1/69, fos. 74 and 143, (LP, v, 742,836); LP, v, 328,611.

21   *Sola fide* was a revolutionary idea in the 1530s. Simply put, it meant that your faith alone could be your path to salvation. Classical thinking had nourished the idea that good works (e.g. endowing churches, monasteries, hospitals) would be a certain path to salvation. This meant that ordinary people were at a disadvantage compared to the rich, and salvation through "good works" was certainly in conflict with Christ's own teaching.

22   Gibbons, op. cit. P. 27.

23   Geoffrey Elton. *The Tudor Revolution in Government.* (Cambridge: Cambridge University Press, 1962) p. 304.

24   Carolly Erickson, *Bloody Mary* (London: Robson, 1978) p. 175

25   Peter Ackroyd. *Tudors.* (London: Macmillan, 2012) p. 99.

26   LP, xi, 10872.

27   Historical Manuscripts Commission, *Bath and Longleat Manuscripts,* Seymour Papers, vol 2 (London, 1907), p. 7

28   PRO. State Papers. 1/170, fo. 201, (LP, v, 1209).

29   LP, vii, 1355-6.

30   Ackroyd, op. cit. p 120.

31   Ackroyd op. cit. p. 125

32   This may not be the end of the story. Various efforts (which are ongoing) have been made to locate the bones of Alfred and his wife. There may yet be a future discovery.

33   Letters Patent xiii Pt. 2 p 155

34   Muriel St. John Byrne, *The Lisle Letters* (London & Chicago, 1981) p. 277.

35   Byrne op.cit.

36   Gibbons, op. cit. p 35

37   Schofield. op. cit. p 361

38   Gibbons, op.cit. p. 53.

39   State Papers of Henry VIII, vol 1, pt ii, 349-50 PRO, State Papers. 1/160, fo 181 (LP, x, 765)

40   H. A. L. Fisher, History of England, Henry VIII (1906) p 434

41   P. Janelle. 'An unpublished poem on Bishop Gardiner' BIHR (1928-9) p.22

42   PRO, SP 1/143, fo. 35v. (LP, xiv, (1),247

43   J. Kaulek, *Correspondance Politique de Mm Castillan et de Marillac* (Paris, 1885). p. 262.

44   CSP Spanish, vi,(2) , 23, 167.

45   CSP Spanish, vi,(2) , 175.

46   LP 35 Henry VIII c 5.

47   John Foxe, The Unabridged Acts and Monuments Online or TAMO (1576 edition) (The Digital Humanities Institute, Sheffield, 2011). Available from: http//www.dhi.ac.uk/foxe [Accessed: 01.03.20]. Vol v, p 434-6

48   G R Elton. *Reform and Reformation.* (London: Edward Arnold, 1977) p. 293.

49   Edward Hall. *Hall's chronicle containing the history of England, during the reign of Henry the Fourth, and the succeeding monarchs, to the end of the reign of Henry the Eighth, in which are particularly described the manners and customs of those periods. Carefully collated with the editions of*

1548 and 1550. London 1809. p 836.

50   Nichols, J. G. ed.. *Narratives of the Reformation.* Camden Society. o.s. 77 (1859) p 255-8.

51   Gibbons, op. cit., p. 180

52   CSP, Spanish, viii, 531; LP. xxi, (2), 568.

53   J.A. Muller, *Stephen Gardiner and the Tudor Reaction.* (London, 1926) p. 298.

54   LP Spanish, Vol. VIII, p. 320.

55   Acts of the Privy Council, n.s., Vol. II, 1547-50, p. 19.

56   APC, n.s., Vol. II, 1547-50, p. 20.

57   Ponet, John. *A short treatise of politicke power,* (Menston: Scolar Press, 1970) p. 131-2.

58   D.E. Hoak. The Kings Council in the Reign of Edward VI (Cambridge: Casmbridge University Press, 2009) p. 253.

59   Hoak. p. 255.

60   CSP. Spanish x, 44.

61   CSP. Spanish x 47

62   Hoak. p 257

63   Charles Wriothesley, *A Chronicle of England during the Reign of the Tudors from 1485-1559.* ed. W. D Hamilton, Camden Society. n.s. London, 1878, vol. ii, p. 42.

64   Jordan, W.K. *Chronicles and Papers of Edward VI*, p. 42.

65   Susan Brigden ed. The Letters of Richard Scudamore to Sir Philip Hoby, September 1549–March 1555 Camden 4th series. p. 143

66   Albert Frederick Pollard. Dictionary of National Biography, 1885-1900 Vol 63

67   Mrs Stopes cites this on page 501 of her book. Apparently this note was discovered in a prayer book once belonging to the family.

68   Kempe 238

69   A.J. Kempe, ed. *The Loseley Manuscripts.* pp. 238-239.

70   Stopes. op. cit. p 523.

71   Joseph Lilly. (1867). A Collection of Seventy-Nine Black-Letter Ballads and Broadsides. p. 260.

72   Stopes p 10, D.S.S.P. Eliz. CCLXXI. 74, July 4-14, 1599, et seq.

73   A Storie of Domesticall Difficulties', Catholic Record Society, Miscellanea, Vol. II, p. 183.

74   ref

75   Stopes, 9

76   Gervase Markham. *op. cit.*

77   Rot. Lit. Claus. (Rec. Com.), 75b.

78   Pope Nich. Tax. (Rec. Com.), 213b; Feud. Aids, ii, 333, 345; Valor Eccl. (Rec. Com.), ii, 24b.

79   Pope Nich. Tax. (Rec. Com.), 213b; Feud. Aids, ii, 333, 345; Valor Eccl. (Rec. Com.), ii, 24b.

80   This estimate comes from Lawrence Stone, . *Family and Fortune.* (Oxford: OUP 1973)

81   A L Rowse. (1965). Shakespeare's Southampton, Patron of Virginia. p. 40.

82   See Appendix 4.

83   Greenfield. op. cit. p. 66.

84   Stone, Lawrence. Family and Fortune. OUP 1973, p. 212.

85   Lawrence Stone. (1973). *Family and Fortune: Studies in Aristocratic Finance in the Sixteenth and Seventeenth Centuries.* , (Oxford: The Clarendon Press, 1973)

86   GPV Akrigg. Shakespeare and the Earl of Southampton. Hamish Hamilton 1968. p. 25

87   Francis Peck. Desiderata curiosa. London 1779. p. 36

88   Lansdowne MS xliii (63).

89   Stopes, op. cit. p. 28

90   Complete Peerage, Vol. XII, Part 1, p. 128.

91   This is speculation. Shakespeare's 'Lost Years' are discussed in Part 4.

92   S.P. 12/233/71

93   SP. Eliz. Xxxiii II.

94   Stopes op. cit., p 46

95   Foley, records of the English Jesuits, iv, 49.

96   Stopes. op. cit., p. 65. 'Lady Bridget Manners' opinion of Southampton as "so young, fantasticall, and easily carried away"'

97   Thomas Nashe. *Piers Pennilesse.*

98   Ref

99   Nicholas Rowe edition

100   Nashe, Works, ed McKerrow, I, 243.

101   cuddle

102   Cecil Papers, 83, 62.

103   lan H. Nelson. His Literary Patrons, in The Shakespeare Circle (eds. Paul Edmonson and Stanley Wells), Cambridge: 2015, p. 287.Cecil Papers, 83, 62.

104   Quoted in R. Savage (ed.), Minutes and Accounts of the Corporation of Stratford upon Avon, 1533-1620, Volume Two, page xlvii.

105   Lansdowne MSS. 830. 12 ff. 111, 113.

106   Frances Yates. John Florio: *The Life of an Italian in Shakespeare's England*. (Cambridge: Cambridge University Press, 1934.)

107   Sidney papers, I, 348.

108   Jonathan Roche. Spanish spies in Elizabethan England. Presentation to Institutio Cervantes and the British-Spanish Society, 3 February 2021.

109   Sidney Papers, II 86.

110   Cal. S.P. Dom., 1598-1601, 90.

111   HMC Salis. MSS. viii, p. 357.

112   Coriolanus has proved to be a difficult play to date, but there are suggestions that it was first staged in 1609, a full ten years after the Essex revolt. There is no strong evidence to suggest that Essex may have been a part model for the stage hero, but it is a possibility.

113   Irish State Papers, CCV 113.

114   Camden Series 82; (Stopes 224)

115   Rose p 171

116   Stone. op. cit. p. 219.

117   Manningham's Diary, p. 168.

118   Birch's James I, pp. 494-5.

119   Shakespeare, x. 69.

120   Add. MS II, 402 (Stopes 286)

121   Bodl. Rawl. MSS., Poet. 26/2. W.H. Long. The Oglander Memoirs, London, 1888, p. 23.

122   Stone. op. cit.

123   Rowse p 236

124   William Shakespeare. The Tempest. Arden Edition, p 315.

125   Rowse p 241

126   It is not known if this was the same ship that sailed from Plymouth or another of that name.

127   Stone op. cit. p. 227.

128   Stone. op.cit. p. 227. In this year there was mention of a lease of 21 years dated 1628 between Sir William Uvedale and Arthur Bromfield, steward to the Earl of Southampton.

129   Stone op. cit. p. 228.

130   Titchfield Parish Register

131   John Mitchell. The Titchfield Canal: A Matter of Interpretation. Titchfield: A Place in History, p. 68-77.

132   Hampshire Record Office. 1M46/1. Plan of Titchfield Haven.

133   John C Lewthwaite. The Sea Lock. Titchfield: A Place in History, p. 82.

134   George Watts. The Canal, Titchfield: A History. p. 68.

135   H.R.O. 5M 53/1129/43

136   HRO 5M 53/331-3328

137   HRO 16M63/14

138   Keith Hayward. Titchfield Haven and New River. Titchfield: A Place in History, p. 86.

139   Mitchell op cit.

140   Arthur Wilson. The History of Great Britain. 1653 p. 161-2.

141   Ackroyd. Civil War p 17. Probably from the Advancement of Learning.

142   Stopes op. cit. p 404

143   Camden Series, Yonge's Diary, July 1621.

144   Venetian papers xvii 75 et seq.

145   Ref

146   Cal. S.P. Ven., 1621-1623, 172.

147   Venetian Papers, xviii 40,41.

148   Sir Thomas Roe's Negotiations, p. 222.

149   D.H. Wilson. *King James VI and I.*, (London: Jonathan Cape, 1956) p. 443

150   SP. James, clv. 77.

151   Parish Register

152   Stopes op.cit.

153   Mrs Stopes cites this on p. 473 of her book. Cheltwood must refer to Chetwode, a small village just to the south of Buckingham. However, any connection between the Wriothesleys and this Chetwode family is not evident. There were two families on the manor; a Chetwode family and a Risley family. There is no evidence in the pedigree of Wriothesleys marrying into either family and the Risley family appears to originate in Northamptonshire in the 13th century and have no apparent connection to the Wriths (Wriothesleys) of London. It may be possible that this Sir Thomas Wriothesley was a descendant of Charles Wriothesley, the Herald. We must note that although Charles Wriothesley was assiduous in recording his ancestors, he left no record of his own children - if he had any. Footnote 7 does note that there may have been other Writh cousins who adopted the Wriothesley name.

154   Parish Register of Titchfield.

155   Illustrations of History.

156   Parish Register

157   Sir Francis Nethersole, quoted in Ackroyd Civil War.

158   She was a daughter of the 1st earl of Southampton, who married Thomas Cornwallis. She had no heirs.

159   Stone op.cit. p. 231.

160   David L Smith. Thomas Wriothesley, 4th Earl of Southampton. Oxford Dictionary of National Biography, 2008.

161   Ibid.

162   Clarendon ref

163   Bodl. Oxf. MS Clarendon 31, fol. 54v.

164   J. Spence, Observations, Anecdotes, and Characters of Books and Men, ed. J. M. Osborn, 1, 1966, 244.

165   Clarendon, Hist. rebellion, 5.211.

166   Clarendon, Hist. rebellion, 2.529.

167   Celia Fiennes. The Journeys of Celia Fiennes, intro by John

Hillaby. (London & Sydney: Macdonald 1983). P. 332-3.

168   (Burnet's History, 1.171).

169   BL., Harleian MS 1223, fol. 202.

170   Burnet's History, 1.280

171   Samuel Pepys. Diary Vol VI.

172   Pepys Diary Vol, IV.

173   Burnet's History, 1.316

174   Life of ... Clarendon, 2.344

175   ibid., 2.345

176   Burnet's History, 1.162.

177   Celia Fiennes. There Journeys of Celia Fiennes, intro byJohn Hillaby. (London & Sydney: Macdonald 1983). P. 332-3.

178   p. 242.Stone. op.cit.p. 242.

179   Pepys Diary

180   Life of Clarendon, 3.229,238

181   Lois G Schworerer, Rachel, Lady Russell. Oxford Dictionary of National Biography, 2004.

182   A. Boyer. History of the Life and Reign of Queen Anne (1722). p. 374.

183   Snitterton is the parish where Richard Shakespeare, William Shakespeare's grandfather, farmed. This fact may be entirely coincidental and has no bearing on the future relationship between the third earl and the playwright.

184   This may be the source of the claim by H. Spelman in his 1895 book *The History and Fate of Sacrilege* that Thomas Wriothesley was granted the manor of St Mary's in York. This was not the case. It was retained by the Crown and eventually leased in 1692.

185   Stone, op.cit. p. 211

186   HRO. Wriothesley deeds, vol 3 p. 230.

187   Leland's Itinerary iii, 111.

188   H Arthur Doubleday, William Page (eds) A History of the County of Hampshire, Vol. 2. pp. 181-186, Victoria County History: 1973.

189   This comes from a report to the Court of Augmentations in 1537,

previously unseen by historians. Reported in *The Times* 6 December 2021.

190   Letters Patent xiii pt 1 51.

191   Dugdale's Monasticon, v 693.

192   VCH Hampshire. Vl 2 p 138

193   Leland, Collectanea (2nd ed. Hearne), v, 354.

194   Benj. W. Greenfield, F.S.A. (1895) "The Wriothesley Tomb in Titchfield Church: Its effigal statues and heraldry." Hampshire Field Club p. 68-69.

A WHO'S WHO

During the preparation of this book it was suggested to me that the number of characters mentioned in a book covering a period of more than a century can be confusing. Accordingly I have prepared this mini-dictionary so that reference can be made if necessary.

Arden, Mary (1537-1608) was the daughter of a Wilmcote farmer. She married John Shakespeare in 1557 and gave birth to eight children, one of whom was William Shakespeare.

Askew, Anne (1521-1546) was born in Lincolnshire to a prominent family. She became a committed protestant and accordingly fell out with her catholic husband. She left for London where she became known as a 'gospeller' and became a prominent thorn in the side of the authorities. They first tried to banish her to Lincolnshire, but she quickly returned to London to continue her mission. She refused to recant, even under torture, and was in the end burnt at the stake as an heretic.

Aubrey, John (1626-1697) was born in Wiltshire to a gentry family. He was an antiquarian and member of the Royal Society, but he is best known for his anecdotal jottings, published as Brief Lives in the 19th Century. Thomas Audley (1488-1544) was a lawyer and judge who was appointed Lord Chancellor by Henry VIII to succeed Sir Thomas More. He coped with the job without incident until ill health forced him to retire. He was succeeded by Sir Thomas Wriothesley.

Bacon, Francis (1561-1626) He was a philosopher and statesman who became Lord Chancellor under James I. He was very influential in devising a methodology for scientific enquiry. He was created Viscount St Albans.

Barnes, Robert (1495-1540) was born in Kings Lynn and became an Augustinian Friar. He was granted the Doctor of Divinity degree by Cambridge University in 1523. He became a follower of Martin Luther and often preached in favour of Lutheran doctrine. After the fall of Cromwell, Barnes was arrested with two other Lutherans and three Catholics. They were all burnt at the stake for heresy under the six articles.

Beeston, Christopher (1570-1638) was an actor associate of William Shakespeare and later a theatre manager.

Beeston, Henry was the eldest son of William Beeston of Posbrooke. He became Master of Winchester College.

Beeston, Sir William (1636-1702) was the second son of William Beeston of Posbrooke. He went out to Jamaica as a young man to make his fortune and rose to become Governor of Port Royal. He was a wealthy man when he returned to England.

Beeston, William was most likely a London merchant. He leased Great Posbrook House near Titchfield at about the time that he married Elizabeth, the daughter of Arthur Bromfield, the earl of Southampton's steward. He died in 1638

Blagge, George (1512-1551) was the son of a prosperous lawyer and land owner. George served as an MP and held various positions at court. Henry VIII liked him and saved him when he was charged with several, others of heresy. He prospered during the protestant reign of Edward VI.

Boleyn, Anne (c 1501 -1536) was the second wife of Henry VIII and the mother of the future Elizabeth I. She secretly married Henry VIII on 25 January 1533 and gave birth to a daughter, Elizabeth on 7 September that year. She failed to produce more children, and more critically the male heir that Henry strongly desired. She was executed for treason on 19 May 1536.

Boleyn, Jane, Lady Rochford (c 1505-1542) She was the wife of George Boleyn and therefore Anne Boleyn's sister in law. She was a Lady in Waiting to Queen Catherine Howard and was accused of facilitating her adultery. She was found guilty and beheaded.

Edmund Bonner (1500-1569) was Bishop of London from 1539-1549 and again from 1553 - 1549. He became a strong opponent of Protestant reforms and led the persecution of heretics during the reign of Queen Mary. He spent his last years in prison.

Brandon, Charles (1484-1545) took as his third wife, Mary, younger sister of Henry VIII., As a military man and a courtier he was influential and was created Duke of Suffolk.

Browne, Anthony (1528-1592) was one of the wealthiest landowners in Sussex and his daughter Mary married the 2nd earl of Southampton. He was a religious conservative during these fractious times, yet he managed to keep his head on his shoulders and held office during three reigns. He was more in favour during the reign of Mary and she elevated him to the peerage as Viscount Montagu in 1554.

Browne, Mary (1552-1607) was a daughter of Anthony Browne, 1st Viscount Montagu. She married Henry Wriothesley, 2nd earl of Southampton on 19 February 1566. She bore three children: Jane, who died before 1573, Mary and Henry, the third earl. In 1504 she married for the second time to Sir Thomas Heneage. Heneage died five years later and she married Sir William Hervey at some time between November 1598 and January 1599. She died in October of November 1607.

Bromfield, Arthur(-1660) was a younger son of William Bromfield of Monkton Farleigh in Wiltshire. With no inheritance he entered the service of the earl of

Southampton, probably in 1594, and in time became the earl's steward. He had entrepreneurial talents and was engaged in a number of business ventures.

Bromfield, Elizabeth Daughter of Arthur Bromfield, she married William Beeston of Posbrooke.

Bruno, Giordano (1548-1600) was a Dominican friar who became a celebrated thinker in his day. He adopted the model of the universe proposed by Nicholas Copernicus and this brought him into trouble with church authorities who accused him of heresy. He travelled extensively in Europe and spent two years, from 1583-1585, in London, where he became friends with John Florio. He then spent some years in Paris before returning to Italy in 1592. From 1593 he underwent various trials until he was finally condemned as a heretic by Poet Clement VIII. In 1600 he was burned at the stake in Rome.

Burbage, Richard (1567-1619) was a celebrated actor in his time and a sharer in the acting company that included William Shakespeare. He took many of the leading roles in plays written by Shakespeare.

de Castelnau, Michel (1520-1592) was a French soldier and diplomat who served as ambassador to England to 1572 to 1585.

Catherine of Aragon (1485-1536) She was a daughter of King Ferdinand of Aragon and Queen Isabella of Castille and first married Arthur, Prince of Wales. After his early death she was contracted to Henry, the second son of Henry VII. Only one of her children survived birth and infancy, Mary, and it was this failure to produce a male heir that prompted Henry to procure a divorce in 1532.

Cecil, Sir William (1520-1598) began his career with the Duke of Somerset, who was for a period Protector for the young king Edward VI. When Elizabeth came to power in 1558, Cecil was already a seasoned administrator and he rose to become her chief advisor, holding such offices as Secretary of State and Lord High Treasurer. His chief policy was to create a Protestant union within the British Isles. He was created Baron Burghley in 1571.

Cecil, Robert (1563-1612) was a younger son of William Cecil, Lord Burghley. He ws a clever man and he assumed his father's political mantle after he died in 1598. He was largely responsible for managing a smooth transition of power to James I after the death of Elizabeth in 1603 and James made him Earl of Salisbury. He served as Secretary of State from 1596-1612 and Lord High Treasurer from 1608-1612. He was a short man and suffered from scoliosis, which caused him to be hunch backed. Although his physical appearance invited ridicule in a less sensitive age, his political acumen was unquestioned.

Chapuys, Eustace (c 1490-1556) He was a Savoyard diplomat who served Charles V as Imperial Ambassador to England from 1529-1545. Almost all his correspondence has been preserved and this provides great insights into the court of Henry VIII.

Chapman, George (1559-1634) He was a poet and playwright who at one time was considered a rival to Shakespeare. He completed Marlowe's poem Hero and Leander, which was left unfinished after the murder of Marlowe. His translation of Homer was well thought of but his body of work has had little following over the centuries.

Chettle, Henry (c 1564- c 1606) He was a London printer and perhaps a writer himself. He was at the centre of some controversy in 1592 when he printed Greene's Groatsworth of Wit which libelled Shakespeare and he was forced to back away from his involvement in that tract.

Cheyney, Jane (c 1510 -1574) She became the wife of Thomas Wriothesley,

1st earl of Southampton. Her family held land around Chesham in Buckinghamshire. She was the mother of the second earl and after her husband's death held considerable influence over the boy.

Cleves, Anne of (1515-47) She was married to Henry VIII on 6 January 1540 and was his fourth wife. She appears to have been a demure lady who was sexually unattractive to Henry. The marriage was annulled on 13 July 1540 and she was pensioned off and sent to live on a manor in Lewes.

Cranmer, Thomas (1489-1556) He became Archbishop of Canterbury in 1533 and was a hugely influential figure in the English Reformation. His Book of Common Prayer, introduced in 1548, became central to the liturgy of the Church of England. He was burned at the stake for heresy in 1556.

Cottam, John was a schoolmaster at Stratford on Avon and taught William Shakespeare when he was a boy. He was a known Roman Catholic.

Cooke, Mildred She was the second wife of Lord Burghley and they married in 1546. She was the mother of Robert Cecil, who succeeded his father as chief statesman to Queen Elizabeth and subsequently King James. She died in 1589.

Crawford, Rowland was one of the commissioner who surveyed Titchfield Abbey in 1537.

Crome, Edward (d 1562) Little is known about his early life but he was educated at Cambridge and in 1516 was the university preacher. He came to national attention when he defended the annulment of Henry VIII's marriage to Catherine of Aragon. He did get into difficulty from time to time and in 1546 was tried for heresy. He was not condemned to death but his licence was taken away. On some later occasions he was arrested but he managed to live out his natural life, dying in 1562.

Cromwell, Thomas (-1540) Sometime soldier and lawyer, he rose from modest beginnings to become Henry VIII's Chief Secretary and architect of government policy during the 1530s. He news created Earl of Essex in 1540, but having run foul of Henry was executed on 29 July 1540.

Cromwell, Oliver (1599-1658) Oliver was descended from a sister of Thomas Cromwell and at some point the family changed its name to capture some of the lustre of the famous Thomas. Although from the landed gentry in Huntingdonshire he was not noticed until 1640, when he made a speech duing the Short Parliament. He grew increasingly influential in the 1640s and his military successes in the civil war propelled him to the forefront of Parliamentary politics. In 1649 he became the Parliamentary leader and effective dictator until his death in 1658.

Culpepper, Thomas (1514 - 1541) He was a courtier at the court of Henry VIII and had a brief affair with Catherine Howard, Henry's fifth queen. For this he was tried and executed on 10 December 1541.

Daniel, Samuel (1562-1619) was a very accomplished poet born somewhere in the West Country. He had a successful career and certainly knew William Shakespeare.

Danvers, Sir Henry (26 Jun 1573-20 Jan 1634) 1st earl of Danby Henry Danvers was born to a well connected West Country family and formed a close friendship with the earl of Southampton. Both he and his brother Charles were implicated in the murder of a local enemy in 1594 and the earl of Southampton helped them to escape. He was pardoned some years later and went on to enjoy a long and successful career as a soldier. He was well regarded by The Stuart kings and Charles I created him earl of Danby in 1626.

Danvers, Sir Charles (c 1568 1601) In 1594 he was involved with his brother Henry in the murder of a neighbour.

Their friend, the 3rd earl of Southampton assisted their escape to France.Both brothers were later pardoned but Charles threw himself into the Essex rebellion of 1600 and like his leader was executed in 1601.

Davenant, Sir William (3 Mar 1506 - 7 Apr 1668) was the son of an Oxford Taverner. He became a successful poet and playwright and was created Poet Laureate in 1638. He liked to claim that William Shakespeare was his godfather.

Denny, Sir Anthony (16 January 1501-10 Sep 1549) was Henry VIII's Groom of the Stool and became a close and trusted confidant of the king. Like Thomas Wriothesley he profited from having an inside track when the monasteries were dissolved and acquired many manors. He was an influential figure in the finalising of Henry's will in 1547.

De Vere, Elizabeth (2 Jul 1575-10 Mar 1627) was a granddaughter of Lord Burghley and he tried to arrange a marriage between her and his ward, the 3rd earl of Southampton. Southampton would have none of it and instead she married William Stanley, 6th earl of Derby.

De Vere, Edward (12 Apr 1550-24 Jun 1604) 17th earl of Oxford. He became a leading figure at court and amongst his many accomplishments was a poet and a playwright. None of his plays survive although there are those who claim that Shakespeare's plays were in fact written by the 17th earl. He intersects with the Southampton story when Lord Burghley tried to arrange a marriage between his granddaughter (Oxford's daughter) Elizabeth and the young 3rd earl of Southampton. Southampton refused.

Devereaux, Robert (10 Nov 1565- 25 Feb 1601) 2nd Earl of Essex. He was talented and charismatic and became a great favourite of Queen Elizabeth, replacing the earl of Leicester, who died in 1588. He enjoyed great favour and prominence and attracted a number of devoted followers, among them the 3rd earl of `Southampton. He was not always successful in his military expeditions and his hubris brought his downfall in 1600 when he rebelled against the old queen. He was executed in 1501.

Devereaux, Penelope (Jan 1563 - Jul 1607) was the older sister of Robert, who became the second earl of Essex. She is believed to be the object of Sir Philip Sidney's sonnet sequence Astrophel and Stella. However, Sidney was not to marry her and instead she was betrothed to Robert Rich. It was not a happy marriage. Penelope gave her support to Elizabeth Vernon after she became pregnant with the earl of Southampton's first child. It was a daughter who was named Penelope.

Drake, Sir Francis (c 1540-28 Jan 1596) was a Devonshire seaman who achieved legendary fame by circumnavigating the world in an expedition that took three years, from 1577-1580. He achieved further distinction in his role in helping to defeat the Spanish Armada in 1588 and a number of piratical raids against Spanish ships.

Dudley, Robert (24 Jun 1532 - 4 Sep 1588) Earl of Leicester. He was a son of the Duke of Northumberland and was involved in the plot to install Lady Jane Grey as Queen. After the failure of that coup he was imprisoned with the rest of his family but escaped execution. During the reign of Elizabeth he became a favourite and a very influential statesman.

Dymoke, Thomas His dates are unknown but he was steward of the Titchfield estates for the second and third earls of Southampton. He was highly regarded by the second earl but seen as an enemy by the countess.

Edward VI (1537-1553) He was born to Henry's third wife, Jane Seymour, on 12 October 1537 and succeeded his father upon his death in 1547. His uncle Edward Seymour acted initially as protector. His reign was noted for its protestant Reformation, but Edward died of tuberculosis in 1553 and was **succeeded by his sister Mary.**

Elizabeth I (1533-1603) She was the daughter of Anne Boleyn and Henry VIII. After the deaths of her brother Edward and her sister Mary, both childless, she came to the throne in 1558 and successfully managed to stabilise a divided country for over 40 years.

Guido or Guy Fawkes (1570-1606) was born in York and ws named John Johnson. He adopted the name of Guido Fawkes while fighting for the Catholics in Spain. In England he became involved in the conspiracy to blow up the Houses of Parliament in 1605 and he was the one caught red-handed as the man planning to set the fuse.

Field, Richard (1561-1624) was born in Stratford on Avon and moved to London to apprentice in the printing trade. Shakespeare knew him well and Field, once he had set up his own printing shop, was able to publish Shakespeare's narrative poems, starting with Venus and Adonis in 1593.

Fitzwilliam, William (1490-1542) was a half-brother to Anthony Browne as a consequence of the remarriage of his mother. He was a capable naval commander, diplomat and government minister. In 1540 he was made Lord Privy Seal by Henry VIII who also made him Earl of Southampton. He died in 1542 without a male heir and Thomas Wriothesley picked up the title in 1547.

Florio, John (1552-1625) was a prominent man of letters in Elizabethan and Jacobean England. He was born in England to an Italian after but raised in Switzerland. He came to England as an adult and established himself as a tutor and writer. In the 1590s he entered the service of the 3rd earl of Southampton and certainly knew William Shakespeare.

Florio, Michelangelo (1515-1566) Italian

Franciscan friar who was early adopter of the teachings of Luther. He settled in England in 1550 but was compelled to flee once Mary came to the throne. He settled in Switzerland near the Italian border. His son John became an established literary figure in England.

Francis, king of France (1494-1547) He was crowned at Rheims in 1515 and his reign ran parallel to the reign of Henry VIII, both dying in the same year.

Frisuthwith (c 650-19 Oct 735) Commonly known as Frideswide, was a Mercian princess, daughter of Dida of Eynsham. She was apparently very devout and founded a monastery. She died at Binsey in Oxfordshire. The Augustinian priory in Oxford that bears her name was dedicated to her and there was a shrine to her. The monastery was dissolved to create Cardinal Wolsey's college, after known as Christ Church.

Garnet, Henry (1555-1606) was a Jesuit priest who became implicated in the Gunpowder plot. He was executed in 1606.

Garret, Thomas was a protestant reformer and supporter of Thomas Cromwell who was executed two days after Cromwell went to the scaffold.

Gardiner, Stephen (1482-1555) was the son of a Bury St Edmunds cloth maker. After studies at Cambridge he became master of Trinity Hall, where he encountered Thomas Wriothesley. He held several high offices of state and was created bishop of Winchester in 1529., He had ambitions to become Archbishop of Canterbury but was passed over in favour of Thomas Cranmer. He was a leading conservative against the reforms in the English church.

Golding, Arthur (1536-1606) was a translator of classical works from Latin into English. He is best known for his translation of Ovid's Metamorphoses, which became the source for Shakespeare's narrative poems.

Greene, Robert (1558-1592) was one of the early figures who tried to make a living out of writing. He was popular but he lived a dissolute life and died in poverty at an early age. He is chiefly remembered for his bitter attack on the rising William Shakespeare published shortly after his death where he characterised the poet and playwright as an 'upstart crow.'

Harrison, John was a London printer who brought out the third edition of Shakespeare's Venus and Adonis

Hall, Edward (d 1547) was a London grocer known for his book *The Union of the Two Noble and Illustre Families of Lancastre and Yorke.* Published a year after his death. It is usually known as Hall's Chronicle and was a source for several of Shakespeare's history plays.

Harvey, Gabriel (1552-1631) was a scholar and writer. He is chiefly remembered for his quarrel with Thomas Nashe who later satirised him in *Have With You to Saffron Walden.*

Heneage, Sir Thomas (1532-1595) was born in Epping, Essex. He held office during the reign of Henry VIII and in 1553 became an MP. He flourished at the court of Elizabeth I. He was the second husband of the Countess Mary of Southampton.

Herbert, William (1580-1630) became the 3rd earl of Pembroke and a prominent literary patron. The First Folio of Shakespeare's plays, published in 1623, was dedicated to him, and some believe that he may have been the young man presented in Shakespeare's sonnets.

Hervey, Sir William (1565-1642) was a soldier and politician, who, at the age of 22, became the third husband of Mary, Countess of Southampton.

Holme, William (d. 1609) He was a London printer who has been put forward as the mysterious 'Mr. W. H.' the 'onlie begetter' of Shakespeare's sonnets. The proposed theory is that he died before publication and the task was taken on by

Thomas Thorpe.

Holinshead, Raphael (1525-1582) was the author of *The Chronicles of England, Scotlande, and Irelande,* a source for several of Shakespeare's history plays.

Hathaway, Anne (1556-1623) was from Shottery, near Stratford upon Avon who married William Shakespeare in 1582.

Hoghton, Alexander (c 1520-1581)was a Lancashire landowner who may have had some connection to William Shakespeare. He employed John Cottam, who had formerly taught William Shakespeare and was a strong Roman Catholic. In his will of 1581 he made a small bequest to 'William Shakeshaft.'

Howard, Henry (c 1517-1547) was the eldest son of Thomas Howard, 3rd duke of Norfolk. He was an accomplished soldier and poet but he often found himself in trouble at court through his intemperate behaviour. He was executed in the last days of the reign of Henry VIII for treason.

Howard, Catherine (1522-1542) She was a daughter of the duke of Norfolk and was deliberately set up by the Howard family to become Henry's fifth queen and the pair were married on 15 July 1540. She unwisely embarked on some extra-marital affairs and once found out was beheaded for treason on 13 February 1542.

Howard, Thomas (1473-1554) ws the 2nd duke of Norfolk and a leading figure in Tudor governments. He was very ambitious and was instrumental in steering Henry VIII towards his nieces Anne Boleyn and Catherine Howard, with unfortunate ending for both women. He was a leader of the conservative resistance against the protestant reforms and was out of favour during the last years of Henry VIII. Nevertheless, he managed to live out his natural life.

Jaggard, William (1568-1623) He operated one of the largest print shops in London and published many of Shakespeare's works over a twenty year period, particularly the edition known as the First Folio.

Jerome, William was a protestant reformer and supporter of Thomas Cromwell who was executed t wo days after Cromwell went to the scaffold.

Jonson, Ben (1572-1637) He was a poet and playwright and something of a literary giant.He never knew his father, who died two months before his birth, and he was brought up by his stepfather, a bricklayer. Jonson was educated at Westminster School and the University of Cambridge. His stage comedies were very successful.

Knyvet, Sir Anthony (1507-1554) He was a follower of the duke of Norfolk and was rewarded with several court appointments. He was appointed Lieutenant of the Tower of London. In 1554 he joined Wyatt's rebellion and was executed.

Lambert, John (d 22 Nov 1538) He was born John Nicholson in Norwich and attended Queens' College in Cambridge. Where he later became a fellow. He was a protestant reformer and finding life uncomfortable at Cambridge he moved to Antwerp, where he changed his name. He returned to England in 1531 where he became increasingly known for his new theological idea. He was prosecuted by the Duke of Norfolk and burnt at the stake in 1538.

Latham, John was one of the commissioner who surveyed Titchfield Abbey in 1537.

Leland, John (1503-1554) He lost both his parents at an early age and was raised by Thomas Myles, who saw to it that he was educated. He attended st Paul's school with Wriothesley, Paget and North and certainly benefited from these contacts. He was granted a number of benefices in his lifetime which allowed him a comfortable living. His lasting achievement was to become the founder of English local history. Between 1533 and 1543 he travelled extensively throughout much of the country and made notes. These notebooks were edited and published in the 18th century as *Itineraries*. He never married. In 1547 he lost his wits and was certified insane in 1550. He never recovered before his death in 1554.

Lily, William (c1468-25 Feb 1522) was born at Odiham in Hampshire. He attended Oxford University and after some years of travels ended up in London as a teacher of Grammar. He also taught Greek. In 1520 the dean of St Paul's, John Colet, planned to found a school and in 1512 appointed Lily as master.

Long, Sir Henry (1487-1556) He was a prosperous Wiltshire gentleman who was Sherrif of Wiltshire on several occasions. He was able to profit from the dissolution of the monasteries through the acquisition of land belonging to Brradenstoke priory.

Lucy, Sir Thomas (1522-1600) was a Warwickshire landowner and magistrate who was reported as whipping William Shakespeare for poaching deer on his Charlecote estate. There is not documentary evidence to support this. Lucy was however, a Protestant reformer and would not have been popular with the Shakespeares.

Manox, Henry He was born c 1515 and hired as a tutor to Catherine Howard. He claimed to have known Catherine's private parts but after her marriage to the king and the eventual scandal involving Thomas Culpepper and others he insisted he had no carnal knowledge. He wss not executed as the affair (if it existed) pre-dated Catherine's marriage to the king.

Marillac, Charles de (1510-12560) was the French ambassador at the court of Henry VIII from 1530-1543.

Marlowe, Christopher (1564-1593) Born in Canterbury, he took an MA from Cambridge and established himself on the London scene as a poet and playwright. He is widely considered to have been Shakespeare's equal before he was murdered in Deptford in 1593.

de Massue, Daniel (1577-1613) He was Seigneur de Ruvigny and a prominent Huguenot and it suited the government of the day to keep him (and the Huguenots) onside. He was the father of Rachel and Henri.

de Massue, Rachel (1603-1640) She was born in France, the daughter of Daniel de `masque, a prominent Huguenot. She married Thomas Wriothesley, 4th earl of Southampton in 1634. She gave birth to five children but died giving birth to the last.

Mekins, Richard (c 1526-1541) He was burned at the stake for making some unwise remark. He was barely 15.

Meres, Frances (1565-1647) He was a churchman and sometime author. He is principally remembered for his commonplace book *Palladis Tarnia, Wits Treasury*, published in 1598, contains some criticism and record of Shakespeare's early plays.

More, Sir Thomas (1478-1535) He was a lawyer who rose to become Chancellor during the reign of Henry VIII and he lost his head because of his opposition to Henry's break with the Church of Rome. He was also an author, known today for his *History of King Richard III* and *Utopia*.

More, Sir William (30 January 1520 – 20 July 1600, descended from a wealthy London fishmonger. He had a large hall at Loseley, Surrey, and for a period held the 2nd earl of Southampton in his custody, as he was trusted by the Elizabethan government. He was a member of every Parliament during the reign of Queen Elizabeth I. More acquired the Blackfriars monastery, part of which he sold in 1596 to James Burbage, who founded his Blackfriars theatre there.

Nashe, Thomas (1567- c 160!) he was the son of an East Anglian clergyman who was able to take a degree at the University of Cambridge. After this he went to London where he tried (and largely succeeded) in making a living from writing. He became known for his prose works, often published as pamphlets, which were of a scurrilous and satirical nature. Unsurprisingly, his career was controversial.

Noel, Edward (1641-1689) married Elizabeth Wriothesley and became the 1st earl of Gainsborough.

North, Edward (1504-1564) Edward North attended St Pul's with Thomas Wriothesley and went to Peterhouse in Cambridge before enrolling in the Inns of Court and becoming a lawyer. He entered government service in 1531 and in 1541 he became Chancellor of the Court of Augmentations, established to deal with the estates accruing to the crown after the monastic dissolution. He was created Baron North in 1554.

Paget, William (1506-9 Jun 1563) was born in wednesbury in Staffordshire, although his fatherhood business interests in the City of London. He was an exact contemporary of Thomas Wriothesley and they both attended St Pauls and Trinity Hall, where he also became a protege of Stephen Gardner. He. Became a Clerk of the Signet in 1532 and was later a clerk of the Privy Council. He achieved higher offices of state and became one of the chief supporters of Somerset during his Protectorate. He was created Baron Paget de Beaudesert in 1549. He suffered a fall from power together with Somerset in 1551 but was reinstated in 1553 and appointed Lord Privy Seal in 1556.

Parr, Catherine (1512-5 Sep 1548) was the eldest child of Sir Thomas Parr of Kendal and Maud Green of Greens Norton. She was first married to Sir Edward Burgh in 1529 and was widoe]wed in 1533. There were no children from this marriage. In the following year she married John Nevill, 3rd Baron Latimer, a man twice her age, and she became a widow again in 1543. Again there was no issue from this marriage. Almost immediately she married King Henry VIII on 12 July 1543. Six months after the king's death she married Thomas Seymour, younger brother of the Protector. By him she entered into her first pregnancy and died after childbirth, probably from puperal fever, on 5 September 1548. The child, a daughter, was named Mary. Catherine Parr was a well educated and literate woman who wrote three books. In her last, *Lamentations of a Sinner,* she articulated Protestant ideas that were anathema to men like Wriothesley.

Peckham, Sir Edmund (1495-1564) held various accounting positions in the household of Henry VIII and rose to become High Treasurer of all the mints in 1544. He was married to Anne, a cousin of Thomas Wriothesley's wife Jane. Like his friend and colleague Thomas Wriothesley he fell from grace during the reign of Edward VI, but regained his position during Queen Mary's reign. Thomas Wriothesley probably learned much about financial management from his older colleague.

Quiney, Richard (1557-1602) He was an alderman at Stratford upon Avon, known to the Shakespeares and he had some correspondence with William Shakespeare.

Rich, Sir Richard (1496-1567) Rich appears to have descended from a London merchant but he began to make his career at court under the patronage of Thomas Audley. In 1536 he became Chancellor of the Court of Augmentations, the court which oversaw the dissolution of the monasteries and was thus able to secure extensive lands in Essex. He was created Baron Rich in February 1547 and succeeded Thomas Wriothesley as Chancellor in the following month. His career spanned the reigns of Henry VIII and his son Edward VI.

Radclyffe, Thomas (1525-1583) was the 3rd earl of Sussex. He married Elizabeth, a daughter of Thomas Wriothesley, 1ˢᵗ earl of Southampton

Raleigh, Sir Walter (1552-1618) was an outstanding character during the reigns of Elizabeth and James I. He was a soldier, explorer, poet and statesman. He was seen as a rival to the earl of Essex and was therefore not favoured by the Southampton household. His career stalled with James I and he was imprisoned from 1603-1616. After his release he led an expedition to the New World to find El Dorado, or the city of gold. He ransacked a Spanish outpost and because he violated a peace treaty with Spain was executed on his return to England.

Russell, William (1616-1700) 1st duke of Bedford and father in law to Rachel Wriothersley.

Russell, William (1639-1683) He was the son and heir to the duke of Bedford and married Rachel Wriothesley. He was executed for treason in 1683.

Sadler, Sir Ralph (1507-1567) He was placed in the household of Thomas Cromwell for his education and seamlessly moved into government office, serving, like his near contemporary Thomas Wriothesley in minor offices and moving up the ranks through demonstrated competence. He served in Henry VIII's government and in that of his son Edward VI. He was pushed into retirement during the reign of Mary but returned to government when Elizabeth came to the throne. His highest office was Chancellor of the Duchy of Lancaster, which he held from 1569 until his death.

Sandys, Sir Edwin (1561-1629) was a close associate of the 3ʳᵈ earl of Southampton in the Virginia Company. He became treasurer of the company in 1619.

Seymour, Edward (1500-1552) was promoted to the Lords after his sister Jane married Henry VIII. He was created earl of Hertford in 1537. During the minority of Edward VI he emerged as Lord Protector but ran into opposition because of his autocratic style of government. He was excluded from office in 1549. He was executed in 1552 for conspiring against the government.

Seymour, Jane (c 1509-1537) She was Henry VIII's third queen and they were married on 30 May 1536. She did give birth to the desired son, christened Edward, on 12 October 1537, but she died twelve days later from puberal fever.

Seymour. Thomas (1508-1549) was the younger brother of the Lord Protector, Edward Seymour. He was ambitious and flirted with the young Princess Elizabeth and then married Catherine Parr, the widow off Henry VIII. She died in childbirth. He plotted against his brother and was executed in 1549.

Shakeshaft, William was mentioned as a servant in the will of Alexander Hoghton in 1581. Some have tried to connect this William Shakeshaft with William Shakespeare.

Shakespeare, Edmund (1580-1607) was the youngest brother of William Shakespeare. He became an actor like his eldest brother.

Shakespeare, Gilbert (1566-1612) was a younger brother of William Shakespeare.

Shakespeare, Joan (1569-1646) was a sister of William Shakespeare. She married a hatter by the name of William Hart and had four children.

Shakespeare, John (c. 1531-1601) was a glover and alderman in the town of Stratford upon Avon. William was one of his sons.

Shakespeare, Richard (1490-1561) farmed at Snittersfield, about 4 miles north east of Stratford upon Avon. He was the grandfather of William.

Shakespeare, William (1564-1616) Born in Stratford on Avon and died there. From about 1588 to 1613 he worked as one of the foremost men of the London stage as an actor and playwright.

Sidney, Sir Philip (1554-1586) was a court, soldier and poet who is now best remembered for his sonnet sequence *Astrophel and Stella*. 'Stella' was Penelope Rich, the sister of the earl of Essex. Henry Wriothesley's first born daughter was named after her.

Stanhope, Sir Thomas (1540-1596) was a Nottinghamshire landowner who made a very generous offer to the 3rd earl of Southampton to marry his daughter. The offer was rejected.

Thorpe, Thomas (1569-1625) was a printer who is most famous for publishing an edition of Shakespeare's sonnets in 1609.

Udall, Nicholas (1504-1556 was a schoolmaster and sometime playwright, remembered for Ralph Roister Doister. He taught at Titchfield and then at Eton where he got into trouble for offences against the Buggery Act of 1533. Thomas Wriothesley saw to it that his sentence was commuted to one year.

Vernon, Elizabeth (1572-1665) was a cousin of the earl of Essex and could claim descent from Thomas Grey, son of Queen Elizabeth Woodville, the Talbot earls of Shrewsbury and the Stafford dukes of Buckingham. She had four children: Penelope, who married William Spencer, 2nd Baron Spencer, Anne, who married Robert Wallop, James who died in 1624 and Thomas, who succeeded to the earldom in that same year.

Wallop, Sir John (1490-13 Jul 1551) was a career soldier and diplomat and for a time the resident ambassador in Paris. In 1541 he became Captain of the garrison at Guisnes and he held that position until his death of the sweating sickness in 1551. He had estates in Hampshire and Buckinghamshire and in 1538 he was granted the manors attached to the dissolved monastery of Berlinch in Somerset.

Robert Wallop married Anne Wriothesley and became an active parliamentarian during the Civil War. He was one of those who signed the death warrant for Charles I.

Wolsey, Thomas (1473-1530) was born in Ipswich, where his father was reputed to be a butcher. He took holy orders and held various benefices before he entered the service of Henry VII in 1507. In the service of his son he rose to become a statesman of great power and wealth.

Charles Wriothesley (1508-1562) was the son of Thomas Wriothesley, Garter King of Arms and became Windsor Herald. He wrote a book entitled *A Chronicle of England During the Reigns of the Tudors, From A.D. 1485 to 1559.*

Wriothesley, Elizabeth (1640-1683) was a daughter of Thomas and Rachel Wriothesley. She married Edward Noel who became the 1st earl.

Wriothesley, Elizabeth (1645-1690) was a daughter of the 4th earl of Southampton by his second wife Elizabeth Leigh. She first married the earl of Northumberland and secondly Ralph Montagu, 1st duke of Montagu.

Wriothesley, Henry 2nd earl of Southampton. (1545-1581)

Wriothesley, Henry 3rd earl of Southampton. (1573-1624)

Wriothesley, James eldest son of the 3rd earl of Southampton. (1605-1624). He died of dysentery while serving with English forces in Holland.

Wriothesley, Penelope (1598-1667) was the first born to the 3rd earl of Southampton and Elizabeth Vernon.

Rachel Wriothesley (1636-1723) was the second daughter of the 4th earl of Southampton. She first married Lord Vaughn and no children survived from that marriage. In 1667 she married William, Lord Russell, heir to the duke of Bedford. By him, she had a son Wriothesley, who became the 2nd duke of Bedford on the death of his grandfather. Lady Russell was prominent in the social and political affairs of her day.

Wriothesley, Thomas (1505-1550) was a son of William Wriothesley, York Herald. He became a rich man in government service and was created earl of Southampton in 1547.

Wriothesley, Thomas 4th earl of Southampton. (1607-1667)

Wriothesley, William (c 1475-1513) was the second son of John Writhe. His son Thomas became the 1st earl of Southampton.

Wrythe, John (d 1504) was a London draper and Garter King of Arms, in which capacity he served Edward IV and Henry VII. His sons, Thomas and William, both became heralds.

Index

134

CPSIA information can be obtained
at www.ICGtesting.com
Printed in the USA
LVHW080548120822
725756LV00008B/197